Dressed in Fiction

Dressed in Fiction

Clair Hughes

Oxford • New York

First published in 2006 by
Berg
Editorial offices:
1st Floor, Angel Court, 81 St Clements Street, Oxford, OX4 1AW, UK
175 Fifth Avenue, New York, NY 10010, USA

Berg is the imprint of Oxford International Publishers Ltd.

Library of Congress Cataloging-in-Publication Data
Hughes, Clair, 1941-
    Dressed in fiction / Clair Hughes.
        p. cm.
    Includes bibliographical references and index.
    ISBN-13: 978-1-84520-171-5 (Cloth)
    ISBN-10: 1-84520-171-X (Cloth)
    ISBN-13: 978-1-84520-172-2 (pbk.)
    ISBN-10: 1-84520-172-8 (pbk.)
    1.   English fiction—History and criticism. 2.   Clothing
and dress in literature. 3.   American fiction—History and
criticism. I.   Title.

PR830.C59H84 2006
823.009'3559—dc22   2005029984

British Library Cataloguing-in-Publication Data
A catalogue record for this book is available from the British Library.

ISBN-13 978 1 84520 171 5 (Cloth)
ISBN-10 1 84520 171 X (Cloth)

ISBN-13 978 1 84520 172 2 (Paper)
ISBN-10 1 84520 172 8 (Paper)

Typeset by Avocet Typeset, Chilton, Aylesbury, Bucks
Printed in the United Kingdom by Biddles Ltd, King's Lynn

www.bergpublishers.com

For George

Contents

Illustrations

Plates

Line Engravings

Acknowledgements

This book owes much to many people: teachers, colleagues and students; scholars in the fields of Literature, Dress and Art History over many years. I would in particular like to acknowledge the importance of Anne Hollander's work for my own, and to salute the memory of the late Adeline Tintner, who gave early and important encouragement. I owe much not only to Mick Carter's books but also to conversation and correspondence with him, and to his comments on this book which were constructive and enlightening. I am very grateful to Kit Constable Maxwell, for technical help with the illustrations, and to Lyn Constable Maxwell who so generously let me use the material describing her grandmother Muriel Stephenson's wedding. Kathryn Earle's and Hannah Shakespeare's unfailingly sympathetic editorial support has been not only a help but an act of friendship.

My greatest debt is to George Hughes – to his unselfish support, his careful, informed reading of my work, and to his own work, *Reading Novels*, which has been a formative influence on this book.

–1–

Dressing for the Reader

'All over town people are putting on their costumes.' The engaging opening to Canadian novelist Carol Shields's collection of short stories, *Dressing Up for the Carnival*, alerts us to a group of people in a particular place – a town and a book – who are preparing their stories and their appearances both for the business of the day and for the entertainment of the reader. To do so, they have to dress up. Dress is perhaps not the first topic we consider when reading a novel or a short story, but as the novelist Elizabeth Bowen has said, '[o]n the subject of dress almost no one … feels truly indifferent … It is dangerous – it has a flowery head but deep roots in the passions.'[1] Descriptions of dress help us fill out our pictures of the imagined worlds of fiction. But, on the other hand, too much information, too great an emphasis on dress, is often felt to be distracting, even suspect. George Eliot, looking back on the failure of her stupendously researched historical novel *Romola*, put it down to over-much detail of this kind – 'my tendency to excess in this effort after artistic vision'.[2]

Mistrust of excessive concern for dress, hostility to fashion's restless consumption, ranges from Old Testament thunder against 'tinkling ornaments' to the studied anti-fashion statement of torn jeans. Mrs Ellis, in her advice of 1842 to the 'Daughters of England', declares the 'power of fashion on the female mind' to be 'the most worthless, the most contemptible and the least efficient of moral agents',[3] and the author of an etiquette book of 1853 abandons his urbane tones to pronounce that 'the best dressers of every age have always been the worst men and women'.[4] By including substantial chapters on fashion, however, both authors acknowledge fashion's centrality to human behaviour. A consumerist love of dress is distinct from a scholarly wish to understand it, and from Thomas Carlyle's insistence in 1832, in *Sartor Resartus*, on the 'unspeakable significance'[5] of dress, many historians, anthropologists, economists have been engaged in the attempt to analyse the phenomenon, and yet, as Anne Hollander says, hostility constantly surfaces in 'pointed neglect, ferocious satire, heavy irony, and sarcastically exaggerated respect'.[6] 'All clothes, no matter what their style', as Mick Carter points out, 'unsettle the split between natural/artifice, that is so important from the Romantics onward. All clothes are barely able to hide their convention-ality ... being dressed never quite achieves the status of the natural'.[7] Furthermore, dress is disturbingly, dangerously protean: '[C]hanging at will, [it] everywhere both reveals and conceals social position.'[8] However, this unsettling ability to arouse the passions, to seduce, disturb, deceive, and to threaten even the wearer with its occult 'otherness' – all adds to the power of dress for the writer of fiction.

Interestingly enough, costume historians have frequently drawn on lit-erature for evidence and information. Literary critics have been puz-zlingly slow to return the compliment – novelists do not, after all, send their characters naked into the world but criticism has often acted as though they do. Virginia Woolf, in *A Room of One's Own*, argued that the values of novels reflect the values of life, '[y]et it is the masculine values that prevail. Speaking crudely, football and sport are "important"; the worship of fashion, the buying of clothes "trivial".'[9] And a century after this remark, we must acknowledge that little has changed in our hier-archy of values. What is it then that dress can do for a text? Why might it be worth not just noting that it is there, but actually looking closer at it?

First of all, references to dress for both reader and writer contribute to the 'reality effect': they lend tangibility and visibility to character and context. From a sociological and historical viewpoint it is worth our while to look closely at descriptions of dress in a novel, because dress is a visible aspect of history, a material index of social, moral and historical change which helps us understand and imagine historical difference: clothes are, as John Harvey says in his study of male dress, 'values made visible'.[10] The French cultural historian, Daniel Roche points out that while fictional works can never coincide 'with the gaze directed at the world and at things, in a reality now gone for ever, ... the relationship to reality ... makes possible a reading of social values and practices in the very codes which organize the fictions and are a part of the communica-tion of the age'.[11] Dress is a social code which can be transmitted across the years through the different codes which organize a period's fictions. Modern dress, its history and its employment in fiction, in particular, allows us to trace the growth of luxury and consumption in the eigh-teenth and nineteenth centuries, as well as the changes in manufacture and publicity in the twentieth century.

Dress is also a language, part of a social system of signs: white clothes may denote purity and virginity, for example; black may be used to represent formality, drama or death. But dress within a novel does not simply follow widely accepted social codes; it can also operate as the author's personal sign-system, conscious or unconscious. References to dress may be plotted by some authors as part of a symbolic pattern – we see this operating particularly in texts of the late nineteenth and early twentieth centuries. Most of my discussion in this book is of fashionable, therefore of middle- or upper-class clothes; dress of the underclass varies little until the advent of the mass market. Thomas Hardy is careful to indicate colour and texture rather than style in the dress of his eponymous heroine, Tess of the D'Urbervilles. Tess's change from working to modish dress – as we see in the last chapter – ironically relates moral judgements to class assumptions about dress. George Orwell remarks that ' clothes are powerful things. Dressed in a tramp's clothes it is very difficult not to feel that you are genuinely degraded.'[12] Dress becomes, in the work of Hardy and Henry James, for example, crucial to the construction of an imagined world, as well as an integral part of the way a novel is constructed as an artwork, part of the novelist's modernist concern with the life of the mind. Descriptions of dress, in general, are often discrete exercises in description (similar to character portraits or descriptions of buildings), and as such offer us one of the *different* pleasures of reading a text – different, that is, from simply following the plot.

If there are some good reasons, then, why it is revealing and often fascinating to consider the topic of dress in relation to novels, there are certain significant points we must also keep in mind when looking at actual examples of fictional clothes. Clothes in fiction are, first of all, rarely described in full. References to dress must be read with the understanding that the general effect is usually 'naturalized', an understood image the writer and a contemporary reader, who knows more or less what is intended without being told; only special effects are usually notable – excess of frills, or brightly-coloured stockings, for example. Gender is, of course, important in relation to this topic: an interest in clothes is often considered only appropriate to, or characteristic of, women. Male interest is generally suspect – and therefore in itself worth noting. In fictional texts describing clothes the colours will often be important, and use of technical terms for costume (when it occurs) will have significance – providing an indication of a historical period or an exotic location, perhaps, or indicating a special audience. Looking at novels we are bound to note that there will often be historical confusion over dress. Novelists sometimes do research on such matters (George Eliot, for example), but often simply follow current perceptions. William Thackeray, for example, set his novel of 1847, *Vanity Fair,* in the

Napoleonic period, but in an early introduction to the novel explained that he had dressed the characters in the styles of the 1840s because the clothes of 1815 were so ugly – a sentiment we might not agree with now. Finally, we must remember that dress, in psychoanalytic terminology, is 'over-determined': that is, it is not possible to give one final explanation, there will always be several possible and different explanations – personal taste, fashionable dictates, unconscious self-images, metaphoric patterns and so forth. An absence of dress references can also be significant – as is an excess of them.

In the Carol Shields story with which I started with, when 'all over town people [were] putting on their costumes', we find that her characters' passions are, directly or indirectly, often related to dress, as indeed the title of the collection, *Dressing Up for the Carnival*, would suggest. For example, the prize-winning middle-aged writer, in the second story, takes a long time and a great deal of trouble to buy a beautiful and expensive scarf for her unhappy young daughter. Through a misunderstanding the scarf ends up in the hands of an unsuccessful, meanly jealous fellow-writer who, when shown the scarf, assumes it is meant as a present for her. The novelist, conscious of the other woman's misery and her increasingly unattractive appearance, allows the mistake to stand, since, she concludes, '[n]ot one of us was going to get what we wanted'.[13]

The significance of the scarf, even in this short story set in the 1990s, is not simple, and it is worth our while, as so often, to attempt a closer examination. Dress is most frequently and critically seen as evidence of expenditure: early and mid-nineteenth-century advice books in particular target the dangers of female extravagance. Mrs Ellis interestingly draws on the novel to urge economy on her 'Wives of England': writers, she says, bestow 'what is gorgeous and elaborate upon scenes and characters with which the best feelings of the heart have little connection; while the favourite heroine is conspicuous in her simplicity'.[14] Later in the century, however, Henry James, answering Mrs Lyn Linton's journalistic attack on the excesses of the 'girl of the period', denies that extravagance is a female monopoly: 'we are all of us extravagant, superficial and luxurious together'.[15] Theodore Veblen's savage satire of 1899 on consumer-capitalism, *A Theory of the Leisure Class*, sees female expenditure on dress as simply an obligatory display of male financial success – Veblen himself dressed resolutely from mail-order catalogues. The woman in Shields's short story, as a consequence of *her* success, is able to buy an extravagant luxury. As dress is also a kind of language, it can speak in terms of seduction, affection or rivalry. This scarf is for the writer's daughter, so it could be seen as an expression of mother-love, or perhaps – since she does not believe any of them will ever fulfil their desires – a substitute for love. It is a bright flag of literary and aesthetic triumph for one woman, or a bitter reminder not only of literary failure but also a failure of looks for the other. In the future, one woman may remember it in terms of an accidental but finally altruistic gesture. And the other? Will she view her rival's gift with envious hatred, or will she be redeemed by the memory of such generosity? In the text's own future, readers may see the 'designer' scarf as typical of the tastes of the last years of the twentieth century, or reading ideologically, see the female values and concerns of the story as, again, typical of the period's political agendas. In fact, the story already has its own after-life, as Shields herself expanded the themes suggested by the story into her last novel, *Unless*, in which the scarf plays its part in the novelist/narrator's relationship with her problematic daughter, a girl who, outdoing Veblen, takes to beggarhood, renouncing all aspects of the material world.

An attention to dress provides, of course, only one way of looking at a text, but it is surprising that so few literary critics have taken the trouble to give such attention in a systematic fashion. There are some exceptions: Richard Altick, gives a chapter to 'The Way They Looked' (on dress, hair and faces) in his survey of the Victorian novel,[16] and Tony Tanner, writing on 'conversation' in *Northanger Abbey*, extracts from the list of conversational topics in the novel 'the matter of dress' and, unusually, gives several pages to the topic. Interestingly, he betrays a kind of shyness about what he is doing by putting a page of his analysis inside brackets.[17] Dress historians, who begin by taking dress seriously, have been able to spot aspects of texts which illuminate subsequent readings. Aileen Ribeiro in her study of eighteenth-century English and French fashions, *The Art of Dress*,[18] makes constant cross-references to the literature of the time, and Anne Hollander, in her interdisciplinary study *Seeing Through Clothes*, draws particular attention to Henry James's use of dress in his fiction. It is not, as Hollander says, that James makes more than the occasional reference to dress, but his consideration of clothing in his fiction may come from his own 'very deep acknowledgement of the power of clothing, of its much greater importance than that of other inanimate objects'.[19] Honoré de Balzac, James's acknowledged master, not only wrote a treatise on fashion but declared dress to be the most powerful of symbols: the French Revolution was, he believed, as much a debate between silk and cloth as it was about politics.[20]

As we see from the example of Carol Shields's work, dress itself can feature usefully as the focus of a short story. Guy de Maupassant famously made a piece of jewellery the subject of his story 'The Necklace', and Elizabeth Bowen borrowed an idea from an early ghost story by

Henry James about rivalry over some dresses to write a ghost story of her own, 'Hand in Glove', about a very desirable collection of gloves. In a full-length novel, of course, over-emphasis on dress might result in a boring, or – at the very least – an oddly unbalanced work. D. H. Lawrence's novel of the 1920s, *Women in Love*, was criticized at the time for over-attention to dress, though on the grounds of frivolity rather than of tedium. It must be admitted, of course, that lengthy descriptions of dress by some nineteenth-century novelists can hold up the narrative and sound like interpolated extracts from a fashion magazine. But even the 'boredom' effect of dress description can be used deliberately: it functions as a distancing device in the recent novel by Brett Easton Ellis, *American Psycho*, where the narrator's obsession with clothes and their brand-names adds to the accumulating horror of the story. However, '[g]reat authors are not fashion writers',[21] as Judith Watt says in the introduction to her anthology of fashion writing, and they are not generally intrusive in their accounts of past or present modes. Dress, according to Roland Barthes, 'must renounce every egotism'.[22]

In the pages which follow I shall be looking at a group of fictional texts, written in English over a period of about 200 years, and placing my focus on scenes of dress. My intention is not to prove that dress is the hidden key to all the mysteries of these texts, but to show how an exploration of the author's employment of dress and its accessories can illuminate the structure of that text, its values, its meanings or its symbolic pattern. The texts are not necessarily chosen because they lay an unusual emphasis on dress, although my first example, Daniel Defoe's *Roxana*, does in fact centre on a dress. Dress references in the two short stories by Henry James under discussion are, by contrast, very economical. But the authors I have selected seem to me to have been deliberate in their deployment of dress, not lazily conforming to the dress stereotypes used by other writers, nor drawing on some generalized memory bank, but rather thinking, feeling and seeing what clothes can mean within a human life, what values they can embody.

In my first example, *Roxana: The Fortunate Mistress* (1724), the plot hangs on the wearing of a Turkish masquerade dress. This central focus on a dress, if not unique – a ball-dress in Charlotte Lennox's *The Female Quixote* of 1752 is another conversation-stopper – is certainly unusual; but then for Defoe to choose a successful courtesan for a heroine is odd, too. Evidence of economic and erotic success, the dress in the novel finally threatens to betray Roxana's identity and murky past, and thus her hopes of middle-aged respectability. While she attracts the romantic attentions of many men, she is herself a hard-headed businesswoman, who subscribes to the new eighteenth-century consumer-capitalist values. We may deplore her ruthlessness, but her beauty, wit and energy are entrancing. We do not want her to be unmasked. And Defoe's conclusion, while suggesting catastrophic revelations, denies us the knowledge of her fate.

In Jane Austen's novel, *Northanger Abbey* – my next example – the heroine Catherine Morland yearns for romance, but her interest in dress is practical and contemporary rather than connected to the seductive and exotic. The young man in this story shows a similar and perhaps greater interest in dress, while his father, who attempts to calculate the 'value' of Catherine's appearance, betrays a moral standard corrupted by the imperatives of full-blown consumerism. Catherine's chaperone, Mrs Allen, and her 'best friend' Isabella Thorpe display an excessive interest in clothes and accessories, which, while providing some of the funniest scenes in the novel, does also indicate the workings of vacant minds, and values that are not merely frivolous but potentially dangerous.

Traditionally, aspects of dress have been used to portray aspects of personality, particularly when a character first enters the story: as for example, when we are introduced to the dandified but old-fashioned outfits worn by Major Pendennis in William Thackeray's *Pendennis*, my third novel. The Major serves as both role-model and warning to Arthur Pendennis, the novel's unheroic hero, whose career across the novel is charted in a series of exquisite outfits which throw no very favourable light on his character. But dress can also itself become the focus of dramatic actions or situations, as for example, the dress in *Roxana*. And no one who has read *Gone With the Wind* or seen the movie will forget the scene in which Scarlett O'Hara, in wartime and without money, makes a dress out of green velvet curtains. Only with historical novels such as *Gone With the Wind* or in earlier historical fictions – by Walter Scott, for example – does the description of a whole garment become crucial to the creation of period atmosphere, and the authors of historical fiction do indeed often go into immense antiquarian detail, sometimes at the cost of the modern reader's attention.

Although neither *Pendennis* nor *Middlemarch*, among the novels I shall be looking at, is a historical novel in the sense of being about the distant past, neither of them is set at the period of the composition of the novel. They are set at a slightly earlier time, within the memory of both author and the contemporary reader. George Eliot is careful to make the distinction between the two periods (1830s and 1870s) clear when describing dress: Thackeray blurs things a little. In both historical and non-historical narratives the more usual way of talking about clothes is to ignore the overall picture and to limit description to extraneous detail: 'ribbons, ruffles, patterns – unfocused finery', according to Anne Hollander, are often focused upon 'to carry the notion of frivolity'.[23] The contrast between the puritanical Dorothea Brooke and the extravagant, flirtatious Rosamond Vincy, in Eliot's realist novel *Middlemarch*, is thus conveyed through a focus on Rosamond's elaborate taste in hair-styles, collars and jewellery, in contrast to Dorothea's austerity. Rosamond conforms to conventional ideas of nineteenth-century female beauty and modesty, as does the wicked Lady Audley, in Mary Braddon's *Lady Audley's Secret* – the focus of my fifth chapter. Lucy Audley is as elaborately got up as Rosamond, and her initial appearance and manner is that of the submissive Victorian domestic 'Angel'. But Lady Audley turns the whole image of the Angel-Heroine dramatically on its head. Although Braddon, like Eliot, was writing within the realist tradition, this is a 'sensation' novel, and, as Lady Audley's criminal career progresses, her dresses are conveyed in a blaze of colour and effects rather than through the small details of finery marking Rosamond's insidious but destructive greed. In both cases these dress-signs conceal and reveal hidden aspects.

Moving toward the Modernist period in the novel, we find an increasing concern on the part of authors such as Henry James, Thomas Hardy or Virginia Woolf to place their narrative within the consciousness of a character, not so much to explore the social or moral 'meanings' of dress as to convey what it is like to wear, to observe, to 'undergo' dress. In *Orlando* Woolf crossed chronological and gender boundaries in her exploration of character and Orlando's experiences of dress are intrinsic to his/her changing sensory perceptions. Similarly, James's aim was to inhabit his character's shell 'as the hand fits the glove', and the dress of the individual, he said, was the 'most personal shell of all'.[24] One could say that James and Woolf are moving toward a 'poetics' of dress. In the two short stories by James at which we shall be looking – 'The Author of *Beltraffio*' and 'The Siege of London' – he employs one of his favourite strategies with costume: the play between the meanings of black and white accents in dress, between negative and positive values, in the appearance of a central female character. He had used this contrast throughout *The Portrait of a Lady* and was to use it again in *The Wings of the Dove*. Here – in two stories written shortly after *The Portrait of a Lady* – we see how these contrasts affect the observers of the pure but terrible Mrs Ambient and the far-from innocent Mrs Headway and what their dress suggests about the way they feel and see themselves, within their circumstances.

The modern representation of character may then include a character's *experience* of clothes, the clothes of others, as well as how it feels to be inside the 'shell' or 'glove' of dress. This in its turn will shape a character's self-image in relation to society. Life surely feels very different inside the rib-crushing whalebone stays and petticoats of Rosamond Vincy in 1830 to the way it feels inside the vaporous draperies of Lily Bart, in the consumer-capitalist New York of 1900 of Edith Wharton's *The House of Mirth*. Yet the imperatives of self-adornment fuelling Rosamond's destructiveness – trapped as she is in her prescribed, decorative role – also consume Lily as she strives to represent an ideal of womanhood which no longer has any real basis. Her self-fashioning – undertaken in a place and period of apparently increased female freedoms – is fatally misinterpreted by a society whose only ideals are cash-based.

As Lily reaches the lowest layers of New York society, she keeps by her the white dress which she believed represented her social role as *jeune fille à marier* – marriage being fiction's fairy-tale ending, and indeed, Lily's only career-option. White dresses may seem to be the most insistent dress-note throughout this study, and the white dress *par excellence* is of course the wedding dress. Present-day designer-fashion shows, maintaining the fairy tale, also always conclude with the wedding dress – the display of the most gorgeous and most symbolic dress of all. So I conclude my study with some wedding dresses in fiction. But here, when we might reasonably expect the realist novelist to indulge in a lavish description of the heroine's happiest moment, what we find, more often than not, is no description at all. Wedding dresses are avoided, or when they are described – as in Charles Dickens's *Great Expectations* – they are not indicative of happiness. On the basis of what we have seen in earlier chapters in this book we should be in a position finally to ask why this is so. These are, after all, the dresses most likely to be put away and treasured, perhaps also those which least reflect the vagaries of a passing fashion. Why are the most expensive, most valuable, most obviously attractive dresses finally so ignorable?

Each of the discussions of texts is accompanied in this book by paintings or engravings of approximately the same date. These are not intended to be illustrations of the novels concerned, but are there to give a general image of the period as well as information on a particular style of dress. They provide information which might have been readily available to a contemporary reader but is less available to most of us now. They should not only help toward an understanding of the text, but in an another way to make the world of the text more tangible, and therefore more accessible to the reader.

Jonathan Bate has remarked on the continuing astonishing popularity of Jane Austen and Thomas Hardy: ' year in, year out their books have gone on selling.... What is the source of their enduring appeal? There is a cynical answer to this question, which could be summarized as *frocks and smocks.*'[25] Bate suggests that our longing for a lost world of empire-line dresses, grand houses and good manners on the one hand, and nostalgia for a simple, timeless way of life among English fields and hedgerows on the other, accounts for this phenomenon. I would also suggest that the recent marked increase in the filming and televising of the novels not only of Austen and Hardy, but also of Henry James, George Eliot and William Thackeray, is at least partly responsible for such popularity, for it has enabled us to experience vicariously the 'feel' of past lives. The year 2000 may have sharpened a general interest in history, but televised and filmed recreations of the past have been for some years an increasingly profitable part of the world of popular entertainment. And, perhaps, not simply popular entertainment. One of a panel of scholars, discussing various film versions of Henry James's novels, wondered 'what it is about the film [*Wings of the Dove*] that I really found very entertaining'. 'Great clothes', said another member of the panel. 'Is that what it was?' 'I think that was it', answered the second critic, and added, 'I think that was the key, the clothes.'[26]

Instead of asking directly what things mean or where they necessarily lead, we might ask – what are things like?[27] Direct questions about what cultural artefacts mean tend to come up with a predictable range of answers dependent on the presuppositions of the questioner. Cultural artefacts may lead in one direction, but there is always the possibility of a counter-current, of a different use, of another unthought-of implication. We are constantly led, of course, toward simple and easily graspable interpretations: in looking at dress in these texts, I shall unavoidably be suggesting from time to time what things might mean or where they might lead, but I also want to avoid the traps of reductivism. I want to ask what this particular thing, 'Dress', is *like*, what is its value as a thing experienced and observed. This is less a question of recording the shifts in the shape or movement of hemlines and collars, but more one of 'impressions', visual, tactile or psychological – never, however, losing sight of the fact that those impressions are governed by material facts. The costume historian Ann Buck, assessing the documentary value of novelistic descriptions of dress, concludes that a novel 'can give more. It shows dress in action within the novelist's world'.[28] I want to give a sense of what it is to be dressed for that world, for the' carnival' of fiction – that cultural phenomenon which is to entertain and enlighten the reader.

–2–

The Fatal Dress:
Daniel Defoe's *Roxana*

In the 1720s people all over town – London, in this case – were putting on their costumes for the carnival. Masquerade balls were *the* fashionable recreation; accounts of the most recent ball jostled for importance with accounts of war and politics in the journals of the time. In Carol Shields's stories people are preparing their costumes to assume their daily lives, as well as their fictional roles for the reader; wealthy people in early eighteenth-century London were buying or hiring disguises from the costume warehouses which had sprung up around Covent Garden, in order to play out their fantasies at masquerade balls, in assembly rooms and temporarily adapted theatres. The costumes on offer were, as Terry Castle explains in her study of the masquerade, 'to some degree conventionalized; ... certain disguises appear again and again'[1] – one of the most popular of these disguises was the Turkish dress. It is on a version of the Turkish dress that the plot of Daniel Defoe's novel, *Roxana: The Fortunate Mistress*, hangs. I propose first to examine Defoe's very 'solidly specific' account of this key dress 'moment' and then to return to the point at the start of the novel where dress starts to become an engine of the plot. This is not the story of single, fixed images, but of dress in movement, in metamorphosis, unpredictable and treacherous.

The Turkish dress is worn at the centre of the novel, at a private, masked party in Roxana's luxurious London apartments. It is when she wears the dress that the name 'Roxana' becomes fixed to the protagonist, and it is this moment that establishes her celebrity as a Court Beauty, and is the pinnacle of her sexual, social and economic success. This is her account of her triumph, at the point where the masked courtiers enter her drawing-room:

[I]n less than half an Hour I return'd, dress'd in the Habit of a *Turkish Princess*; the habit I got at *Leghorn*, when my *Foreign Prince* bought me a *Turkish* Slave ... with this *Turkish* Slave, I bought the rich Cloaths too: The Dress was extraordinary fine indeed, I had bought it as a Curiosity, having never seen the like; the

Robe was a fine Persian, or India Damask; the Ground white, and the Flowers blue and gold, and the Train held five Yards: the Dress under it, was a Vest of the same, embroider'd with Gold, and set with some Pearl in the Work, and some Turquois Stones; to the Vest, was a Girdle five or six Inches wide, after the *Turkish* Mode; and on both Ends where it join'd, or hook'd, was set with Diamonds for eight inches either way, only they were not true Diamonds; but no-body knew that but myself.

The Turban, or Head-dress, had a Pinnacle on the top, but not above five Inches, with a piece of loose Sarcenet hanging from it; and on the Front, just over the Forehead, was a good jewel, which I had added to it.[2]

We should note that the perspective of this description is different from that of the narrative action: Roxana is not recording her dress as she saw herself or was seen in it, but remembering, with the sensuous recall of the wearer, intimate details and secrets: its exoticism, its volume, its fastenings, its colours and most especially its jewels. These jewels are both genuine and fake – only Roxana knows which is which: a secret she keeps until the 'now' of her narration. The memory of the dress is therefore a part of the private, confessional framework of the narrative as well as a crucial, public moment in the story itself. It is, as David Blewett puts it, 'a device linking the public immorality of the masquerade party, Defoe's vivid example of the moral and social decay of his age, directly to the destruction of private individuals'.[3] Roxana tells us that she must relate her story 'as if I was speaking of another-body' (6). What is conveyed here, importantly, is a sense of the occult 'alterity' of clothes: for Roxana, her Turkish dress is a desirable, intimately familiar object, but when wearing it, she takes on another identity – the dress, it would seem, has a life of its own. It is first seen as a triumphantly beautiful image, defining her social body; once it is taken off, it becomes the hidden body within her lodgings, then finally, taking an uncontrollable and subversive hold of the minds of the characters, it waits, an assassin in the shadows.

As an exotic disguise, of course, the dress itself obscures her identity. One of the objects of masquerade costume, as Terry Castle explains, 'was to gratify, horrify or seduce'; the other was to define 'a second self at the furthest remove from the actual'.[4] Roxana first attracts the attention of a masked stranger and dances with him, but refuses a partner for her Turkish dance, claiming that such was the 'Mahometan' custom. Her guise is thus successfully seductive, but she extends 'Turkishness' beyond dress to Islamic religious taboos, confusing the rules of masquerade, which assumed an absolute opposition between the disguise and the real individual beneath. Disguised as a lascivious 'houri', she advertises the good Christian Englishwoman beneath, for whom dancing is perfectly proper. Castle characterizes masquerade dress as essentially ironic, but Defoe's use of it seems doubly even trebly ironic: Roxana performs as the 'stage' oriental seductress, but she insists she is untouchable according to *actual* Islamic custom. Is she therefore really a promiscuous Englishwoman beneath? In insisting on the dress as moral signifier, however, with a meaning *beyond* masquerade, she risks taking on aspects of the dress which, as we shall see, cannot be put on and off at will.

Independent of male direction, Roxana controls her own performance. Unlike her guests, however, she is not masked, and is thus unable to control the association of face with dress, a triumph now, but a danger to come. For the moment, however, her attractions are enhanced by her dance, which is actually new and French, although 'they all thought it had been *Turkish* ... one Gentleman had the Folly to expose himself so much, as to say ... that he had seen it danc'd at *Constantinople*; which was ridiculous enough' (176). The fake is more pleasing than the real thing, performed later by other ladies attempting to steal Roxana's thunder: 'as mine had the French Behaviour under the Mahometan Dress, it ... pleas'd much better' (179). At the end of the dance Roxana is uproariously applauded, 'and one of the Gentlemen cry'd out, *Roxana! Roxana!* by —, with an Oath; upon which foolish Accident I had the Name of *Roxana* presently fix'd upon me' (176).

The name is the one she chooses to use throughout the narrative, and the title of Defoe's book, but like the diamonds and the dance, it is false. It may be a name borrowed from any one of several Heroic tragedies with exotic settings; or it may be intended to recall Alexander the Great's mistress. Roxana even uses the name generically, contemptuously calling herself 'a meer Roxana', distancing herself from her 'other', indecent body. Only once does she let her real first name slip, when her maid Amy contacts Roxana's lost daughter – '*Amy* and Susan (for she was my own Name) began an intimate Acquaintance' (205). But we never learn her full name, or those of her two husbands, whose names she would also have borne. As Roxana says herself at the end of her story, 'secrets shou'd never be open'd without evident Utility' (326).

David Blewett's account of *Roxana* sees the protagonist as 'passively evil'[5] and the novel as conveying a cumulative sense of tragedy, charting Roxana's 'secret hell within'. The abrupt reversals of the final short paragraph of the novel certainly speak of catastrophes; but like the details of her name, explanations are frustratingly withheld: she has, after all, only just said that 'telling all' is a bad risk. To the last, she delights in her deceptions, not just for their own sake, but because of the power they confer, over the reader – who must share her delight – as much as over other characters. Her zest in 'counterfeiting' is, however, interwoven with penitential interpolations – the 'hell within'. Repentance usually accompanies *deteriorating* fortunes, but here Roxana's self-castigation is undermined by further successes. Repentance itself could be read as counterfeit, what she herself calls 'Storm-Repentance' (128), inserted retrospectively into the narrative after the final, unexplained calamity.

We might refer to the theatre here – since so much of Roxana's story is performance – and to the comedic tradition from late Shakespeare, to Jonson, Wycherley and Congreve, where we find time and again that the last laugh is with whoever holds the last secret. Roxana's story is one of successful manipulation of adverse circumstances, until the final, abrupt reversal torpedoes any kind of resolution – tragic or comic. It has not after all been a story of unalloyed triumph; there was a hidden, corrosive fear threading its way through the story, enslaving and imprisoning: fear of *not* holding the last secret, fear of exposure by way of the Turkish dress: fear that sacrifices natural affection to social and economic security, and which culminates in bitter regret and untold disaster. We do not finally know the circumstances of the dénouement, whether there was an uncovering of a body, a name, or a dress; I suggest that the narrative disintegrates into chaos, rather than moving to a tragic reckoning.

Roxana the novel has a muddled early history, remaining anonymous for fifty years and, until late in its career, like Roxana herself, it was denied respectable attention. Although rarely the subject of critical comment, its manifestly unsatisfactory ending was frequently expanded or rewritten by successive editors. Publishers felt free to amend, and critics to ignore the novel, because it appeared to fall into the popular but ignoble category of 'secret history', of which Eliza Heywood's *The Unfortunate Mistress*, was an obvious predecessor, although the two novels share little beyond a similar title. These 'secret histories' titillatingly chronicled the lives of criminals and prostitutes, the private vices underlying public lives of the Restoration Court, and as John Richetti notes, they describe 'a fascinated and envious condemnation of "aristocratic" decadence ... a world of upper-class violence and sensuality where women are the main victims'.[6]

Roxana, despite the claims of the original title page to be a 'History of the Lady Roxana in the Time of King Charles II'[7] does not really follow this 'secret history' pattern. It employs a shifting location and time-frame which contains the Restoration court *and* the city-merchant life of the 1720s, Defoe's purpose being to warn his own age against falling into 'the same vile debauch'd Taste of King Charles the Second's Reign'.[8] Roxana is not only the languishing beauty of Sir Peter Lely's portraits, panting for a little victimization, but also a brisk businesswoman of Hogarth's early eighteenth-century London, who manages her assets with the finesse of the new consumer-capitalist middle classes. Rather than being a prurient peep at the scandals of a libertine court, *Roxana*, like so many of Defoe's narratives, is more of a survival manual: an account of a lone woman's success in the business jungle of the eighteenth-century city, just as *Robinson Crusoe* is an account of a practical man's management of an untamed wilderness.

Roxana's dance before the courtiers also combines the fashionable recreations of the two periods. Defoe exploits the current commercial craze for masquerades, but elides it with the earlier Stuart Court Masque, an elite and elaborately costumed affair, which concluded with a dance between performers and courtly spectators. The Turkish costume was a favourite among masquerade disguises, but costume designs by Inigo Jones, for example, for the Stuart masques of the early seventeenth-century, also frequently featured Oriental styles. In a masque, words, music and costume are imposed on the performer – Roxana, however, controls her own scenario, and invents her own costume. A watchful clear-headedness marks the marketing of herself – 'we were no more than two Adulterers, in short, a Whore and a Rogue' (43), she says of herself and the first of her lovers. If success lies in displaying her dress, security lies in concealing its place in her history – she must be constantly alert to its moral import as well as its seductive powers. The threads of meaning which form the dress lead both back and forward in time, and to unravel their significance we need to turn to the rags which start the narrative journey.

If dancing celebrates Roxana's triumph, it is also the cause of her disastrous first marriage. At the time of this marriage she recalls that she 'danc'd, *as some say,* naturally, lov'd it extremely' (6). John Richetti draws attention to Roxana's mockery of 'natural' talent – these are 'social acquirements'.[9] She is launched into society, lacking 'neither Wit, Beauty, or Money'; but these advantages lead to marriage with a fool, an 'Eminent Brewer … [who] danc'd well, which, *I think,* was the first thing that brought us together' (7). His dancing talent proves no guide to his general abilities, being his only talent, and he runs through her money and his own, playing the aristocrat and neglecting his brewing business. Social accomplishments are exposed as artificial and useless, as we see when Roxana, abandoned by her bankrupt husband, is responsible for her own and her children's survival: 'one single woman not bred to Work … to get the Bread of five Children, that was not possible' (15).

Roxana, then, is not an adventuress from the underworld of the 'secret histories', a Moll Flanders born in Newgate, but a genteel young woman who might, in future, step from the novels of Jane Austen or Fanny Burney, and who, through no fault of her own, tumbles overnight from middle-class comfort to face the realities of starvation in the city's lower depths. When her family refuse help, we see Roxana in tears, in an empty parlour, 'sitting on the Ground, with a great Heap of old Rags, Linnen and other things about me, to see if I had any thing among them that would Sell or Pawn' (17). Before the nineteenth-century democratization of fashion we might remember that clothes represented a substantial investment. Dresses were passed down in wills, people went to prison for stealing handkerchiefs. The main criminal trade in John Gay's *Beggar's Opera* (1728) is in clothes. For all but the upper-classes, clothing was acquired second-, third- and even fourth-hand. Roxana is therefore viewing her few remaining assets: it is at this point that the novel's one named central character steps in – the maid Amy.

Roxana at first calls Amy 'this poor girl, my Maid', praising her 'Kindness and Fidelity' (16); but then describes her as a 'cunning Wench, and faithful to me, as the Skin to my Back' (25), adding to the conventional image of a loyal servant the more complex intimacy of an alter ego, a second skin, the one constant beneath changing dresses. Amy is, as John Mullan says, both Roxana's accomplice and her 'bad angel.... Her role is to have thoughts which her mistress cannot have allowed herself to entertain.'[10] Roxana, after all, is not Moll Hackabout of Hogarth's *Harlot's Progress*, imitating the modes and mores of 'high life'; she possesses, as Ronald Paulson points out, 'a genteel sense which sets [her] off from the other denizens of [the] underclass'.[11] Amy proposes that Roxana start to retrieve her fortunes by disposing of her children. '[T]he Misery of my own Circumstances', she says in her confessional commentary, 'hardened my Heart against my own Flesh and Blood', but, evading the reality of her heartlessness, she leaves 'the Management of the whole Matter to my Maid, Amy' (19).

Through trickery Amy foists the children onto relatives, and then prepares Roxana for the next step to survival in a man's world, the seduction of their landlord to secure board and lodging. To Roxana's conventional protests about her honour, Amy replies 'I think Honesty is out of the Question, when Starving is the Case' (28). So, like Judith preparing to slay Holofernes, Roxana organizes supper and then does what she can with her appearance; 'I had dressed me as well as I could, for tho' I had good Linnen left still, yet I had but a poor Head-Dress, and no Knots [ribbons], but old Fragments; no Necklace, no Ear-Rings ... However, I was tight and clean, and in better Plight than he had seen me in a great while' (29). To sell herself, the packaging has to be right.

The moral values of white linen, cleanliness and neatness would not have been lost on Roxana's landlord, a middle-class, propertied, London jeweller, whose trade takes him to Holland. Holland was home to those Protestant virtues linking cleanliness to godliness and thrift, and in 1688, its royal family had sent Prince William to sit on the English throne, a sober replacement for Stuart libertinism. Roxana's charms, bereft of ornament, but enhanced by a white linen cap, collar and cuffs on a dark ground, are precisely those to attract such a man. The values she represents here are genuine enough – she is indeed poor, still honest and husbandless. The sad austerity of her appearance – her landlord assumes she is widowed – counteracts and conceals the imminent indecencies of her enterprise and his desires: we might see her as Lely's Nell Gwyn dressed to join the housewives of De Hooch or Terboch. Anne Hollander, noting the way that black 'with a touch of white linen' takes over in seventeenth-century Holland, sees this as 'adding the idea of modesty'[12] to the bourgeois and professional values of dark clothing. Roxana's talent for social performance is now turned to good account.

The business of seduction is approached with many protestations of 'Honesty', 'Virtue', and 'Affection', but Amy hard-headedly points Roxana to the inevitable end of all this polite foreplay: 'Come, pray Madam, let me go air you a clean Shift; don't let him find you in foul Linnen on the Wedding-Night.' (37) This may be shameless adultery, but at least the underwear is clean. It is characteristic of Defoe's narrators, as Mullan remarks, 'that while striving to survive in a world of reductive commercial values, they still keep up a sense of other values – even as they betray them'.[13] With the various guises that she puts on, Roxana recognizes and mimics the values they represent, believing they can be discarded, like collars, cuffs and shifts.

This is only the first 'betrayal'. So far, Amy has been the instigator and director of Roxana's actions, but in a subsequent extraordinary scene, Roxana makes sure that Amy is truly her 'second skin': 'I fairly stript her, and then I threw open the Bed, and thrust her in' to the waiting arms of the landlord-lover – 'as I thought myself a Whore ... my Maid should be a Whore too, and should not reproach me with it' (46, 47). By this perversely brutal act (without so much as a clean shift), Roxana establishes a kind of moral superiority over the landlord, with his cosy social pretence that he is their 'lodger', and Amy, with her faith in a no-nonsense view of their situation. Roxana has re-defined the situation, invented, as Richetti says, a 'new reality', a tableau of literally naked truth, and has denied the pair 'their respective claims on Roxana as ideological masters'.[14]

A *modus vivendi* is established, until, some years and several children later, Roxana and her lover make a business visit to Paris. Leaving the bulk of his jewels and wealth with Roxana, the jeweller sets out for Versailles to meet a potential buyer. He is, however, robbed and killed. She has described her relations with the jeweller warmly, so we have no reason to discount her sorrow at his death, but the pages itemizing the wealth she now possesses outnumber those describing her 'Excesses of Grief'. Indeed, she is swift to secure her possessions, instructing Amy in London to sell the furniture and remove 'all the Plate and Linnen' (55) from the house before her lover's family can (rightly) claim their inheritance, letting it be thought in Paris that the robbers had made off with most of her 'husband's' wealth and jewels. She is now in the interesting situation of a young, beautiful 'widow' in distress in foreign lands – her real wealth, in London and Paris, is concealed.

As she is the innocent victim of the tragic outcome of the jeweller's transactions, his intended customer, an unnamed 'Prince' at Versailles, proposes to compensate Roxana for her misfortune. Like a Tragedy Queen, she prostrates herself in tearful gratitude before him, 'dress'd in a kind of half-Mourning ... and my Head, *tho' I had yet no Ribbands or Lace*, was so dress'd, as fail'd not to set me out with Advantage enough, for I began to understand his Meaning' (61). Having quickly discarded full mourning, which she describes as 'a most frightful thing' (57), she will now be in softer colours: greys or mauves with touches of white – and richer materials. 'Subdued patterns and even silk fabrics were allowed',[15] replacing the unattractive dull crepe of full mourning. In fact, Lou Taylor records that mourning dress had become quite chic by the end of the seventeenth-century: Samuel Pepys, in 1666, 'commented on the appearance of "my Lady Falmouth ... now in second or third mourning and pretty pleasant in her looks"'.[16] The Prince, indeed, declares Roxana 'the most beautiful Creature on Earth' (61), and the way is open for her most successful career move.

In relation to events, Roxana's mourning is genuine, but as a sign of grief it is belied by her real motive – seduction. Mourning-dress marks the independent status of widowhood, but, of course, it also signals her renewed availability. This time the preliminaries are brief, though once more they involve a change of costume, to an inner 'packaging', which clarifies the availability suggested by half-mourning. After a late supper, Roxana retires to undress but returns 'in a new Dress, which was, in a manner, *une Deshabile*, but so fine, and all about me so clean and agreeable' (64). Incongruously bourgeoise even at this point, she reminds us of the value of cleanliness.

'*Déshabillé'*, or 'undress', was not in fact underwear as we know it, but informal, relaxed clothing for indoor use. In the early part of the eighteenth century, 'undress' was standard morning-wear, though, in keeping with the low moral tone of the Restoration period, 'undress' at Charles II's court was generally *de rigueur*: Lely's portraits of the 'Windsor Beauties' showed them 'undressed'. Undress also involved an element of role-playing: Lely's ladies in their tumbling, provocative draperies could pass themselves off as classical goddesses, even Christian saints – Nell Gwyn was represented as St Agnes. There was, however, an etiquette involved: 'a person of inferior rank had to be fully and formally dressed when attending a person of superior rank',[17] Roxana's dress therefore suggests a change of status in her relationship with the Prince, as well as her recognition of the Prince's 'meaning' – undress always had its wanton aspects. Undress also anticipates Roxana's Turkish dress, being loose and often oriental in style – '"It is only a loose Habit, My Lord," says I' (64). It would be nice to think that the pun was intended, as the paragraph ends in bed.

The picaresque novel of sixteenth-century Spain measured the progress of its heroes by changes of costume. With her middle-class origins, Roxana is not, strictly speaking, a *picara*, but her spectacular career move in becoming the Prince's mistress is registered, like the career of the *picaras*, in an expanded wardrobe. She carefully points out that the Prince's gifts are unsolicited, as she is already (secretly) 'Mistress of ten Thousand Pounds' (65); but she revels in the dresses he sends her: 'a Suit ... of the finest Brocaded Silk, figur'd with Gold, and another with Silver, and another of Crimson; so that I had three Suits of Cloaths, such as the Queen of France would not have disdain'd' (70). 'I had no less than five several Morning Dresses besides these,' she crows, 'so that I need never be seen twice in the same Dress.' (71)

' Yet', she says, 'I went out nowhere.' (70) Her dresses are, in fact, *not* seen, for the jaws of the trap she is creating for herself are closing round her. Because of the Prince's position, his wife, his other mistresses, she must live immured in secret lodgings. Concealment from the jeweller's family, business associates, or even disappointed robbers, is also essential, for exposure of her real wealth, her real relation to the jeweller, would put an end to this enjoyable new prosperity. The imperatives which drive her are no longer those of survival, but an appetite for gain on the one hand, and the fear of disclosure, on the other. Luxury – the pursuit of 'anything unneeded' – as John Sekora's study makes clear, was in eighteenth-century England a 'volatile and political'[18] issue. Social and economic changes challenged Biblical definitions of luxury as the ultimate vice – it did after all provide 'a market for the nation's goods and increased the circulation of money'. While Defoe maintained throughout his writings that 'the new freedoms won by the middle orders could never reasonably be called luxury',[19] Roxana has clearly overreached herself and is physically and morally at risk. She is safe only indoors, where she can parade her trophy-wardrobe for her master alone. Even before she displays her Turkish dress, she is a slave in the seraglio.

This luxurious if reclusive existence is brought to an end after some years by the Prince's remorse at the death of his wife; but not before two apparently disconnected events foreshadow the climactic masque dance. First, a glimpse of her husband (who was not dead after all) at court underlines the danger of exposure. Subsequently, on a Grand Tour with the Prince, Roxana acquires some Turkish clothes and learns 'the Turkish Language; their Way of Dressing and Dancing' (102). After the Prince's departure, Roxana decides to leave France. She is now rich, 'richer than I knew how to think of' (110), but the problem is how to take it all with her – money and plate are heavy stuff. Shrewdly assessing her limitations, she turns to a Dutch merchant for help. Whether it is the persuasiveness of Roxana's physical or fiscal charms, we don't know, since she does not record any seductive costume moments. Later, however, when in bed with him, having got what she wants, she admits she had 'resolv'd from the Beginning he shou'd Lye with me' (143).

In her first encounter with the English jeweller, Roxana had simulated bourgeois Dutch virtues, and now she is offered the real thing – marriage with a Dutch merchant. Little stands in her way – her husband has vanished, she is rich, and fond of this notably kind man. But she turns him down in a proto-feminist argument for independence: 'a Wife must give up all she has ... whereas a Mistress makes the Saying true that what a Man has is hers, and what she has is her own' (132). Marital affection, for a woman, is a kind of slavery, she believes, a denial of self: 'a Woman gave herself entirely away from herself in Marriage ... the Marriage Contract was ... nothing but giving up Liberty, Estate, Authority, and every-thing, to the Man, and the Woman was indeed a meer Woman ever after, that is to say, a Slave' (147, 148). But liberty and greed are not her only motives; 'her ultimate ambition lies in a powerful androgyny'[20] – 'seeing Liberty seem'd to be the Men's Property, I wou'd be a Man-Woman; for as I was born free, I wou'd die so' (171). While rejecting the realities of life as a 'meer Woman', she fails to see that the reality of a mistress's role is also slavery – confined by fear of disclosure, and enslaved by the need to flatter and seduce. She is not wrong in her damning assessment of women's status, but her belief that she can free

Figure 1 Illustration to *The Beautiful Turk*, trans. from the French, *A Selection of Novels and Histories*, London: John Watt, 1729.

herself from the Female, and assume the Male, like another dress, is illusory.

Looking ahead thirty years, to Charlotte Lennox's *The Female Quixote*, of 1752, we find Lennox's heroine, Arabella, similarly trying to find an alternative to the mundane realities of a sensible marriage. It is not that the man in question is unacceptable, but that she identifies with the heroines of her favourite French Romances, set in some far time and place, for whom marriage is the *grande finale* to an exciting series of adventures, in which a beautiful heroine is the untouchable object of male worship. Arabella is waiting for these adventures to begin so that she can fulfil her heroic role; she knows that, once married, a heroine's independence vanishes, subsumed into the identity of another. Interestingly, her career-plans are also signalled in two exotic dresses: one is vaguely oriental in style, featuring a jewelled belt, and making teasing play with a veil. The other, although 'Roman', echoes Roxana's Turkish dress in its looser, *déshabillé* mode; it, too, causes a sensation at a ball, and sets a fashion. Both Arabella's dresses are based on styles she believes appropriate to 'Romance' heroines – as though the correct dress will somehow set her 'story' in motion. Roxana's dress, as we shall see, sets *her* story on its downward spiral.

Unlike Roxana, however, Arabella's illusions are naive and unworldly – she really believes that life is a French Romance. Her dresses are not calculated to serve any material or sexual end. They represent her bid for an independent identity, for an alternative female story, but the narrative ends in capitulation to social norms and marriage, and her recognition that she has been deluded by literature. The dresses are put away – forlorn flags of independence.

Roxana's declaration of independence, however, causes a breach with the merchant, and she moves back to London to try her fortunes, a venture culminating in her dance in the Turkish Dress. I have already suggested that she is deluded in her belief that the role of mistress buys a life of freedom: her appetite for wealth (and therefore men) and need for secrecy, build prison walls. Furthermore, she tells us that she bought her

Figure 2 Frontispiece to 1724 edition of Daniel Defoe, *Roxana: The Fortunate Mistress*, London: Constable, 1923.

Turkish dress from the booty of a ship captured off Leghorn. The dresses had belonged to Turkish ladies who were then sold into slavery. As Linda Colley's *Captives* makes clear, slavery in the Mediterranean, around 1700, was a two-way trade: 'Malta's sea-going Knights of St. John routinely preyed on Muslim vessels, seizing their crews and passengers and selling them in the open market'.[21] But Europeans were equally terrified of capture and slavery by Barbary corsairs: '[c]aptives and captivities were the underbelly of British Empire'.[22] Clothes – especially ones with other owners – can have occult aspects. The stolen Turkish dresses take revenge, reducing Roxana to the slavery of their rightful Muslim owners.

How would Defoe's readers have envisaged Roxana's masquerade dress? What images were current? 'One of the paradoxes of Barbary captive-taking', according to Colley, 'was that it not only exacerbated pre-existing hostility to Islam, but also increased the volume and variety of information available about it in Britain.'[23] The defeat of the Ottoman Empire in Vienna in 1683 had both lessened its threat and opened it up to the West. Volumes of *The Arabian Nights* were best-sellers between

Plate 1 J. B. Vanmour, *Lady Mary Wortley Montagu and Her Son.* 1713. National Portrait Gallery, London.

1704 and 1717; accounts and pictures of Turkish life were widely circulated, the best-known of these being Lady Mary Wortley Montague's letters from her travels in Turkey, as wife of the British ambassador. There was also a flood of painted and engraved portraits of Lady Mary in her Turkish dress – every female portrait in vaguely exotic costume was given her name. Of the many portraits of Lady Mary, two by J. B. Vanmour of 1713 – one with her son and Turkish servants, and the other a single, full-length – stand out as relevant, as Vanmour had lived in Turkey at the end of the seventeenth-century.

The harem, was by definition a hidden subject, and therefore '[a]ny study of the West's relations with the harem must be in large part a study of the imagination'.[24] The erotic thrill of forbidden glimpses of slavery and polygamy, jewelled and scented luxury, played a large part in the phenomenal appetite for images of Turkish women, but the authenticity of these early visions of '*turquerie*' must of necessity have involved a good deal of fantasy, drawing on illustrations to popular Romances (of the kind read by Lennox's Arabella), theatrical costume, as well as engraved and painted portraits, such as those of Lady Mary. For a reasonably accurate representation of Turkish dress we have look ahead to the Swiss artist, Jean-Etienne Liotard, 'who painted sitters in Constantinople and in fashionable western European capitals, dressed *à la turque*'.[25] His portrait, of 1754, of the Countess of Coventry, for example, features a white Robe, covered with small embroidered flowers, very like Roxana's 'India Damask: the Ground white, and the Flowers blue and gold' (174).

Lady Mary Wortley Montagu, however, seems to have adapted her Turkish garments to English fashions of *c.*1715. Her dress in the portraits by Charles Jervas, though featuring a blue *anteri* (an over-robe) over a white *salvar* (under-dress), is in silhouette and arrangement not very different from the contemporary European robe and petticoat. It is the turban and pointed slippers that lend exoticism. The two Vanmour portraits feature a rather different and possibly more authentically Turkish costume. Vanmour had published engravings of Turkish scenes and costumes in 1712, and the dress which Lady Mary wears in her portraits follows these closely, with its *décolleté*, relatively uncorseted bodice, white *salvar*, red under-vest, gold *anteri* and *kirk* (a furred over-robe). A turban, sometimes with 'a Pinnacle on the top', and a jewelled belt are important features of all the portraits and engravings. The voluptuousness of this image contrasts with the more angular lines of the fashions of 1715, and of the Jervas portraits. Vanmour's engravings of Lady Mary are a good deal more suggestive than the paintings, and may well be the images with which Defoe's readers were familiar, because more generally available. Turning to the engraved frontispiece of the 1724 edition of the novel, it is difficult not to conclude that the engraver has copied a Vanmour portrait and simply added jewels to the neck and fullness to the skirt, in the style of 1724. The come-hither look he has added to the face is justified by Lady Mary's own description of the erotic charge of Turkish dances: 'the motions so Languishing ... halfe falling back and then recovering themselves in so artfull a Manner that I am possitive the coldest and most rigid Prude upon Earth could not have looked upon them without thinking of something not to be spoke of'. Montagu also comments on the freedom the Muslim veil gave to women to move around – a freedom which, of course, depended on concealment – as well as their freedom from corsets, which she witnessed in the women's baths; but, as an antidote to such voluptuous attractions, she warns the recipient of her letter that ''tis no less than Death for a Man to be found in one of these places'.[26]

In decoding Roxana's Turkish dress, therefore, we need to look not only at Vanmour's portrait and the novel's frontispiece, but also at Lady Mary's own comments on Turkish women – at the tensions between a freely displayed eroticism in loose and revealing dresses and a life which was fiercely restrictive, excluding all male contact other than a single master. Having rejected the conventions of marriage which establish mutual contractual obligations, and set herself up in 'business' in London's expanding West End, Roxana's life appears to be the very opposite to that of an enslaved Turkish odalisque, or a powerless European wife. Yet her ambition leads her to wear the fatally revealing Turkish dress in an erotic display calculated to seduce the highest male in the land – 'the KING himself was in my eye' (172). Is she not courting the very sexual slavery she has scorned? – a slavery which the dress and its history certainly contains, and which is fixed on her by the name 'Roxana'. Turkish imagery was already suggestive, and it would not require a great imaginative leap for Defoe's readers to undress the image further. Roxana does it for us, in fact, by describing her discomfort after too much dancing: 'I wou'd have withdrawn and disrob'd, being somewhat too thin in that Dress, unlac'd, and open-breasted, as if I had been in my Shift.' (181) Later, she says she cannot wear it in public because 'it is not a decent Dress ... it was one Degree off from appearing in one's shift' (247). While these later descriptions are more intimate than the first, Roxana has grown uneasy with the dress; there is something unreliable about it.

As so often happens in Roxana's narrative, we never know the identity of the mysterious stranger who takes her as mistress – whether in fact it was the King, as she suggests. At any rate, her season of success culminates in three years of 'most glorious Retreat' 'with a Person, which Duty … obliges her not to reveal' (181). We might pause at the oxymoron, 'glorious retreat': 'glory' requires publicity, after all. Emerging from her 'retreat', with substantial spoils, she settles for a 'Lord', and lodgings chosen for 'Privacy' where 'I might live very handsomely, and yet not so publickly' (186). But life in this seraglio palls: the Lord 'grew worse and wickeder the older he grew' (199), and, with middle age upon her, Roxana begins to search for her children, sending Amy out into the city to trace their whereabouts. Having broached the walls of her seclusion, in the hope of re-entering society on respectable terms, her appearance will have to be reconsidered.

Amy's search uncovers the children's fates – some dead, a boy apprenticed, a girl unaccounted for and one in service, whom Amy finally traces. Alarmingly, she is a servant in Roxana's own household and therefore witness to her life as courtesan. Amy conceals her discovery, however, and, as controller of the household, dismisses the girl. As Roxana's 'second skin' she is a practised deceiver, and so acts swiftly when her own position is endangered by this new claim to Roxana's affections. Amy finally tells Roxana of the girl's existence, and though she cannot afford to give in to maternal feeling and reveal herself, Roxana sends money to the girl, with instructions to 'put herself into a good Garb … and fit herself to appear as a Gentlewoman' (204).

We have seen how pursuit of personal freedom and consumer goods – especially dress and most especially the Turkish dress – has resulted not in liberty and happy prosperity, but in fear and confinement. True happiness, she now suspects, may come from the shared pleasures of family life. It is time therefore for a change of values, location and dress. A proxy relationship with her daughter is not enough, and Roxana longs to be acceptable to her children and to society – but 'what Family of any Character will visit or be acquainted with a Whore?' (208) Her answer lies in the complexity and fluidity of the booming, early eighteenth-century city. Charles Saumarez Smith, describing the new importance of the location of dwellings in London of 1720, sees this reflected in novels, which 'stimulated the imagination of the reader into conjuring an appropriate location for the events which were described'.[27] Certain areas of London were associated not only with particular trades, but also with particular social groups: when the American painter Gilbert Stuart came to London in mid-century, he found lodgings in a Quaker area. To move to such an area, Roxana believes, would be to start a new life – to 'transform ourselves into a new Shape' (209) – and she sends Amy out to prospect. Amy

Figure 3 Puritan Dress – *Frontispiece* to *Cutter of Coleman Street: A Comedy* (anon.), London, 1727.

finds 'handsome' lodgings, in the old City with a 'Female Family ... nothing very gay; the People were Quakers, and I lik'd them the better' (210).

Roxana not only likes her new landlady but decides to *become* her: 'I pretended ... to be extreamly in Love with the Dress of the Quakers, and this pleas'd her so much, that she wou'd needs dress me up one Day in a suit of her own Cloaths; but my real Design was, to see whether it wou'd pass upon me for a Disguise ...'Why you look quite another-body", Amy declares, '"more than that, it makes you look ten Years younger".' (211) Roxana goes out into the town to test-run her new outfit – 'there was not a Quaker in the town look'd less like a Counterfeit than I did: ... this was my particular Plot ... that I might depend upon not being known, and yet need not be confin'd like a prisoner, and be always in Fear' (213). Roxana is in some ways returning to the costume in which she first seduced her landlord – her charms veiled in sober stuffs, but set off and rejuvenated by the flattery of white linen, an echo of seventeenth-century dress. In *Roxana*'s double time scheme, Roxana's Quaker dress in 1670, would be a risky statement of religious belief, but by 1720, Puritanism, which 'had been one of the major forces attacking dress as sinful, was no longer of major importance'.[28] Both views of the dress are possible. Roxana is right to see in Quakerism a release from slavery – the first voices against the slave trade were Quaker. But in assuming not only Quaker dress but also Quaker language, Quaker family life, she is adopting values that cannot be lightly laid aside. To exploit spiritual meanings is again to play with occult fires.

Roxana's metamorphosis into yet 'another-body' is a further instance of her successful role-playing, a packaging of herself for new 'customers', but it can also be read in terms of the masquerade. 'Fashion', as Terry Castle writes of the masquerade, 'is endlessly separable from truth', and what, under one dispensation, was a marker of religious faith, could mislead, or mock faith in another: in masquerades, or in life, 'one is always free to wear misleading dress, dress that is either playfully or criminally inappropriate'.[29] In eighteenth-century masquerades ecclesiastical dress was regularly mocked; often that of the Catholic Church, but 'Quakers, Methodists and other "Fanatick" sects had their impersonators too'.[30] She has chosen an identity diametrically opposed to that of 'a meer Roxana', and so, if she is still playing at masquerades, her Quaker dress now conceals a whore. Roxana, however, is *not* operating under the licence of masque or masquerade any more – she is supposed to have renounced such things in order to fit herself for re-entry into society and recovery of her children. But her 'playful' attitude to her Quaker dress, comparable to her delight in her Turkish guise, runs counter to any serious intent. Her amorality is not yet 'criminally inappropriate', but one could say that the bow is bent and drawn.

Taking on the outward show, if not the morals, of Quakerism, she thinks wistfully of the Dutch merchant's offer of marriage – Quaker values are essentially family values. Through a maze of coincidence the merchant arrives at the Quaker's house in search of Roxana, for he too has settled in this area of the City. For the first time, she is nonplussed. She needs him to carry out her plans for respectable family life; but this scheme depends on her credibility as a Quaker, and the merchant has known her as his materialistic and free-living mistress – knowledge that threatens her new identity. Deciding to see him, she swiftly accounts for the intervening years by claiming that she had piously retreated from the world, 'liv'd remote from London ... even my Dress wou'd let him see, that I did not desire to be known by any-body' (225) – resting her credibility on the contrast her present appearance makes to her earlier persona of a very wealthy, very Merry Widow.

What we see here is a version of one of the effects of the new consumer culture on women, identified by Bernard Mandeville in *The Fable of the Bees*, and discussed in G. J Barker-Benfield's *The Culture of Sensibility*. The increased availability of fashionable clothing could give all women 'an outward identity which invoked courtesy, civility, and "Esteem" from others, specifically a man',[31] an esteem previously accorded only to the upper-classes. Roxana gives this process an extra twist, securing the merchant's esteem by 'dressing-down': she embodies Protestant house-wifely thrift rather than courtly luxury. She must, however, burn or bury that Turkish dress, evidence of the reality of those hidden years, that very impious 'retreat'. Instead, during the Quakerish celebrations of her marriage – 'no Musick at-all, or Dancing' – Roxana gives in to her love of finery and unearths her 'great-many rich Cloaths'. She tells the merchant she will surprise him by dressing herself so 'that he wou'd not know his Wife when he saw her' (246). And she then appears in the Turkish dress, loaded with jewels, 'charming' the Quaker, and leaving the merchant 'perfectly astonish'd'. Roxana explains that the dress was bought for her by her 'husband' (the murdered jeweller), but that she will only wear it in private; a request that appears both sentimental and modest, but is in fact vital to her security.

After Roxana's Quaker/Turk double-act, we appear to be moving into the novel's concluding and happiest passages, detailing the couple's wealth and plans for a future in Holland. But Roxana has riskily disclosed her private 'body' to her new husband and to her friend, and she admits that she is 'Hag-ridden with Frights' (264). Now Roxana's 'heart' gnaws at her, and draws her into danger, to the progeny she has scattered with such apparent carelessness across her life, and in particular to Susan, the daughter who carries her name, and who, as Christopher Flint says, 'comes to represent all the children who have been neglected in Defoe's fiction'.[32]

At the point where she is poised to leave England with her new husband, Roxana starts to weave back through her narrative fabric to pick up the threads of Susan's story. Through a chance meeting, Susan has claimed Amy as her mother, and linked her with the celebrated courtesan she once served. Amy and Roxana are puzzled and terrified, for although the girl is 'quite wrong in some things, she was yet so right in others' (269). Amy persuades Susan that she is not her mother, but then Susan cries that 'if she were not her Mother, Madam Roxana was her Mother then'; and concludes by threatening, 'with a kind of Smile ... I know how it all is, well enough' (270). Reporting back, Amy horrifies Roxana by proposing that they murder the girl. Roxana threatens violence to Amy herself, if anything of the sort should happen, but confesses 'I wou'd not have been seen, so as to be known by the Name of Roxana, no, not for a Thousand Pounds' (271) – not just at the point where respectability and safety in Holland lie within her grasp. The threads of the narrative thus draw together for a dark version of a comedic dénouement, where children find parents, secrets are revealed, marriages made and justice done.

The wife of the Captain – whose ship is to take Roxana and her husband to Holland – has befriended Susan. Mother and daughter coincidentally meet when Roxana and the merchant come to view their shipboard accommodation. Roxana is terrified that Susan will identify her if she sees her with Amy, or worse still, if she associates her with the Turkish dress: 'it was the only valuable Secret in the World to me'. Her emotion at the formal kiss of greeting with Susan is the most powerful in the novel – this reunion with her child is what she has wanted – and yet 'the whole of my Prosperity' (275/6/7) depends on concealment. Roxana carries it off, until, in 'a Thunder-Clap', the Captain's wife and Susan both swear they have seen her before. Roxana persuades them that this is impossible, but, as she says, 'I am not come to the worst of it' (282).

The threads tighten when the Captain's wife and Susan call unexpectedly at Roxana's lodgings to find her '"in a kind of *Dishabille* ... a loose Robe ... after the Italian Way ... showing the Body in its true Shape, and perhaps, a little too plainly, if it had been worn where any Men were to come'. The 'revealing' aspects of the dress grow alarming, when the girl says that Roxana's loose robe is 'just such a Thing as I told you ... the Lady danc'd in' (284), and to Roxana's horror, the others beg Susan to tell them more. She prolongs her story unbearably, picking up past threads with menacing circularity, talking of having seen Roxana 'several times in her *Dishabille*' (287), and goes on to describe the Turkish dress, which proves 'so compleat an Account of every-thing in the Dress, that my friend the Quaker colour'd at it, and look'd two or three times at me ... for (as she told me afterwards) she immediately perceiv'd it was the same Dress that she had seen me have on' (288–9). Ironically, Susan lavishes praise on Roxana; 'nothing but an Angel was like her ... her Hair and Head-Dress ... shone like the Stars' (290). What we witness is a replay of Roxana's first performance for the male courtiers, but now experienced through a spectator's eyes, rather than in Roxana's secret memory. The dress is reconstituted for the reader in Susan's narrative, and freshly evoked for the fictional listeners – women, whose attention to detail will be close and precise.

Struck by Susan's description, the Quaker 'innocently began a description of *mine*; and nothing terrify'd me so much as the Apprehension lest

she shou'd importune me to show it' – which of course she does, supported by the others. Quickly, Roxana explains that the dress is packed
for the voyage, but should they happen to be in Holland, 'they shou'd see
me dress'd in it' (291). For the moment, the situation is saved; but Susan
returns to question the Quaker, convinced that the dress is the key to her
mother's identity – 'the Girl was in a great Passion when she talk'd of the
Habit ... she wou'd go over [to Holland] on purpose' (293). Roxana post-
pones her journey and leaves London in a panic, but the girl swears she
will follow her. The pursuit of lost children has, with savage irony, become
a flight from 'this impertinent Girl, who was now my Plague' (302) – not
a term used lightly by the author of *A Journal of the Plague Year*.

Imprisoned by fear of exposure, dependent on Amy (who knows all her
secrets) and on the Quaker (who knows none) for news of her daughter,
Roxana is powerless to control events. After further threats of violence
against Susan, she throws Amy out, an action that only leaves her more
helpless and prey to worse nightmares – 'Sometimes I thought I saw
[Susan] with her throat cut, sometimes with her Head cut, and her Brains
knock'd out' (325). Suspecting that Susan is dead, and having lost sight
of Amy, Roxana sends the Quaker, her new alter ego, as a beneficent
emissary to her remaining daughter, before leaving for Holland. When
Roxana meets her last daughter, 'I was dress'd-up in a Quaker's Habit,
and look'd so like a Quaker, that it was impossible for them, who had
never seen me before, to suppose I had ever been anything else' (329).
Pleased with her final 'counterfeit', she arrives in Holland 'with all the
Splendor and Equipage suitable to our new Prospect' (329). The dénouement, a 'Blast of Heaven', strikes Roxana and Amy in the final seven lines
of the novel – but whether this 'blast' is the exposure of Roxana's identity, Susan's body or the Turkish dress, we never know.

Although Roxana's last guise is one of sober virtue, the Turkish dress
is still there, packed in a trunk. The dress moves, shadowing her, always
there – fixed to her name and her face, contained in all her guises, meta-
morphosing into its Puritan opposite, kept and worn not once but many
times. Looking ahead 150 years, to one of Henry James's early ghost
stories, 'A Romance of Certain Old Clothes', we might find an echo of
Roxana in its strange conclusion. James's protagonist is found, horribly
dead, in front of a trunk full of her sister's dresses; a sister whose death
she has willed, and whose dresses she coveted and tried to possess. It is
in fact an awkward ending since we are bound to question the mechanics
of a dress as killer. Defoe, however, having represented Roxana's dress
with Jamesian 'solidity of specification', and repeatedly impressing it on
our memories, omits its final role in a catastrophe whose narrative

decomposes rapidly, as though some Last Trump has sounded to devour 'this crumbling pageant' at its 'last and dreadful hour'.[33]

'The masquerade', as Terry Castle says, 'itself masquerades. Ostensibly the scene of pleasure, it is actually a scene of snares – a region of manipulation, disequilibrium and sexual threat.'[34] Roxana manipulates her contradictory disguises with seeming success, but since she is unable to relinquish that triumphal symbol of her sexual power, the Turkish dress, the dress itself takes over, moving in on her moral disequilibrium – the fears that corrode her security. Even when the dress is absent, when Roxana herself sits talking like a good Quaker wife, she is its prisoner.

A dress represents alterities, other lives. Fugitive too from an earlier life, the heroine of Milan Kundera's novel *Ignorance* returns to her native country and, needing warmer clothes, tries on a dress in a shop. Like Roxana, she is seized by panic: 'through the magic power of a dress, she saw herself imprisoned in a life she didn't want and from which she was unable to escape. It was as if, once, at the start of her adult life, she had had before her several possible lives, amongst which she had chosen the one that led to France. And as if those other lives, disowned and discarded, lay always ready for her, jealously waiting in the shadows. One of these now seized her, and pinioned her in the new dress, like a straitjacket.'[35] Kundera's heroine frees herself from the dress, but all that we know of Roxana's fate suggests that something waiting in the shadows finally and fatally emerges – like the vengeful dresses in James's trunk. Contained in 'the magic power of a dress' are the lives of lost and rejected children, of discarded husbands and lovers, the distant shade of a Turkish captive, and Roxana's own vortex of identities.

As the dress is to Roxana, so Roxana is to society – a 'potentially disruptive or socially unstabilized energy', one of those 'displaced figures' of the early English novel, identified by Tony Tanner as threatening social institutions 'whether by the indeterminacy of their origin, the uncertainty of the direction in which they will focus their unbounded energy, or their attitude to the ties that hold society together'.[36] Roxana and her dress are unstable, unstoppable and beautiful. If Roxana was to serve as an object lesson of where the primrose paths of aristocratic, Restoration *mores* led, as opposed to the ways of the 'Enlightened' middle classes, then which path are we to suppose she took? Defoe, her declared historian, seems to vanish and leave us with the spectacle of her final decomposition – her return to the rags from which she had once so efficiently risen.

–3–

Talk About Muslin:
Jane Austen's *Northanger Abbey*

Sarah Byng, the heroine of one of Hilaire Belloc's *Cautionary Verses*, refuses to learn to read, and subsequent events confirm her 'instinctive guess/That Literature breeds distress'. The debate about the propriety of novel-reading for young women, a subject for comic verse at the end of the nineteenth-century, was a very real one in the second half of the eighteenth-century. If Arabella, the heroine of Charlotte Lennox's *The Female Quixote* of 1752, had contented herself with the usual female occupations of 'Dressing, Dancing and Tattling over Tea-tables' rather than devouring French Romances and dressing herself like a fictional heroine, she might happily have accepted marriage and a life of insignificance, and not longed for adventures which get her into such trouble. Unlike the case of Roxana, her adventures are not motivated by the need for survival, but by an active imagination bored and frustrated with her empty – if comfortable – life. Arabella's reading frees her to imagine worlds beyond her own dull one (to which she must finally capitulate), and this makes her a more complex character – Sarah Byng was, after all, as Belloc tells us, 'a most uncultured gal'.[1]

Catherine Morland, heroine of Jane Austen's novel of 1798, *Northanger Abbey*, although another enthusiastic Romance-reader, is, unlike Arabella, only sketchily educated. Her naive imagination has been fed by the novels of Ann Radcliffe, a contemporary of Austen, whose Gothic novels – *The Mysteries of Udolpho, The Romance of the Forest* and *The Italian* – were best-sellers. Mrs Radcliffe's heroines are beautiful, pure and persecuted. These young and unprotected women, fleeing through landscapes of ruined castles, dense forests, towering mountains and bottomless ravines, were subject to multiple threats. Murder, incest, concealed passages, supernatural phenomena, wicked nuns, monks and uncles ensured that no Radcliffe heroine ever has a decent night's sleep nor a moment to change her dress – which was nonetheless invariably becoming (especially when disarrayed) and usually white. In the interests of credibility, everything in her novels was vague: the setting was southern European – such horrors only being possible in Catholic countries – and the period sixteenth or seventeenth-century. Dress details in Radcliffe's novels were therefore sketchy, with an occasional slashed sleeve to provide historical colour, or a cloak for disguise. Veils, however, were in constant use and there was a particularly exciting one in Catherine's favourite, *The Mysteries of Udolpho*.

Despite the length of Radcliffe's novels and their extensive descriptions of scenery and buildings, she has little interest in dress. The dress and art historian Anne Hollander has noted that the design of garments, and the way they look when worn, is nearly always missing from the 'literary mirror' when held up to nature; it is a pre-existent image assumed by the author to be familiar to the reader. Dress is invoked principally in connection with dramatic conditions or actions – disarrayed gowns or noisy armour in Radcliffe's novels, for example. Action in these novels is all externalized, and so hectic that the underpinnings of normality have no place at all in the lives of her heroines; only a bed, in which to sink, exhausted, at dawn, seems necessary.

Although Austen would be unlikely to have read *Roxana*, categorized as it was with the scandalous 'secret histories' of prostitutes and criminals, she had read and admired Lennox's *The Female Quixote* and we might guess that she found the unstoppable Arabella more entertaining than Radcliffe's girls with their over-wrought sufferings. 'Run mad as often as you chuse', advises Sophia, in Austen's juvenile parody, *Love and Friendship*, 'but do not faint'.[2] Although *Northanger Abbey* is both a Gothic novel and a parody of one, not a great deal happens to Catherine that could be described as an 'adventure', nor (at first) does she have any of the requirements of a heroine – although in leaving her unromantically large family to visit Bath, invited by the rich but inadequate Mr and Mrs Allen, she does in fact become vulnerable. Anticipated supernatural thrills and dark crimes, however, never materialize; instead very real threats to Catherine's emotional and even physical well-being emerge first from the daily social round in Bath and then in the family life of the Tilneys at Northanger Abbey. It is the effect of these events on the education of Catherine which concerns Austen, and Catherine's drama is thus more internalized than either that of Roxana or that of Radcliffe's interchangeable heroines.

Compared to Austen's later heroines, Catherine has been criticised for not showing much psychological development; she still seems very young and naïve at the end of the novel.[3] She does, however, undergo a process of enlightenment about herself and others, and in the process she falls in love and finds her love returned. Clothes play their part in this process. Dress was certainly important in Austen's own life, but it has to be said, there are few precise descriptions of dress in the novels. This is not because her heroines are uninterested in dress, but, as Penelope Byrde points out, because dress 'was not considered a suitable or interesting topic for general conversation'[4] – and decorum is a key virtue in the novels. It is, therefore, what the characters reveal when they *talk* about dress rather than the way they *look* that is significant. Austen herself discussed dresses, hats, caps, shoes, gloves and petticoats upside down and inside and out – but only in her letters to her family and friends, whose essence is the often quite indecorous trivia of daily life. She seems, as Byrde notes, 'to have had a weakness for stockings',[5] especially silk ones. Descriptions of dances, dinner and tea-parties play a large part in these letters and the dress of others is subject to a lively, indiscreet and highly critical commentary. When she writes to her sister Cassandra, she frequently commissions her to buy dress materials and trimmings, or describes those she herself has bought for Cassandra. Changes in fashion are commented upon, usually with a view to altering existing garments – sadly, for most of her life Jane Austen had not the means to fully indulge her love of clothes.

Mrs Allen, of *Northanger Abbey*, has, however, indulged Catherine with a new dress for her first ball in the Bath Assembly Rooms, where Catherine meets Henry Tilney. Bath was now *the* fashionable city of the late eighteenth-century; a spa town for health cures and leisure activities, for dancing, gambling and theatregoing. It had lately undergone a frenzied building and rebuilding programme and was now an elegant city full of shops for the consuming middle-classes, and of places to display their purchases. One of these arenas for display was the Assembly Rooms, where Henry and Catherine have their first crucial conversation, at the end of which a remark of Henry's makes Catherine giggle – '"How can you ... be so – ", she almost said strange.'[6] A rather bold thing for a heroine to say to a hero at their initial meeting, but then he has just had a very odd conversation with Mrs Allen. Mrs Allen's passion, we are told, is dress. The difference between Austen's own passion and Mrs Allen's is that nothing else occupies Mrs Allen's mind, a fault which, Austen warns us, will 'tend to promote the general distress of the work' (18). It *is* 'strange', therefore that a key topic of Henry Tilney's first conversation with Catherine, developed at length in the subsequent exchange with Mrs Allen, is also dress – in this case muslin. In this, as in all Austen's novels, characters like Mrs Allen, whose conversation runs on clothes and fashion, are shown not only as silly but also morally deficient. Are we then to consider Henry also in a negative light? And what are we to make of the fact that all this talk about muslin for ladies' dresses comes from a young *man*?

Henry starts by making Catherine laugh with his teasing parody of what a young man says to a young woman at a ball, and then imagines how she will record their meeting in her Romantic Heroine's journal: 'went to the Lower Rooms; wore my sprigged muslin robe with blue trimmings – plain black shoes – appeared to much advantage; but was strangely harassed by a queer half-witted man' (24). Of course, what Henry has cleverly done is to compliment Catherine on her appearance, but saved his remark from the triteness of standard compliments by self-mockery. He has also crossed the unspoken barrier between male and female worlds in the matter of courtship behaviour – young men are not supposed to know that young ladies write about them in their journals. Henry's subsequent exchange with Mrs Allen on the practical aspects of muslin takes his venture into female territory even further.

When Mrs Allen interrupts Henry's and Catherine's conversation, wailing over the torn sleeve of her muslin dress which cost nine shillings a yard, Henry astonishes her by saying '"[t]hat is exactly what I should have guessed it, madam." "Do you understand muslins, sir?" "Particularly well … my sister has often trusted me in the choice of a gown. I bought one for her the other day, and it was pronounced to be a prodigious bargain by every lady who saw it. I paid but five shillings a yard for it, and a true Indian muslin."' Mrs Allen is 'quite struck' and pursues the topic, asking Henry his opinion of Catherine's muslin gown. '"It is very pretty, madam … but I do not think it will wash well; I am afraid it will fray."' (25, 26) He reassures them, however, that muslin is so useful that Catherine will be able to use it for handkerchiefs or caps. The topic of muslin continues until the dancing starts again, and, as far as Catherine can see, Henry is perfectly polite and serious throughout.

In decoding this conversation from a modern standpoint we must recall that muslins were to the late eighteenth-and early nineteenth-centuries what synthetic fibres were to the mid-twentieth-century – they transformed life. Up to the end of the eighteenth-century, formal clothing for both men and women with any claims to prosperity and fashion was of silk, satin or velvet. Wool or fustian (a coarse linen and cotton mixture) was worn further down the social scale, or for informal, country-wear. Silk or linen lace was used to edge sleeves and necks not only because the touches of white or cream were flattering, but because lace was also washable, whereas the other costlier, heavier materials were not. Muslin is a light, fine, washable cotton, but from 1721 until 1774 cotton textiles had been banned in England, to protect the silk industry. People with money found ways round the legislation, of course, and Indian muslin – which the law excluded – began to be very popular from the 1760s.[7] After 1774 cotton was imported and cotton cloth manufactured in England, providing the impetus for the enormous growth and eventual dominance of the British textile industry, but real Indian muslin – as Henry Tilney makes clear – had greater chic. The French – for political reasons perhaps – preferred the Indian variety and what was French was fashionable.

Muslin was ideally suited to reproducing the draped effects of antique statuary. Whether the increasing popularity of a light and restrained neo-classical style of dress was a result of muslin's special properties, or whether muslin became popular *because* it lent itself so well to this style, is a chicken-and-egg question; but certainly by the time Catherine attends her first ball in Bath in the 1790s everyone who can afford it is wearing muslin and this continues to be true well into the next century. Muslin was relatively cheap and easy to work with, though, as Henry points out, quite fragile. It was thus possible to own more than one

Figure 4 Day and Evening Muslin Dresses, *The Lady's Monthly Museum*, Vol. 12, 1804, London: Vernor & Hood.

muslin dress without straining the budget. But because muslin garments soiled easily and had to be washed and changed often, extensive indulgence in this fashion involved the employment of several servants. A muslin dress, however, could be altered at home and, because it was cotton, it was easier to dye than heavier fabrics. Jane Austen and her sister, both on limited incomes, tended to keep their muslins for special occasions. Jane complains about the poor laundering of a new dress despite having asked that care should be taken, and she writes of dyeing an old muslin gown a darker colour. As they get older the sisters seem to favour the tougher wool and silk mix of bombazine for daily use.[8]

Because muslin was washable, it was possible for the fashionable woman to pursue the analogy with classical statuary even further by favouring white or light pastel colours. When white muslin began its career it was associated with children, but Mrs Allen, we note, as well as Catherine, wears muslin. On the older, plumper figure this sometimes had an unfortunate babyfying effect, as caricaturists of the period, such as Thomas Rowlandson, were quick to point out – and I suspect Mrs Allen may have fallen into this category. But as we can see in the painting by Rolinda Sharples of *The Cloakroom, Clifton Assembly Rooms*, of 1817, the general effect of these simple, light-coloured gauzy dresses is elegant and flattering to most women, especially when seen against the dark, sharp outlines of formal, male evening wear. The dresses here are a little later than those described in *Northanger Abbey*, and we see the beginning of an expansion of the hemline in the addition of flounces. Austen writes to Cassandra in 1813, 'You really must get some flounces', and in the following year tells her friend Martha Lloyd that dresses are 'generally, though not always, flounced'.[9] Austen may have revised *Northanger Abbey* around 1816 (it was not published until after her death), but she didn't add flounces to Catherine's dresses.

In Rolinda Sharples's painting some of the older women are wearing darker muslins – notably the plump lady in sprigged grey muslin in the foreground – but the light-coloured dresses draw the eye. Eleanor Tilney, a model of good taste and elegance – and, as we have seen, encouraged by her brother – always wears white. Austen in her letters frequently refers to the prettiness and suitability of white. White, of course, can have a symbolic function as a sign of purity and innocence in the dress of children and young women, and this will be taken very far in later nineteenth-century dress requirements for unmarried girls: something Henry James makes frequent use of in his fiction.

Although Austen is no 'symboliste', when Mrs Allen is asked by her husband what she thinks of young women driving together with young

Plate 2 Rolinda Sharples, *The Cloakroom, Clifton Assembly Rooms*. 1813. Bristol Museum and Art Gallery.

men in an open carriage, she answers, "'[o]pen carriages are nasty things. A clean gown is not five minutes wear in them. You are splashed getting in and getting out.'" That is not the problem, her husband says; the problem is that it looks 'odd'. Catherine is mortified; "'[W]hy did you not tell me so before? I am sure that if I had known it to be improper, I would not have gone with Mr Thorpe at all.'" (93) What Catherine actually wants from Mrs Allen is not fashion but moral guidance as to the propriety of such an excursion with the pushy John Thorpe. Mistakes in propriety – 'stains' on the purity of a girl's reputation – are less reparable than mud on white muslin. Elizabeth Bennet's muddy dress in *Pride and Prejudice*, we might remember, meets with Darcy's approval not censure, because it is a sign of Elizabeth's good heart, evidence that she has tramped across fields to be with her sick sister. We see here how Mrs Allen's obsession with dress, though comic in its effect, could indeed promote the 'general distress' of the work. Her prattle on dress is, as Tony Tanner says, perhaps harmless, 'but it can involve an inversion of values'.[10] If Catherine were to be guided by Mrs Allen she would order her conduct according to its effect on her clothes rather than on her moral standing. An outing with John Thorpe would be doubly dangerous: Catherine's physical welfare would be threatened by his reckless driving, and her reputation put at risk by being seen in his dubious company.

Why then is Henry Tilney's interest in dress different from that of Mrs Allen? We might reply that Henry's conversation with Mrs Allen on muslin is first made out of kindness and good manners: Henry sees that dress is her sole concern and so he unselfishly tailors his conversation to her interests. He does not expand on the topic of dress with anyone else. Mrs Allen, however, for all her good-heartedness, is, as we have seen, insensitive to others and harps on dress inappropriately – even dangerously. Henry's interest is also in the practical aspects of muslin, its price and wearability, not in the latest style or colour. More importantly, perhaps, it is a signal to Catherine of his denial of the separation between male and female spheres. He knows about dress, he is interested in it, he helps and advises his motherless sister in these matters and is happy to extend his expertise to Catherine. We are assured at the end of the chapter that Tilney is a clergyman of respectable family – in case we thought he was in the cloth-trade. But he is nevertheless strange for his time: Evelina, the eponymous heroine of Fanny Burney's novel of 1778, makes fun of the expertise of male shop assistants in London : 'so finical! so affected! They seemed to understand every part of a woman's dress better than we do ourselves; they recommended caps and ribbands with an air of so much importance, that I wished to ask them how long they had left off wearing them.'[11] We have to look to the end of the nineteenth-century for a similar denial of the female monopoly of an interest in dress, to Henry James, who declared that 'we are all of us extravagant, superficial and luxurious together'.[12] John Thorpe's leering and self-interested pursuit of Catherine, his 'macho' boastfulness, is much closer to the norm. But Catherine is never in any doubt as to which of the two men she prefers.

Henry's sensible remarks on dress are not only contrasted with Mrs Allen's silly ones but also with those of Isabella Thorpe, John Thorpe's sister. Catherine, endearingly if unguardedly naive, warms to Isabella's gushing overtures of friendship. They share an interest in Gothic novels, parties and clothes and arrange to spend time together. Catherine is awed by Isabella's ability to compare the fashions of Bath with those of London, and Isabella is happy to 'rectify the opinions of her new friend in many articles of tasteful attire' (30). They meet in Bath's Pump Rooms and Isabella immediately overwhelms Catherine with a torrent of inconsequential chatter, ending in a jumble of fashion and literature: '"Do you know, I saw the prettiest hat you can imagine, in a shop window in

Milsom Street just now – very like yours, only with cocquelicot ribbons instead of green: I quite longed for it. But my dearest Catherine, what have you been doing with yourself all morning? Have you gone on with Udolpho?"' (36) Miss Andrews, a 'particular friend' of Isabella's knows all the Radcliffe novels; "'you would be delighted with her. She is netting herself the sweetest cloak you can conceive. I think her beautiful as an angel, and I am so vexed with the men for not admiring her!"' (37)

If Henry has given courteous attention to the problems of muslin, Isabella's prattle leaps from novels, her hats, her friend, to Catherine, and then to cloaks and her men, revealing that her concern for her friends (or for literature) is as profound as for her hats. Her reference to the hat's 'cocquelicot ribbons' does also, incidentally, place the novel in the 1790s, rather than the period of its revision around 1816, since bonnets in 1816 were small, fairly modest affairs compared with the immense confections of the 1790s. Isabella's final comment on Miss Andrews is pure malice. Catherine is much too candid and impressionable to see this as yet; but when Isabella's engagement to Catherine's

Figure 5 Hats and Caps, *The Lady's Monthly Museum*, Vol. 3 1807, London: Vernor, Hood & Sharpe.

brother James proves to be as enduring as cocquelicot ribbons, Catherine may wish she had noticed these signs of a fickle heart before.

This contrast between Isabella's self-centred superficiality and Henry's polite seriousness appears to be counteracted by a little sermon that Austen reads us on the foolishness of taking clothes too seriously. Catherine, in bed and thinking of what she will wear to the cotillion ball the following evening, lies awake 'ten minutes ... debating between her spotted and tamboured muslin'. 'Dress', Austen writes 'is at all times a frivolous distinction, and excessive solicitude about it often destroys its own aim. Catherine knew all this very well; her great aunt had read her a lecture on the subject only the Christmas before.' She longs to buy a new gown, but this 'would have been an error of judgement', as her brother might have told her; 'for man only can be aware of the insensibility of man toward a new gown'. The heart of man is unaffected 'by what is costly and new' in a woman's attire, and indifferent to 'the texture of their muslin'. This sounds like Austen's own voice, but when she ends by saying that 'not one of these grave reflections troubled the tranquillity of Catherine' (67), we remember that Catherine fell asleep in ten minutes and therefore did not actually allow the business of dress, or moral reflections about it, to trouble her overmuch. These 'grave reflections' have been delivered by a great aunt, but we know that Henry Tilney did in fact give considerable attention to the texture of Catherine's muslin. We might conclude that Austen, in self-mocking aunt mode, causes Catherine to fall asleep during her lecture, secure in the knowledge that, on the contrary, Henry does care about the way she looks.

Catherine's education and discrimination has advanced sufficiently to judge and reject the advances of the crudely bullying John Thorpe, and she escapes his threats to her happiness when she leaves Bath to stay with the Tilneys at Northanger Abbey. But she thrills to the prospect of other imagined 'Gothic' dangers among crumbling ruins and the super-natural possibilities of a medieval Abbey, a fantasy which Henry teasingly encourages on the journey there. Catherine is a little crestfallen when Northanger turns out to be a light, airy house, the subject of a costly modernisation scheme being undertaken by Henry's father, General Tilney. 'Improvement' of land and property was very much a part of the ethos of the new consumer and leisure society, and generally met with Austen's approval: Darcy is a model 'improving' landlord in *Pride and Prejudice*. But General Tilney's schemes are motivated by snobbery and ostentation, as is his desire that Henry should court Catherine, for he believes, mistakenly, that she is an heiress.

The kindness of the Allens has introduced Catherine to the delights of this new consumer culture, and, for the occasion, has provided her with several muslin frocks – something which has presumably impressed General Tilney. She has more frocks than she strictly needs, as General Tilney has a good deal more chinaware than *he* needs He brings Catherine's attention to his breakfast service, bought two years before, which he then dismisses as 'old', and owns he is contemplating the purchase of another. This – unexpectedly perhaps – makes Tilney a typical product of the Romantic period. The social historian Stana Nedanic has pointed out that while Romanticism was critical of brute commercialism, it also encouraged focus on the self 'and the cultivation of unstated emotions'. 'A permanently unfocused dissatisfaction, a longing for some hard to define emotional fulfilment', transferred itself to a longing 'for those material objects that could act as proxy for the emotions and thus make them real'.[13] Earlier religious and moralistic associations of luxury with vice, or with the corruption of a wealthy elite, had been replaced by economic considerations – shopping was good for the national economy. Furthermore, '[l]uxury objects denoted a refinement of taste and expressed civility'.[14] There is of course a difference between Catherine innocently dropping off to sleep while thinking about a new dress, and General Tilney's plans to secure Catherine's imagined fortune to further his upwardly mobile aspirations. Austen, as Alistair Duckworth points out, is 'deeply aware of a threatened change from a stable society based on Christian principles to a society in which money, or the appearance of money, is all that counts'.[15]

Catherine does not like General Tilney, and senses his children's unease with him. Stimulated by her reading and by this Gothic setting, her overactive uneducated imagination translates her dislike into a belief that the General has murdered his wife. Trembling in delicious fear, she opens an old chest in her room, only to find a neat white cotton counterpane instead of mouldering bones; and, in a stormy midnight, by guttering candlelight, she extracts a roll of papers from a black cabinet. In morning light this turns out to be not a bundle of blood or tear-stained letters, but a collection of recent laundry lists featuring such sinister items as shirts, stockings and cravats. Washable white cotton prevails again. When Catherine shortly afterward betrays her lurid view of his father to Henry, his response is to urge on her his image of the security, openness and sanity of contemporary English life, as a reproof and a rebuttal of her fantasies, and a final, humiliating enlightenment.

But, of course, this isn't her final enlightenment, and Catherine is right to dislike the General, though she does so for the wrong reasons. It is not the late Mrs Tilney who is finally the victim of the General's brutality, but Catherine herself. She is after all the heroine of a Gothic novel of a sort.

Catherine is a transparently nice girl, who has obviously won the affections of both Tilney's children, but when it emerges that her 'appearance' as heiress to the Allens's fortune is a mistaken speculation of John Thorpe's, passed on to the greedy General, her virtues go for nothing, and she is bundled unceremoniously out of the Abbey to find her own way home. No murder, rape or torture takes place, but she confronts an emotionally and psychologically devastating experience nonetheless, and in practical terms, her return home is a risky journey for an unprotected female. Dr Johnson felt that one of the purposes of novel-writing was to teach the young how to avoid the snares laid by 'Treachery for Innocence'. Mrs Radcliffe had filled Catherine's fairly empty mind with images of quite the wrong 'snares', but Henry was also wrong to conclude that no snares exist in modern, sensible, well-washed England. Catherine's final educated judgement of the General's behaviour is a personal one, free of melodramatic prototypes, and Henry's speedy journey across country to claim Catherine's hand and admit his father's wrongdoing is an acknowledgement of the insufficiency of his earlier sanitized view of English society.

Catherine, of course, marries Henry – one of Austen's most attractive heroes. Henry can be pompous and patronizing at times, especially when undertaking the aesthetic education of Catherine, but, as we have seen, he unhesitatingly, in Gothic hero fashion, 'rescues' Catherine from the consequences of his father's ill-treatment and declares his love for her. Is he, as Catherine nearly said, 'strange'? As Marilyn Butler points out, Austen uses commodities, and dress in particular, to establish not only social and income distinctions but also moral differences: 'Mrs Allen', Butler says, 'damns herself in the reader's eyes by using anything so trivial as lace and muslin as her yardstick of quality.' Nevertheless, 'it is the appearance of commodities and their sophisticated treatment, that is deeply interesting ... [e]veryone in Bath becomes involved in the display or reading of signs'.[16] Tony Tanner, however, has made the interesting point that Austen does not seem to see dress-signs as part of a strategy in flirtation or courtship: 'The emphasis is on narcissism not on seduction.'[17] Henry quickly notices Catherine's dress and comments on it, which may be a signal of his appreciation of her, but unlike both John Thorpe and his own father, he does not read into her appearance her likely financial expectations. His teasing conversations with Catherine are like those with his sister and advance their intimacy; but he is also trying to 'read' whether Catherine is capable of going beyond the formulaic exchanges between the sexes, and, although he sees the extent of her ignorance (as she does herself), he also establishes that she has a lively and educable mind. He finds that she is natural, honest and funny, and their conversation begins to sound, in fact, very much like Jane Austen talking to Cassandra.

Henry is happy to give considered and informed attention to muslin, even although this appears an eccentric – even indecorous – topic for a young man meeting a young woman for the first time. But also, he demonstrates that, unlike John Thorpe, he is equally well informed on the contemporary novel, or on recent ideas about art, and he shows that he would happily discuss politics at length with Catherine – if she wants to, which she doesn't. In short, he denies that there is some mysterious barrier between male and female concerns, and that a girl, if reasonably informed, is not capable of a sensible discussion on grown-up subjects, and that topics such as dresses or novels cannot be treated seriously as well as amusingly, if the occasion warrants. When Austen said she enjoyed nothing so much as choosing a sponge cake, she was both making fun of herself and being perfectly truthful. There is a time and a season for taking sponge cakes – and muslin – seriously. Butler sees Henry as a 'mysterious, almost allegorical figure, who stands for androgynous ideas, youthful play, the comic spirit, romance ...'.[18] She sees him, in fact, as Austen's double or perhaps as her brother – inventive, playful, sharing an intimacy in which it is understood that hats or novels can be enjoyably discussed without losing a sense of discrimination. We should recall that if *Northanger Abbey* has much about muslin, it also contains Austen's famous defence of the novel as a serious art form.

Mrs Allen's and Isabella's obsession with clothes and headgear is not only boringly self-centred for others to listen to (although entertaining to read about), but indicates a lack of proportion – 'a displacement of concern'.[19] When Mrs Allen hears of the General's brutality to Catherine, she deplores it in the same breath as she tells Catherine that she has had 'that frightful great rent in my best Mechlin [a kind of lace] so charmingly mended' (207). Commodities are not, however, wicked in themselves, and to read sermons about them is also boring. We leave Catherine generously provided for, and, we can assume, about to embark on a burst of shopping for herself and her new home. The discussion of muslin brought Catherine and Henry together; his 'strange' unabashed interest in the topic was perhaps the very thing marking him out as the man to fall in love with. Being something of a pedant, he will educate her, but because they share that sense of the ridiculous that marked their first conversation, it will not be the repressive pupil/teacher relationship we are to see in George Eliot's *Middlemarch* sixty years later. Catherine will enjoy that rare privilege of having a husband who can choose dresses with her, as well as swapping novels and commenting on them. Austen may have been sparing in her fictional descriptions of dress – as in conversation, these things can be overdone – but her interest in the topic persists. As Tanner says, dress in Jane Austen's novels 'at once reveals and conceals'.[20] And we might recall that her last written words, in a letter to a friend, were to recommend the wife and sister of a Captain Clement, who were 'all good humour and obligingness, and I hope (since the fashion allows it) with rather longer petticoats than last year'.[21]

–4–

Unrepentant Dandies:
William Thackeray's *Pendennis*

Dress in many novels is conventional. It is rarely uninteresting, since even when writers simply follow what other writers are doing with fictional clothing, they show some features of their style and view of the world in describing it. But when dress does become important in novels it is normally, as we have seen in earlier chapters of this book, women's dress that is the focus; although Jane Austen, as we saw in the last chapter, sees no reason why the subject of dress, within the general decorums of conversation, should not be as interesting to men as to women. Modern men (despite all the evidence that we still have around us, from male boutiques to wildly expensive Saville Row tailors and the appalling intricacies of regimental and club uniforms) are generally supposed not to care what they wear. In fact, as Christopher Breward makes clear in his study of nineteenth-century masculinity and fashion, the 'underlying insistence on the un-manliness of the whole clothing business in general, actually positioned men right at the centre of a debate concerning fashion and modern life'.[1]

It is of particular interest, then, when a novelist breaks this pattern and masculine fashion becomes the focus of a novel, when what a man wears becomes the topic and the index of a novel's social criticism. Victorian men retain for us the popular image of men in suits, conformists with whiskers and top-hats. But that is only vulgar modern prejudice: for them, as always in the modern world, dress is a form of consumption, a badge of class, a possible mark of originality and a form of self-creation. Even for Victorians (or perhaps especially for Victorians) it is of interest and importance. In the troubled world of the male Victorian Bildungsroman, dress may be a key index of the social chaos of modernity. This, at least, seems to be how it functions for Thackeray in *Pendennis*.

The way men looked changed radically at the turn of the nineteenth-century. If the aspiration of the elegant female of 1800 was to be a classical nymph in soft light drapery, fashionable males in the following decades – inspired by the newly-discovered Parthenon sculptures – hoped to recall the nude forms of Greek deities, with cropped hair, skin-tight pantaloons and manly chests decked in clean white linen. Henry Tilney had taken a grave interest in the washability of Catherine Morland's muslin dress, but by 1820 – if still interested in fashion – he would have been more concerned with his own laundry.

The consumer boom of the late eighteenth century had seen a 'downward spiral of fine dressing',[2] as a result it became possible for anyone, with the means, to display luxury in dress. For a 'gentleman' to maintain a distance between himself and his social inferiors, some new criterion of elegance had to be found. The pear-shaped eighteenth-century male silhouette, in an often ill-fitting velvet or silk ensemble of coat, waistcoat and breeches, its surfaces shimmering with costly decorative effects, needed replacing. In Europe as a whole the spectre of revolutionary egalitarianism also had to be acknowledged – the display of privilege itself could now be seen as provocative, and prudent Frenchmen during the Revolution adopted the working man's buckskin pantaloons and the Englishman's sporting coat in woollen cloth, to save their necks.

The British monarchy under an ailing George III and a profligate Prince Regent also had its problems in the early years of the nineteenth-century. It was a friend of the Prince, Beau Brummell, who laid down the rules for a new style which looked superior but not obviously exclusive: a dark, tailored cloth coat, plain pale waistcoat, light close-fitting pantaloons, flawless footwear and a clean shirt. If you wanted to achieve his 'look', all you needed, Brummell said was 'fine linen, plenty of it, and country washing'.[3] Clean linen indeed became a new symbol of male elegance: in 1853 the author of *The Habits of Good Society, A Handbook of Etiquette for Ladies and Gentlemen* ruled that 'if you are economical with your tailor, you can be extravagant with your laundress'.[4] The 'look' developed at this time has in fact been the bedrock of male dress until very recently, and is only gradually giving way now to the predominance of a casual, 'sportswear' look, to jeans and trainers as the mark of the up-to-date, successful, modern male. Beau Brummell popularized a 'natural', classical, masculine look – monochrome, with visible seams, and a cut which clarified the silhouette. Perfection in such matters was, as always in matters of dress, not easily achieved and required a maintenance team of tailors, bootmakers, valets and laundresses – plus a large personal expenditure of time. As Ellen Moers has said, in her study of the Dandy, it was an essentially ironic style: the Dandy's 'arrogant simplicity was an affirmation of the aristocratic principle, his way of life an exaltation of aristocratic society; but his terrible independence proclaimed a subversive disregard for the essentials of aristocracy. The Dandy, as Brummell made him, stands on an isolated pedestal of self.'[5] But it could claim also to be democratic; no ancestors, titles or any obvious display of expenditure were needed to look like this. Money, in fact, was not to be talked of. It was something of an irony that Brummell fled England in 1816, like any aristocratic rake in a Restoration comedy, pursued by his creditors.

On the first page of William Thackeray's novel *Pendennis*, Major Pendennis, uncle to the novel's hero, Pen, is introduced to us 'in the best blacked boots in all London, with a checked morning cravat that was never rumpled until dinner-time, a buff waistcoat which bore the crown of his sovereign on the buttons, and linen so spotless that Mr Brummell himself asked the name of his laundress'.[6] The Major's appearance as Regency Buck and 'a military man en retraite' (1) is thus a compound of two heroes – Brummell and the Duke of Wellington. *Pendennis*, of 1850, like Thackeray's novel of three years earlier, *Vanity Fair*, is a novel without a hero – or even a heroine. Nevertheless, in Bildungsroman pattern, we follow the education of Major Pendennis's nephew, Arthur, or Pen, from childhood, through youthful mistakes, to his wedding-day, when he gets the 'good' girl, Laura Bell, and a decent income. He has, however, done nothing to earn either. During the course of the novel, in the sole cause of personal adornment and a good time, he has run through his own, his mother's and Laura's money, but demonstrations of penitence have been intermittent; we leave him, on his wedding day, hardly a better man, but dressed to kill in an entirely new outfit.

'[O]urs ... is a selfish story', Thackeray confesses toward the end of the novel; and Pen has 'devoted himself to himself' (719–20). Thackeray not only leaves Pen unpunished, but goes on to appoint him narrator of *The Newcomes* four years later. Two related Dickensian narratives of heroes in search of gentility – *David Copperfield* (1850) and *Great Expectations* (1862) – end more conventionally: the virtuous David gets his girl and the money, while the snobbish Pip has only a distant prospect of either, or, in the novel's alternative, almost tragic ending, nothing at all. What merit could there have been for Thackeray in the ambitions of a dandy? Ellen Moers has pointed to an ambivalence in Victorian attitudes in general: while frivolity in dress was clearly 'wrong', there was something attractive, even nostalgic, about the way the Dandy 'made a success (however despicable and trivial) of *absolute selfishness*'.[7] Looking at the sequence of scenes in which Thackeray foregrounds clothes and accessories in *Pendennis*, as markers in Pen's (selfish) 'Progress', we gain a clearer view of the sense of nostalgic dissatisfaction, which, though 'far from a tragic response'[8] as Barbara Hardy says, may be Thackeray's intended conclusion.

The chronological placing of Thackeray's picture of male fashion in *Pendennis* is a delicate business. Thackeray illustrated the first edition of *Pendennis* himself, in a style close to that of George Cruickshank, a caricaturist of the 1820s. In Cruickshank's own pictorial Rake's Progress – *The Adventures of Tom and Jerry in London* – a dandiacal young Jerry is guided in his adventures by the older Tom, an elegant roué with a military air and a Wellingtonian nose. This 1820s world of Tom and Jerry was that in which Thackeray placed the start of *Pendennis*, something which presented him with a problem similar to that which he had faced in *Vanity Fair* – set in and around 1815, but essentially a satire on the *mores* of his own society. Richard Altick, in his study of the Victorian novel, *The Presence of the Present*, has examined the problem of 'lapses of time' in such Victorian novels that are not really historical novels, but, as they trace the career of a hero or heroine, must of necessity start some twenty years before their close. Altick points out that in the 1840s it was 'the vogue to be voguish',[9] and the 'Silver Fork' novels of the 1840s even advertised their modishness in the use of 'Modern' and 'New' in their titles. To identify details such as costume too closely with an earlier period would thus have been to lose saleable topicality, as well as the bite of contemporary satirical comment. Pendennis, as Thackeray said in his Preface, was to be a 'gentleman of our age'' (lvi). But all the same, it was central to Thackeray's project not to lose sight of that earlier, Regency age, and its Regency bucks.

Illustrations exacerbated and pointed up Thackeray's problem. With words it was possible to render effects rather than details, and details could be chosen to avoid anachronism, but engravings in the sharp style of Cruickshank could not easily be blurred. Thackeray had opted for anachronism in *Vanity Fair*, confessing in a note to the first edition that he had not 'the heart to disfigure my heroes and heroines by costumes so hideous [as those of 1815]; and have ... engaged a model of rank dressed according to present fashion'.[10] This freed him to put his engraved characters in modified crinolines and frock coats, while leaving the text in the earlier period. In the 1862 serialization of *The Adventures of Philip*, he pursued the problem in an address to his 'fair reader', concluding that 'these anachronisms must be',[11] and shuffling the responsibility onto this reader's alleged demand for high fashion. In *Pendennis* (of 1850), however, Thackeray's double portrait of a dandy, young and old, meant that fashion was, even more than elsewhere, his focus, and blurring the edges would be more difficult.

The Major, as we have seen, is described in the text as a figure from the era of Waterloo. In the illustrations he wears Brummell's tight trousers strapped under the instep, rather than military breeches, and light shoes, not boots. The great change in men's dress, the shift to a dandyesque style, had already happened during the first years of the century, and no radical change of costume took place in the 1830s and 1840s. The Major's general appearance in the illustrations therefore remains credibly smart, if a little dated and conservative, until his last appearance, where we shall see a significant change. With female dress, however, the problem was more complex, since the silhouette of the late 1840s unmistakably anticipated the horizontal crinoline, while that of the 1820s and early 1830s had more in common with the high-waisted verticals of the Empire style. In an illustration of the very young Pen with Helen, his mother (15), Thackeray places Pen – properly dressed in a 'skeleton' suit[12] of the 1820s – against Helen's skirt in an attempt to downplay its crinoline tendencies. As it is Pen's appearance that counts, Helen can remain a background figure both in text and in illustration. It is only with the arrival of Blanche Amory that crinolines cannot be suppressed.

Figure 6 Pen and Helen. Thackeray's illustration to 1850 edition of *Pendennis*.

Despite his strenuous cultivation of the gentlemanly ideal, the Major's origins, while respectable, are modest. A career in the Indian army has given him status, but his younger brother, Pen's father, had been an apothecary. By moving to fashionable Bath (of the Austen period), old Mr Pendennis had become successful, married well and replaced his 'black breeches and stockings' with 'a bottle-green coat and brass buttons with drab gaiters just as if he had been an English gentleman all his life' (11). Black clothing – which was to become the male uniform across all classes in the second half of the century – was more modestly the colour of trade and commerce in 1800. What the upwardly mobile Pendennis Senior adopts, in bottle green and brass, is the costume of the English country gentleman, derived from hunting dress, the move up from trade to the look established by Brummell. The next step on the social ladder was the purchase of a country estate, followed by the expensive education of a male heir. It was at this point that Pen's father died, leaving Pen in the hands of his mother and uncle.

Owing his own status and income to the army, the Major naturally tries to set Pen on the same path. Pen is drawn to the idea when he sees an old schoolfellow arrayed 'in crimson and gold, with an immense bearskin cap on his head, staggering under the colours of the regiment ... talking familiarly to immense warriors with tufts to their chins and Waterloo medals' (28). Traditional masculine aggression has become ritualized, sentimentalized and confused with colourful dressing up. Pen's vision of heroic happiness in the military is brief but of its time: Fabrice, the hero of Stendhal's *La Chartreuse de Parme* of 1839, yearns for the opportunities for glory of the Napoleonic era; but Baudelaire, in the 1840s, knows that the hour is past and that heroism must be sought in modern life, among top hats and sombre suits. 'For the military glory that their fathers enjoyed,' Anita Brookner explains, 'the sons sought a compensating glory in an artistic or literary career ... this is the generation that codifies the cult of dandyism'.[13] Stendhal's hero longs for heroic *action*, whereas Pen longs for heroic *costume*. In giving in to his mother's pleas against army life and taking the Baudelairean path, Pen is only sacrificing 'his visionary red coat' (28), not a whole way of life. But he annoys the Major, whose remembrance of time past becomes a nostalgic threnody to the novel.

Having allowed the feminine to prevail and rejected the military, masculine aspects of the Major, Pen now encounters another old friend, Foker, who appears before Pen 'in one of those costumes to which the public consent ... has awarded the title of "swell"' (36). The 'swell' would have been familiar to a *Punch*-reading audience of 1850, as 'the dandy's leisured middle-class imitator'[14] – but almost anachronistic here, since he did not appear until the 1840s. The 'swell' adopted the dandy's extravagant obsession with dress, but stripped the look of its refinement, and 'vulgarized it with loud colours and fancy, eccentric cuts'.[15] Foker wears a 'scarlet shawl neckcloth' with a pin representing '[a] bulldog in gold, ... a fur waistcoat laced all over with gold chains, a green cutaway coat with basket buttons, and a white upper coat ornamented with cheese-plate buttons' (36–7). Thackeray obviously enjoys the comedy of technical terms such as 'basket' and 'cheese-plate' applied to the fastenings of men's coats – and if this novel were to be characterized by a single item of dress it would be such outlandish buttons.[16]

According to *Punch* in the 1850s there were varieties of 'swell', but all lacked the dandy's *ton*, and Foker's conversation is larded with slang as vulgar as his outfit. In his illustration of Foker and Pen together (41), Thackeray gives checked trousers and a cane to Foker, identifying him as a 'Languid' swell, one of those who, according to *Punch* , wore 'hugely checked trousers ... and [carried] excessively slim canes'.[17] The text, however, dwells on details more characteristic of the 1830s and early 1840s: his jewellery, neckcloth, and variously buttoned coats. A cigar is added and also features in the illustration, for cigar-smoking, according to Altick, was the favourite vice of the 'swell' as well as of the socially inferior 'gent'. Pen's reaction to Foker is confused, for he is 'not much more refined than in his school-days' (39), but he listens with respect to lively accounts of Foker's university life. The effect of the illustration is to show Foker as amiably vulgar, in a loud outfit that will soon date, while Pen retains his pared-back Regency style, discreetly up-dated by a pale stovepipe hat and bow-tie of the 1840s. 'Simplicity is the only distinction which a man of taste should aspire to', the *Handbook of Etiquette* rules; 'the charm of Brummell's dress was its simplicity'.[18]

After a very 'Regency Buck' episode with an actress, Pen decides to cram for Oxbridge at a local school, where he is hated because 'he did not wear corduroys' (172), the countryman's practical leg-wear. Trousers continue to bother Pen at Oxbridge, where he is 'rather annoyed that one or two very vulgar young men, who did not even use straps to their trousers ... beat him completely in the lecture room' (212). The dislike of village hobbledehoys was one thing, but it was less easy to sort out the mismatch between sartorial and intellectual expertise at Oxbridge, the training ground of gentlemen, for the trouser-strap was *de rigueur* for fashionable young men until trouser-bottoms widened in the late 1840s. Pen, however, does not allow intellectual pursuits to prevail over fashion, and when he returns home to his mother and cousin, Laura Bell, for

Figure 7 Pen and Foker. Thackeray's illustration to 1850 edition of *Pendennis*.

Christmas, Laura notes the 'quantity of fine new clothes he brought with him'; Helen 'admired his improved appearance'. Further improvements are noted in the summer vacation when Pen brings home 'more smart clothes; appearing in the morning in wonderful shooting-jackets, with remarkable buttons; and in the evening in gorgeous velvet waistcoats, with richly embroidered cravats, and curious linen'. Laura snoops around his room, marvelling at his 'beautiful dressing-case, with silver mountings, and a quantity of lovely rings and jewellery. And he had a new French watch and gold chain, in place of the big old chronometer.' (213) We see a paradigm shift here from the Brummell/Major Pendennis model to a new concept of the Dandy – one modelled on the Count D'Orsay.

The French-born Count, who with Lady Blessington ruled London society in the 1830s and 1840s, brought softness, colour and the gleam of jewellery to Brummell's exacting austerity; as Moers says, 'his dandyism was made from weaker stuff'.[19] Pen is not made of very stern stuff either, and if he has not adopted Foker's style wholesale, he has indulged in a coloured cravat and waistcoat, and an excess of buttons and jewellery. Anticipating the shift from the male Regency regime to that of Victoria, Brummell's manly verticals were softened by D'Orsay into feminine curves: 'Inside the open curve of the coat lapels could be seen the curve of the waistcoat lapels, a curve accentuated in turn by a gold watch-chain which ... curved across his chest.'[20] In Thackeray's vignette of Pen and a fellow-student at Oxbridge, we see precisely this change: their open coats curve backward, waistcoats curve across white linen, each appears to have a patterned bow-like cravat, and Pen's friend displays a large watch-chain (218).

In contrast to Brummell's studied reserve, D'Orsay's appearance excited public comment, for unlike Brummell, D'Orsay was strikingly handsome, a born self-publicist and exuberantly good-natured. Ellen Moers suggests that D'Orsay was just 'too amiable',[21] but his amiability was needed and cheerfully exploited in his career as social arbiter and parasite. Thomas Carlyle's anti-fashion polemic of 1834, *Sartor Resartus*, was directed at D'Orsay; and while *Fraser's Magazine* made him the constant butt of jokes and attacks, the same magazine employed Daniel Maclise to produce a series of engravings celebrating not only D'Orsay but Bulwer Lytton and Benjamin Disraeli, dandies of the 1830s, who modelled themselves on D'Orsay. Thackeray joined in the fun against

Plate 3 Daniel Maclise, *Benjamin Disraeli. 1833*. National Portrait Gallery, London.

dandies in his *Yellowplush Papers* for *Fraser's*, but the ambivalence of his attitude was evident in his friendship with D'Orsay and Lady Blessington, and when debts finished them, he wept.

The image of Pen, from Oxbridge onward, then, owes much to D'Orsay: his auburn curls, his saving grace of charm and his career as fashion leader. Thackeray, commenting on Pen's metamorphosis from imitator to imitated, notes that 'he exhibited a certain partiality for rings, jewellery and fine raiment of all sorts; and it must be owned that Mr Pen, during his time at the university, was rather a dressy man and loved to array himself in splendour ... They said he used to wear rings over his kid gloves, which he always denies.' (217) The shift here from authorial to reported comment suggests the fame of gossip-columns – but readers of 1850 would also have recognised Disraeli as the dandy known to wear rings outside his gloves. Disraeli not only modelled himself on D'Orsay, but wrote a novel in 1826, *Vivian Gray*, in which the hero's dandyism conceals his immoral pursuit of political power. The image of Pen therefore has literary as well as fashionable resonances, but is a reminder of darker uses of looks and charm.

In his second year at Oxbridge, Pen has become 'one of the men of fashion in the University.... When the young men heard at the haberdashers' shops that Mr Pendennis of Boniface, had just ordered a crimson satin cravat, you would see a couple of dozen crimson satin cravats in Main Street in the course of the week – and Simon, the jeweller, was known to sell no less than two gross of Pendennis pins.' (219) The *Handbook of Etiquette* of 1853 seems to frown on jewels for men – 'the man of good taste will wear as little jewellery as possible' – but then does produce a substantial list of them. They should be 'real and good', however, and simple, not shiny: if you have a diamond ring 'you may wear it on great occasions', but never more than one ring at a time. Jewellery is acceptable, if it is neither showy nor excessive. In the text Pen errs on both counts: in the illustrations, however, little more than watch chain and buttons are visible. It is as though Thackeray senses that Pen can survive mockery in the text but not caricature in the illustrations.

While Thackeray does not hesitate to itemize the enormous expenditure of this dilettante life, he also emphasizes its brevity and generous pleasures: 'He had his fill of pleasure and popularity ... Pen's jovial wit, and Pen's songs, and dashing courage, and frank and manly bearing, charmed all the undergraduates.' (221) In contrast to Vivian Gray's cynicism, Pen has that 'impeccable *naiveté*'[22] which, according to Baudelaire, was required in the Hero of Modern Life. Nemesis arrives, nevertheless, in the form of unpaid bills; Pen fails his degree, and returns home to

Fairoaks once more, this time bereft of 'every single article of jewellery except two old gold sleeve-buttons'. Helen 'had cruelly to pinch herself' to settle the jeweller's bills, but Thackeray pleads that Pen is not 'a hero or a model, only ... a lad, who, in the midst of a thousand vanities and weaknesses, has yet some generous impulses and is not altogether dishonest' (237).

Pen, in failing to gain the qualifications necessary for a productive life of work, has rejected Victorian middle-class values and has instead cultivated the fashionable éclat of an *ancien régime* grandee. His glamour, however, evaporates with his dismissal from Oxbridge; at home, indulged by two women, he becomes childish. It is not only Helen who has been 'pinched' to pay for Pen, but Laura, who has to sacrifice her small savings to allow him to return, with debts paid, to retake his degree. Pen at Oxbridge has not abused his charm or money to harm others, but he could be said to have deprived Helen and Laura of any fashionable pleasures they might have had. As Barbara Hardy remarks, 'there is very little innocent enjoyment'[23] in Thackeray's fiction. Pen has confused education with learning to wear clothes stylishly. And while learning such things was once a highly significant part of a courtier's education in the societies of the *ancien régime*, he has failed to notice that in modernity one is also supposed to learn how to earn the money to buy the clothes. He has ruined the women who supported him. Thackeray underscores the harm consequent on so much female indulgence: 'What made Pen at home such a dandy and a despot? The women had spoiled him ... they had cloyed him with obedience, and surfeited him with sweet respect and submission' (677). Toward the end of the novel, the less indulgent Laura, looking back, tells Pen, 'I often thought our dearest mother spoiled you at home, by worshipping you; and that if you are ... what you say [selfish], her too great fondness helped to make you so' (864).

Pen, more dispirited than penitent, is soon bored by country life and female worship, and Helen declares he must go to London and be freed 'from the dull society of two poor women. It *was* dull – very, certainly.' (257) It is at this point that Blanche Amory – flitting seductively between town and country – breaks the tedium, for Pen's dandyism has not only drained his womenfolk financially, it has also drained them of a share in the novel's life and colour. Such descriptions as there are of the women, are of their pious modesty, not their dress. In Willett Cunnington's categories of nineteenth-century women, Helen and Laura are women of the 'Romantic '30s', versed in improving literature, 'trained in a strict discipline ... in order that [they] might learn to obey.' For the male, this ideal woman was 'sedately charming, submissive and innocent, and equipped to perform what he did not care to do himself, such as making him comfortable'. The ideal gradually softens until 'a sweet prettiness is attained, suggestive of a Sunday doll'.[24] By the 1840s piety had become a performance of sensibility, and, encouraged by advice and etiquette books, young ladies went in for poetry, tears and an interesting pallor. Blanche Amory models herself on the languorous 'Beauties' of the illustrated Annuals, such as Lady Blessington's *Keepsake*, appearing 'meek in dove colour, like a vestal virgin' (271). She plays up the idea of pallor in her name, her clothes, her food, and writes poetry in a velvet-bound book, entitled *Mes Larmes*, quickly spotting the dewy-eyed enthusiasm for literature that will draw Pen. Although Laura is now financing Pen's law studies, she is overshadowed by Blanche. Pen, after a dutiful but tepid proposal of marriage, which Laura rejects, leaves for London.

Thackeray concedes that in London Pen has given up 'some of [his] dandified pretensions' (369), but he impresses his city acquaintance 'as a man of ton', with his 'superior looks and presence' (372). Although the Major believes he is reformed, Pen has by no means settled to a life of study: theatres, pleasure gardens and parties occupy him. However, a new and salutary influence is introduced – George Warrington, with whom Pen shares lodgings. The Major is at first surprised by Warrington's appearance, 'dressed in a ragged old shooting-jacket ... drinking beer like a coalheaver'; but, to his relief, Warrington re-appears to play host 'dressed like a gentleman' (362–3). All Warrington's possessions bear the mark of long usage, in contrast to Pen's room, which was 'rather coquettishly arranged' and, according to Warrington, typical of a dandy: '"[he] has got curtains to his bed and wears shiny boots and [has] a silver dressing-case"' (364). Warrington represents a new and thoroughly Victorian version of the gentleman – the Man in the Jacket.

As Ellen Moers points out, the thinness of Carlyle's proposition in *Sartor Resartus* that clothes now replaced the man could be covered by 'the eloquence of rage', but in 1841, in a piece for *Fraser's Magazine*, 'Men and Coats', Thackeray had painted himself into an absurd corner in which the 'manly, simple and majestic' jacket becomes a moral symbol: it is the costume of a gentleman, 'simple, steady, and straightforward ... a man IN A JACKET is a man. All great men wore jackets.' By 1850, in fact, the slender cut-away coat was being replaced by the shorter, fuller, more sombre frock-coat – a less sexy, less revealing garment, as Anne Hollander notes.[25] The working man's short-waisted, thick cloth jacket, a relative of Thackeray's rural 'worsted-net jacket ... with pockets all over'[26], was also beginning to work its way up the social scale, until by the century's end it had become the main component of the ubiquitous, dark, three-piece suit. Thackeray's evangelical leanings found such homespun sobriety appealing, but in his fiction his satirist's nose for the absurd collides with his reductivist ideals, and he never quite allows worthy, decently jacketed fellows, like Warrington, to set the tone.

When Warrington learns of Pen's current set of unpaid debts and of 'how great the son's expenses had been, and how small the mother's means', he scolds him: 'You will discover what a number of things you can do without when you have no money to buy them. You won't want new gloves and varnished boots, eau-de-Cologne ... You have been brought up a molly-coddle, Pen, and spoilt by the women.' (393) These bracing remarks – an inspiration for reform, surely? – have no effect whatever on Pen's tastes, not even for a wilderness of jackets. A vignette, featuring Warrington rescuing the manuscript of Pen's novel from the fire, shows him in a short, stout jacket set against a wilting Pen in a longer, slimmer coat. The success of the rescued novel, however, saves Pen from the fire of Warrington's advice and he becomes something of a literary lion at evening parties. At one of these parties, he strikes another

Figure 8 Pen and Warrington. Thackeray's illustration to 1850 edition of *Pendennis*.

guest as 'one of those little Mayfair dandies ... with his very best chains, shirt-studs and cambric fronts' (435), indicating that, by way of personal adornment, Pen has sacrificed nothing. We might also see in Thackeray's increasing focus on Pen's jewellery the typical novelistic preoccupation with extraneous detail 'to convey the notion of frivolity'[27] which Anne Hollander has described in relation to female dress in fiction. If Pen has learnt to make money at last, he has also learnt how to waste it on frippery. His dandyism has drifted from self-creation to egregious self-indulgence. He has not become a useful member of society, but he has learnt how to penetrate Mayfair circles and display his 'fine linen' in public.

Pen, in London, pursues his rakish way with women, carrying on a sentimental flirtation with Blanche, encouraged by the Major, who has his sights on the Amory cash, while Laura is relegated to a rural, fall-back position. Foker reappears as Pen's rival with Blanche, and it is here that Blanche's crinoline is allowed full illustrative reign, although textually she remains meekly dove-coloured. Foker's own over-the-top tendencies in dress – 'pantaloons in many different stripes, checks and colours' –

Figure 9 Blanche and Foker. Thackeray's illustration to 1850 edition of *Pendennis*.

and his anxiety to achieve a D'Orsay hair-style – 'curly-moi un pew' (497) – culminate in an illustration, where his outfit of an enormous bow-tie, two waistcoats and a widening pair of trousers, matches that of Blanche, who rises demurely out of an ocean of flounces. What we see here are the fashions of 1850: the replacement of the cravat with the bow, the dark two-piece suit, and the wider trousers. Blanche's skirts have reached the greatest width possible in petticoats, before the mid-century invention of the cage-crinoline.

In the early part of the century the simple, clinging verticals of female dress, followed (and frequently revealed) the lines of the body beneath, and had its equivalent in the new, pared-down, slim male silhouette – there was a kind of egalitarianism between the sexes in these styles. The voices of women in social reform, in literature and even to some extent in politics, seemed to be strengthening. But the accession of Victoria to the throne paradoxically returned women to docility and secluded domesticity. Female fashions ballooned into the rounded horizontals of the crinoline skirt, concealing the body yet emphasizing its fertility; hair

Figure 10 Pen and Fanny. Thackeray's illustration to 1850 edition of *Pendennis*.

drooped and shoulders sloped submissively downward, impeding movement and implying a general lack of muscle. The invention of chemical
dyes in the 1850s added rainbow colouring to this voluminous female
form. Conversely, male dress became increasingly angular, severely vertical and monochrome; shoulders thickened and sharpened in heavy
jackets and coats, and dark trousers replaced light pantaloons and
breeches, relegating them to either servant's uniform or ritualized court
dress. Macho musculature and sombre austerity offset and formed a
background to an exaggerated and colourful femininity, visibly
embodying the separation of male and female worlds. Pen is not shown
with Blanche in the illustrations in the latter part of the novel – her 1850s
modishness and burgeoning skirts might overwhelm Pen's languid elegance as a latter-day Regency Buck – for she is a foreground, not a background figure. The comedy of Foker's parvenu fashion excesses in the
illustrations lends Pen's appearance dignity and taste by contrast– unjus-
tified, perhaps, but to retain sympathy for Pen, readers would have to
recognize in him the gentleman of the 1850s, as well as the Regency Buck
– 'a man whose dress is neat, clean, simple and appropriate'.[28]

Blanche is perhaps too much competition for Pen as Sex Object. He is
more comfortable when patronizing a Cockney *grisette* – Fanny Bolton. It
is with Fanny that Pen comes closest to falling from the grace of a dandy
to the disgrace of a cad. Having rescued Fanny and her mother from
embarrassment in Vauxhall Gardens, he then squires them around and
finds his vanity tickled by the significant leers they receive from Lord
Colchicum, an ancient buck of the Major's vintage. Pen pursues the flirtation, and in an illustration of Pen with Fanny we see how his slim elegance in a tail coat and pale waistcoat retains the Brummell ideal, while
a bow tie, the lengthened points of the waistcoat and wider trousers bring
him subtly up-to-date. Fanny's demure, un-crinolined skirts do not challenge Pen in any way.

Fanny, indeed, just adds to the narrative another and, for her, more
dangerous form of worship of Pen. Parading with him in Temple Gardens,
she thinks how '[h]is white duck trousers and white hat, his neckcloth of
many colours, his light waistcoat, gold chains, and shirt-studs, gave him
the air of a prince of the blood' (626).[29] When his visits unaccountably
stop she agonizes: 'Pen was not wicked and a seducer. Pen was high-
minded in wishing to avoid her. Pen loved her: the good, the great, the
magnificent youth, with the chains of gold and the scented auburn hair!'
(650) The smooth transition from moral esteem to chains of gold and
scented hair is revealing. In truth there is nothing high-minded about his
absence – he is ill. Fanny devotes herself to nursing him, but when Helen

and Laura discover her in Pen's room, she is dismissed as a vile seductress – ironically, in view of Pen's erotic impact on Fanny. As Barbara
Hardy says, 'we are never quite sure what Thackeray is doing with the
problem of Pen's sexual innocence ... but what Pen is on the brink of in
the Fanny episode is not the loss of virginity but the seduction of a poor
virgin'.[30] Pen knows that the pleasures of Vauxhall, the theatre and walks
in public gardens are not innocent; if he has not seduced Fanny with his
peacock display, he has certainly compromised her.

The collision between the values of early and mid-century, which
underlies the fashioning of Pen, here surfaces in the Major's outrage,
when Helen suggests that if Pen is 'guilty' he must marry Fanny: '"Good
God! are you mad?" screamed the Major.' (690) Pen, a chip off the old
Major's block, has in fact never had any ideas of the sort, and while
Fanny breaks her heart, the convalescent Pen takes off for Europe, with
his family and Warrington. If the Major has been less active during the
central sections of the novel, he now returns to conclude it; and if he is
– as Barbara Hardy suggests – 'the prime agent in the corruption of Pen',
the 'representation of all things wordly',[31] then that conclusion, to satisfy
Victorian readerly desires, should see the Major defeated by Warrington
in his jacket – representative of mid-Victorian codes of manliness,
morality and restraint. But Pen and the Major are in fact envied by
Warrington: 'He found himself looking at the young bucks ..., Pen
amongst them, with their calm, domineering air, and insolent languor:
and envied each one of them some excellence or quality of youth.' (720)
And the Major? – 'When [he] travelled he wore a jaunty and juvenile travelling costume; to see his back still you would have taken him for one of
the young fellows whose slim waist and youthful appearance Warrington
was beginning to envy.' (721) In a vignette we see Warrington (in a jacket),
at Helen's side, gazing wistfully at a distant group of young men and
women, a pictorial expression of the sense of premature elderliness which
aligns him to Helen. It might be worth remembering here, since the
vignette highlights the point, that Victorian social codes had become by
the 1840s the province of women; rackety dandies like D'Orsay and
Disraeli were representative of a past age. Woman was the civilizing force,
the moral and spiritual centre of Victorian life, to whom the male might
turn from the wicked world of work to be restored and tamed. So
Warrington turns to Helen, while Pen, the young buck, continues to
stray.

When Helen's death follows the European trip, that influence is removed.
The Major has already reintroduced Pen to opposing and more amusing
definitions of 'gentlemanliness' than domesticity and thick jackets when he

draws his attention to the exploits of the Marquis of Steyne in Paris, an ancient rake and survivor of *Vanity Fair*, who has broken the bank, gambling three nights running 'without showing the least emotion at his defeat or victory – "And that's what I call an English gentleman, Pen, my dear boy."' (722) And indeed, when we next view Pen in costume, it is at Epsom races through the eyes of Fanny Bolton. Pen is in mourning still, but a mourning in which sex appeal is the calculated effect:

> There he stood, about whom she was going to die ten months since, dandified, supercilious, with a black crepe to his white hat, and jet buttons in his shirt front: and a pink in his coat that someone else had probably given him; with the tightest lavender-coloured gloves sewn with black; and the smallest of canes ... the trinkets at his watch-chain, the ring on his hand under his glove, the neat shining boot (748).

The devil, one could say, is in the details – the pink flower, the black trim to the lavender gloves, the fact that the ring is now under the glove. (Disraeli has become middle-aged and respectable.) *The Handbook of Etiquette,* in an argument with itself over cost and taste, concludes that light colours, because easily soiled, are 'proofs of expenditure ... light gloves are more esteemed than dark ones, and the prince of glove-colours is undeniably lavender'. This leads the author to remark that a white hat indicates 'fastness'[32] in a man – an association which we have lost, but which seems significant here. The focus on such luxurious detail is almost shocking, given the novel's depiction of Helen's self-sacrificial devotion to Pen, and the fact that the scene follows a sentimental one where Pen and Laura go through her effects. But Fanny's disillusioned eye records the scene with the realistic clarity of William Frith's painting of *Derby Day*. That was how Pen looked: this is the chaotic clash of modern moral and fashionable values. In terms of perspective and description in the Realist Novel there is, however, a curious contradiction: Fanny stands at a distance observing, but unseen by Pen. Yet what she records is minute, and the minutiae are crucial to the effect. The closeness of her gaze, unreal on the one hand, lends a bitter sexual intensity which is psychologically wholly real, on the other.

If Pen seems to have achieved at last a Baudelairean heroism as a *flâneur* among the hats and suits of Modern Life, he is no hero in Victorian Fanny's eyes. One could say that the Major's out-dated definition of an English gentleman – the cold-hearted Regency Buck – has finally triumphed. 'You are your uncle's pupil' (795), declares Warrington. But no one triumphs long in a Thackeray novel and the Major has had intimations of mortality, for all his jauntiness in Europe: 'To say the truth, the old gentleman's reputation was somewhat on the wane'; society now cared little for his traditions '"of the wild Prince and Poyns", and of the heroes of fashion' (871). Thackeray constantly undermines heroic pretensions, and yet he still yearns for the past: he is 'anti-romantic but not satisfied with the present', as Mario Praz observes, and it is from the depths of Thackeray's 'disillusioned meditations upon mortality and the impermanence of all human things ... that a breath of poetry most often arises'.[33] As he flits on his parasitic way from house to house to grouse-moor in the autumn hunting season, the Major reflects on Seasons of the past: 'the Regent's Lady Lorraine ... beautiful, gorgeous, magnificent in diamonds and velvets, daring in rouge'; and 'today's Lady Lorraine – a little woman in a black silk gown, like a governess'. And what of 'the wits of the world', 'the old polished gentlemen'? 'the breed is gone – there's no use for 'em: they're replaced by a parcel of damned cotton-spinners and utilitarians, and young sprigs of parsons with their hair combed down their backs. I'm getting old: they're getting past me.' (872–3)

In his gloom he grows tetchy with his valet Morgan, the single, bullied and over-worked member of the Major's fashion-maintenance team. Not only is no man a hero to his valet, but the novel itself was begun in 1848, the Year of Revolution, 'a period of high alarm for the middle-classes'.[34] And Morgan, alarmingly, revolts. He is in fact now the owner of the Major's lodgings and furniture, and, as one of a new breed of 'capitalists', rather wealthier than the Major himself. Morgan declares he will bear his treatment no longer: 'I'm tired on it: I've combed your old wig and buckled your old girths and waistbands long enough, I tell you.' The Major is oddly impressed by this fighting talk, but regrets the loss of Morgan's receipt for boot-varnish, 'which was incomparably better and more comfortable to the feet than any he had ever tried' (879–80). The old soldier rallies, however, and next morning before his departure, he not only flourishes a pistol at Morgan, but reveals that this revolt has been far from rationally democratic; over the years Morgan has been pilfering the Major's wardrobe and he is now planning to make off with a velvet cloak, a gold-headed cane, and – of course – 'some fine lawn-fronted shirts' (888) – Morgan's ambition is to *become* the Major, not inaugurate a socialist dawn. Accompanying the scene is a final illustration (889), where the point is vividly made: the Major faces Morgan, as in a mirror, and ironically, his frock coat and wide trousers are more modish than the younger man's narrow tail-coat, expansive white shirt and skin-tight pantaloons – a moral, physical and sartorial victory for the 'old breed'.

With a pistol, as well as the new Victorian force of law and order held over him, in the person of a policeman, Morgan is forced to acknowledge

Figure 11 The Major and Morgan. Thackeray's illustration to 1850 edition of *Pendennis*.

his thefts, release his landlady from debt and pay back the ruinous interest he has been charging her. For the moment the Major's old-fashioned ways with a pistol, his gallantry to a lady, have triumphed, although he is still homeless and Morgan is still rich. But the Major's real defeat, the defeat of his political ambitions for Pen – to be financed by Blanche's fortune – comes at Pen's own hands. In a burst of new-found Victorian probity, Pen decides to reject the money, when it is discovered that Blanche's paternity, and therefore her cash, is not all it seems. Illegitimacy poses no problems for the Major's *ancien régime* standards, but, despite his pleas, Pen, in a piece of fine rhetoric, declares that though he will honour his engagement to Blanche he will not degrade himself with her money. Quite what he thought he had done with Laura's money is another question. As he is by now making a living as a writer, he has no urgent financial need, and is happily saved from a misalliance with Blanche when, in a rather milquetoast rerun of Rawdon Crawley's confrontation with Becky and the Marquis of Steyne in *Vanity Fair,* Pen surprises Blanche in the act of receiving a costly bracelet from Foker.

Resigning her to Foker, Pen rushes off to propose to Laura – who accepts him.

There is a decidedly hurried air about these last pages; as though the reader must not have too much time to consider what Henry James called the 'distribution at the last of prizes, pensions, husbands, wives, babies, millions, appended paragraphs and cheerful remarks'.[35] The wedding day arrives and for his last stand as a dandy, Pen is 'attired in a new hat, a new blue frock-coat and blue handkerchief, in a new fancy waistcoat, new boots, and new shirt-studs ... made his appearance at a solitary breakfast table' (972). Thackeray repeats 'new' five times here, and if we consult *The Handbook of Etiquette* on the question of 'newness', we find that 'while freshness is essential ... a visible newness in one's clothes is as bad as patches and darns'. Worse still, newness is vulgar: 'to be in the extreme of fashion, with bran new clothes ... does not differ immensely from being badly dressed'.[36] We might also ask if it is possible to be a dandy without spectators. Brummell stood aloof, but on a pedestal, *for* an audience; Pen parades alone at the breakfast-table. As the wider world of male imitators and female admirers retreats and the narrow walls of virtue and domesticity close round him, we might note that Pen's new coat is the unsexy frock-coat. Warrington, in a congratulatory letter conjures up a future of nurseries and 'uncle' George, and on the last page we see the poor Major being read aloud to by Laura – no doubt from an improving text. It is a dispiriting line-up for a final tableau.

But this dissatisfaction is a contradictory mix. Pen, in good Bildungsroman fashion, becomes integrated into his society. We may still wonder how it has been done, and what he has learnt. He has behaved fairly badly all round – especially to Laura – but she has married him. Is Laura a punishment or a prize? In *Vanity Fair*, it could be said that Amelia – an earlier 'Laura' – will be Dobbin's dull burden for life, a 'reward' for his spiritlessness. Laura has already warned Pen that she is less indulgent than Helen, and as a Ruskinian 'Queen' in her 'Garden' she will be a damper on any Regency Buck tendencies. If Pen's image on his wedding day is triumphant, his peacock preening is also complacently solipsistic; furthermore, his glossy consumerist show looks vulgar by the standards of the Victorian world which he is now entering. We might ask why Laura accepts him – perhaps her biological instincts are responding to Pen's 'display characteristics', which in the bird-species, according to neo-Darwinian biologist, W. D. Hamilton, 'have evolved in response to the female need to assess the male's state of health'.[37] As a Regency Dandy his gorgeous, ever-changing wardrobe and irrepressible behaviour have entertained the reader for over 900 pages; but as a Victorian paterfamilias there will be an end to larks with girls in Vauxhall – as, in fact there was shortly be an end to Vauxhall.[38] These last pages are thoroughly unsettling, for it seems Pen will become dull – as indeed he does, in *The Newcomes* – and that is not a comforting way to resolve social problems or integrate young men into the adult world.

Gordon Ray in his biography of Thackeray, points out that Thackeray had 'come to know London society in the final period of aristocratic predominance',[39] and while he fiercely satirized this 'ornamental society', in figures like the Major, he did not warm to the new Victorian dispensation and regretted the passing of the 'old breed'. Mario Praz calls Thackeray's attitude toward modern progress 'elegiac and melancholy': the most successful parts of his novels 'are always descriptions of the protagonist's youth'.[40] There is, as Ellen Moers says, a strong personal element to Thackeray's chastisement of Pen, 'as though going over his own career. ... He had wanted to be Pen; what his mature self chastens in the novel is the dream world of his younger self.'[41] His own youthful extravagance had not made him a handsome buck, but, as he wrote to Mrs Brookfield, '[m]y vanity would be to go through life as gentleman – as a Major Pendennis you have hit it'.[42] Thackeray cannot therefore seriously punish Pen for fulfilling his own dreams of what might have been. Nor can he damn the Major, the figure Thackeray sensed he might have become, had his vanity been satisfied: solitary, selfish and worldly, certainly – but gallant and even convincing in his belief that the glamorous figures and the pleasures of the past constitute a lost Arcadia. And Warrington is, of course, the Man in the Jacket that Thackeray felt in theory – in 1850 – he ought to be.

Warrington's hirsute aspect and rough jacket herald a Victorian prototype, and John Sutherland, in his Introduction to the novel, suggests that it is his figure which has had the most lasting influence, pioneering 'the physically powerful, hairy, philistine chauvinist "Tom Brown" ideal of English masculinity on which the Empire was built'.[43] But Thackeray never had much truck – though a lot of fun – with nabobs (Jos Sedley) or military adventurers (Barry Lyndon and George Osborne) in his fiction. Warrington's stout hairy jacket pales before Pen's slim distinction. Warrington has an adulterous wife, bribed to stay away from him, and is therefore denied Laura, whom he loves, and who of course loves the unworthy Pen. Everyone, in fact loves Pen. Pen is handsome, charming and infectiously bent on worldly pleasures, confident that he deserves success and getting it. His confidence and appeal is derived largely from his appearance, and Thackeray, for all his mockery of dandyism, is careful to maintain Pen's beauty in both text and illustration to the last.

The 'effortless effort of Brummell's style',[44] as Anne Hollander says, packs a strong erotic charge. Pen has been a Sex Object throughout this long novel, and enjoyably so. But under a Victorian dispensation, Woman must be the decorative object, focus of the desiring male gaze.

If Thackeray, as Moers concludes, withdraws the gift of heroism from Pen as punishment for vanity and self-regard, there is, nevertheless, no other recipient for the reader's sympathies. The only real alternative is that older roué, the Major, who, while almost 'past it' by the end, in both text and picture, recalls a youth that parallels Pen's – an evocation of Stendhal's *chasse au bonheur*. He had and still has that '*gaîté de coeur*' that puts him among Stendhal's Happy Few: he might say at the last, with Julien Sorel, 'Leave me to enjoy my ideal life.'[45] His skinny frame, in a discreetly updated costume, has an absurd but touching courage that contrasts with the portly, démodé Morgan, in the novel's final illustration of the two men. Morgan, Foker and Warrington, representatives of the new Victorian order, tending to embonpoint, are the captives not captors of women and sartorially out-of-date, vulgarly over-done, or boringly homespun.

But even the Major cannot be left to his 'ideal life', and he is finally reduced by Laura to an inactivity appropriate to his years. Anne Thackeray Ritchie recalls that her father 'had a certain weakness for dandies ... Magnificent apparitions used to dawn upon us in the hall, glorious beings ascended the stairs.'[46] He knew he should strive to be Warrington in his Jacket – unselfish and indifferent to ornament – but in spirit, as Thackeray wrote of himself, 'I am walking about in 1828 ... in a blue dress-coat and brass buttons, a sweet figured waistcoat, looking at beautiful beings with gigot sleeves.'

What makes this novel most alive, then, obsessively concerned as it is with question of male fashions in a borderland between the *ancien régime* and industrialized modernity, is its inability to make sense of the world it brings to life. Thackeray could contrive no satisfactory compromise between the decorative and the virtuous life: 'There is an enjoyment of life in these young bucks of 1823', Thackeray wrote of Cruickshank's images of Tom and Jerry, 'which contrasts strangely with our feelings of 1860.'[47] Loyalty to that *douceur de vivre* is a stronger motive in Thackeray's fiction than zeal for moral reform, and his urge to get his half-hearted sop to Victorian moralizing over quickly is justified by the novel's enduring and exhilarating double image of a Dandy – the Major defying the conventions and realities of old age with wigs and corsets, and Pen, Fashion Icon and Sex Object, in a succession of gorgeous outfits, celebrating the pleasures of youth. There is a kind of satisfaction in Thackeray's defeat of his better-self.

The Woman in White and the Woman in Colour: Wilkie Collins's *Woman in White* and Mary Braddon's *Lady Audley's Secret*

Laura Bell, Thackeray's 'good' girl, is colourless in every sense. She is not seen in white, however; not even at her wedding, where only Pen's wedding clothes are described. Thackeray's maiden in white is of course Blanche, who has spotted that for marital purposes the image of the pallid, submissive angel is an idea whose time has come, and she plays the part to the hilt. Blanche, though a fraud, is a comic creation, therefore not a serious contender for the hand of the hero, and she poses no threat to the hold which this ideal retained in the period's life and literature. As John Harvey points out in his study of *Men in Black*, 'colour died in menswear in the nineteenth century' and the 'stark formula of black men and bright women, seems another of that century's sharpened severities'.[1] The introduction of aniline dyes in the 1850s brightened the palette of female dress, but as we see in the paintings of the period – in the work of Manet, Tissot, Whistler, for example – white was also very much in fashion. Its connotations were not simply virginal or bridal, but could suggest festivity, formality and refinement; on the other hand, it was also the colour of mourning, shrouds and ghostliness.

Mary Braddon, in a magazine interview, acknowledged the debt her best-selling novel of 1862, *Lady Audley's Secret*, owed to Wilkie Collins's popular Sensation Novel of 1860, *The Woman in White*. Collins – as his title suggests – had fixed on the period's central image of the feminine and played on its nuances, although focusing on the association of white with passivity and death rather than with youth and festivity. In Braddon's novel the central situations of *The Woman in White* are reversed: the criminal is female, her victims male; Anne Catherick and Laura Fairlie, Collins's two heroines, are rescued from a lunatic asylum, Lady Audley is finally locked up in one. But as Toru Sasaki has pointed out, 'she was also expressing opposition to [Collins]. ... Lady Audley was clearly meant as a protest against the passive and angelic heroines of the period.'[2] Extending the idea of reversal or protest to the novel's title image of a Woman in White, Lady Audley, I suggest, is a Woman in Colour, and the colouring of her appearance is bound up with her 'secret' – a secret contained in Braddon's images of her, images closely allied to pictorial 'sensations' of the period.

Even Collins's admirers must have found Laura Fairlie, the heroine of *The Woman in White*, irritating. A helpless victim of the men around her, Laura, like so many of Collins's heroines, is bleached into almost non-existence. She is pale, fair-haired, with eyes of 'liquid, turquoise blue', and the bleaching effect is redoubled in her paler alter ego, Anne Catherick, the first woman in white we meet. The frequent confusion of the two women with ghosts further undermines their physicality and provides several of the novel's more alarming moments. In the novel's first chapter, the hero, Walter Hartright, crossing Hampstead Heath at night (never a good idea), is stopped by a hand on his shoulder: 'there, as if it had that moment sprung out of the earth or dropped from the heaven – stood the figure of a solitary Woman, dressed from head to foot in white garments ... her hand pointing to the dark cloud over London, as I faced her'; her face is 'colourless', her hair 'a pale brownish-yellow'. She is, as Harvey says, 'ghost, angel, moon-goddess, corpse, bride, mourner, virgin'[3] all at once. A further disturbing option presents itself when at the end of the chapter we hear that 'she has escaped from my Asylum. Don't forget: a woman in white.'[4]

Collins leaves the mystery unexplained for some time, adding to it by introducing a second woman in white, Laura Fairlie, also seen at night, on the terrace of Limmeridge House, where Hartright is now her tutor. 'My eyes fixed upon the white gleam, of her muslin gown and head-dress in the moonlight,' (WW 59) and it is here that he first notices her disquieting resemblance to the woman on Hampstead Heath, now identified as Anne Catherick. White, like black, is a denial of colour – but paradoxically while these non-colours can be denying and self-effacing, they are also dramatic. Characters dressed in black or white on the stage immediately draw the eye. Walter's attention is in fact caught by the two women's white dresses. Laura's white suits her, but, as Harvey observes, she also uses white, as men did black, to avoid class and wealth distinctions. Walter comments that she is almost 'poorly dressed in her plain white muslin', a choice that reflects her 'natural delicacy and ... aversion to the slightest display of her own wealth' (WW 54); Laura and Anne are all innocence and goodness: yet Anne seems hopelessly distrait, and Laura leaves an impression on Walter of 'something wanting in her' (WW

51). White is an absence, a blank sheet waiting to be filled. Anne always wears white and dies young. Laura's single gesture to colour is in the 'delicate' blue stripe on one of her white dresses – and for the evening before her dreaded marriage to Sir Percival Glyde she wears blue silk.

Thereafter Laura is wisely kept out of most of the novel's action. She could be said, as Harvey points out, 'to personate femininity as absence'.[5] Often too weak to leave her room, ill, believed dead, in a lunatic asylum, and then finally reduced to such childishness that she is unable to speak, she becomes what Alfred Hitchcock called 'the MacGuffin' – a reason for others to act. One of the most attractive of those others is Marion Halcombe, her dark and voluptuous half-sister. Marion dresses more interestingly and colourfully, in rich yellow silk for evening-wear; and when she climbs out of her window to eavesdrop on Count Fosco's plot against Laura, she compounds the unfemininity of the action by removing not only her silks but her petticoats – of which there were many in the 1860s – to stand in the rain in the more masculine colouring of dark flannel and a black cloak. Count Fosco is one of literature's more appealing villains, not least because he admires Marion, 'this magnificent woman' whom he compares with 'that poor flimsy pretty blonde' (WW 331), Laura. But Collins quickly scotches Marion's sexual attractions for Walter, and confuses gender stereotypes by giving her a moustache. If this masculine attribute frees her to become the intelligent and resourceful protagonist who rescues Laura, it does not radically challenge the blonde/brunette oppositions of popular literature. In ending the novel with Walter installed in a *ménage à trois*, however, Collins seems to have recognized that as a companion for life, the infantilized Laura, without Marion, was an unpromising prospect.

Collins himself seemed to be pleading against such formulae in 1856 when he wrote that he wanted to 'revolutionize our favourite two sisters … Would readers be fatally startled … if the short charmer with the golden hair appeared before them as a serious, strong-minded, fierce-spoken, miserable, guilty woman?'[6] Readers, as we know, were in fact delighted in their millions when in 1862, Mary Braddon gave them Lady Audley, a heroine with Laura Fairlie's looks and Count Fosco's wicked ingenuity and energy. Laura/Anne had been the Woman in White; how then would Helen Maldon/Lucy Graham/Lady Audley/Madame Taylor colour her multiple personalities? The colouring, is, as I hope to show, principally a matter of dress, but also of description, representation and associated properties.

Braddon's heroine wears the white summer dress appropriate to a young unmarried woman when, at the sunny start of the novel, as the humble governess to the Dawson family, Lucy Graham, she wins the love of Sir Michael Audley. Her response to his proposal is her one almost-truthful moment, her one white dress: she falls at his feet, 'her thin white dress clinging about her, her pale hair streaming over her shoulders, her great blue eyes glittering in the dusk, and her hands clutching at the black ribbon about her throat'. She warns him that in her impoverished circumstances, her answer '*cannot* be disinterested'; when he goes on to ask if she loves anyone else, her reply – 'I do not love anyone in the world'[7] – is truthful but adroitly open. Accepting the situation as she defines it, he repeats his offer and she accepts. Whether she is like the disturbed, lower-class Anne Catherick, or the pure, refined Laura accepting a loveless union under pressure, her physical and material resemblance to Collins's doubled heroines is evident.

Lucy Audley does not precisely have a double, but Phoebe Marks has followed Lucy from the Dawsons, to become her maid at Audley Court. Phoebe 'might have been pretty ... but for the fault [of] an absence of colour': she has 'dull flaxen hair' and 'light grey eyes', even her dress shares this faded quality – 'the pale lavender muslin faded into sickly grey, and the ribbon knotted round her throat melted into the same neutral hue' (25). Each detail, down to the ribbon, is a faded restatement of Lucy's appearance; even Lucy's ability to cross class-boundaries is echoed in Phoebe's figure, which 'in spite of her humble dress ... had something of the grace and carriage of a gentlewoman'. More threateningly, however, Phoebe shares Lucy's upwardly mobile aspirations, and comments enviously on Lucy's luck to her loutish sweetheart, Luke, who fuels her envy. She recalls that Lucy had been a servant like herself, with 'shabby clothes ... worn, patched, and darned, and turned and twisted', but, she adds, – in a surprising coda of appreciation – 'always looking nice upon her, somehow. She gives me more than ever she got from Mr Dawson.' (27) Phoebe is less a double than an ambiguous shadow to Lucy, made dangerous by Luke. Luke himself is a coarsened version of Lady Audley's nemesis, Robert Audley – Sir Michael's nephew and heir (until Sir Michael's marriage), coincidentally the friend of George Talboys, Lucy's first, vanished husband. Robert is also the pursuing detective figure, soon to become a fixture of the Sensation Novel.

After her marriage, Lucy, now Lady Audley, appears in a sequence of highly-coloured, lavishly dressed set-pieces. The change in style and colour of dress reflects, on the most superficial level, her altered social and (apparent) marital status, from poor spinster governess to wealthy aristocratic wife; but the way Braddon dwells on these scenes, in a novel she wrote at high speed, suggests there is more to it than this. Collins's title concealed the fact that there were *two* women in white; equally Braddon's title teased the reader with the question of just *what* was Lady Audley's awful secret? – there seem to be several: she's a bigamist; possibly a murderer; she has had a baby, her father is an alcoholic, she's a forger, she may be mad – but most of these facts are revealed well before the end. Only hereditary madness is offered with any sense of revelation. Under that first white dress, she wears a trinket on a black ribbon, 'but whatever the trinket was, she always kept it hidden under her dress' (8): it is in fact the ring from her first marriage to George Talboys, who unexpectedly returns from Australia, causing her to push him down a well.

While working on *Lady Audley* Braddon was also writing *Aurora Floyd,* a novel in which Aurora's appearance is frequently noted, but the focus is almost entirely on hairstyles and headgear; dress is registered in brief colour-notes. Aurora too has her secret, but it is not really bigamy she conceals; it is a traditionally angelic heart beneath a hoyden's surface. Elsewhere Braddon chose to describe dress precisely enough to date a novel. For example, the costume in which Lesbia intends to elope in

Figure 12 Fashion plate of rose-coloured satin robe. *The What-Not or Lady's Handy-Book*, 1862. London: Kent & Co.

Phantom Fortune (1884) is described minutely from her 'little blue silk toque' down to the toes of her 'dainty little tan-coloured boots'.[8] And in my final chapter, looking at another Braddon novel of 1884, *Taken at the Flood* (see pp. 238–40), I shall be examining her detailing of the heroine's wedding outfit to signal disaster. In *Lady Audley's Secret*, however, Braddon gives us neither single telling details nor fashion-plate jargon, but instead focuses on dramatically loaded effects. Henry James accused her in a review of 1865 of 'getting up' her 'photograph' of Lady Audley with 'the small change ... [of] her eyes, her hair, her mouth, her dresses, her bedroom furniture'.[9] it is not, however, photography she has in mind but, quite specifically, Pre-Raphaelite painting. The deliberate references in the novel to this other, earlier popular 'sensation' in the arts seem worth exploring.

Before Robert Audley actually meets Lucy Audley, he and George Talboys – just returned – enter her apartments while she is absent. Making their way through the intimacies of discarded dresses and untidy toilet-table, they penetrate her boudoir, where they face not her but her portrait. The narrator, generally absent from the book, interrupts the narrative here to comment on the painting: 'I am afraid the [painter] belonged to the pre-Raphaelite brotherhood, for he had spent a most unconscionable time upon the accessories of this picture – upon my lady's crispy ringlets and the heavy folds of her crimson velvet dress.' (69) First Robert, then George, looks at the picture:

> No one but a pre-Raphaelite would have painted, hair by hair, those feathery masses of ringlets with every glimmer of gold and every shadow of pale brown. No one but a pre-Raphaelite would have exaggerated every attribute of that delicate face as to give a lurid lightness to the blonde complexion and a strange sinister light to the deep blue eyes ... I suppose the painter had copied quaint mediaeval monstrosities until his brain had grown bewildered, for my lady, in his portrait of her, had something of the aspect of a beautiful fiend.
>
> Her crimson dress, exaggerated like all the rest in this strange picture, hung about her in folds that looked like flames, her fair head peeping out of the lurid mass of colour, as if out of a raging furnace. Indeed, the crimson dress, the sunshine on the face, the red gold gleaming in the yellow hair, the ripe scarlet of the pouting lips, the glowing colours of each accessory of the minutely painted background, all combined to render the first effect of the painting by no means an agreeable one. (70–1)

We should note that the demonic hints in these paragraphs are the narrator's. The focus is on colour but is selective, what the French critic Denis Apothéloz terms a *découpage*: that is, a description in which

certain details or effects in the text are 'cut off from [their] surroundings'[10] in order to give them particular significance. Here, face, hair and
dress are selected, but the background is described only as 'minutely
painted'. The dress is 'exaggerated', and taking into account the already
expansive skirts of the 1860s, so much crimson might well strike an
alarming note. George Talboys says nothing, Robert Audley says he dis-
likes the portrait; nevertheless, in the novel's final pages, visitors to
Audley Court admire 'the pretty, fair-haired woman' (446) in the portrait.

Braddon was evidently familiar with the work of the Pre-Raphaelites,
who had first shocked the London art world in 1848. Though they were
controversial and claimed to be radicalizing British art, in their first
phase they simply brightened and intensified its colour range, removing
the statutory layers of brown varnish that had washed over British art
after the Romantic period. Their choice of subject matter created a rage
for medieval themes on the one hand, and minutely realistic documents
of modern life on the other. Otherwise they continued to produce the moralizing narratives that typified nineteenth-century British painting. In
fact, with Ruskin's support, they were soon fashionable, though they
maintained a profitable reputation for outrage and modernity. It is worth
asking just which Pre-Raphaelite paintings Braddon could have seen,
with which works she might expect her readers to be familiar, and what
associations these would have had.

As we now know from Jennifer Carnell's biography, at the time of the
Pre-Raphaelite exhibitions of the 1850s, Braddon was pursuing a career
as an actress, mainly in Brighton, but with occasional appearances in
London and the north,[11] so she could have visited any London exhibitions in which she was interested. That she had more than a passing
interest in art is suggested by the fact that in 1865 she wrote a letter to
a fringe-Pre-Raphaelite, Alfred Elmore, suggesting titles for a work of his
which she had evidently seen before it was offered for exhibition.[12] In
Elmore's picture, *On the Brink*, a woman is the focus of a morally
ambiguous drama, the kind of scene characteristic of Pre-Raphaelite
work after 1860. Pre-Raphaelite images of women before this betray few
obviously sinister aspects: Rossetti's early pictures feature pure if etio-
lated virgins: Holman Hunt's seductive shepherdess, in his much-dis-
cussed *Hireling Shepherd*, is a cheerful, bouncing brunette.

Braddon's focus, in Lady Audley's portrait, on a meticulously painted
head of golden hair, blue eyes and a pale face against a brilliant dress
does recall, however, two of the most popular works exhibited by the Pre-
Raphaelite Brotherhood (PRB) at the Royal Academy, Arthur Hughes's
April Love of 1856 and his *Long Engagement* of 1859. Ruskin rhapsodized

Plate 4 Arthur Hughes, *The Long Engagement*, 1856. Birmingham Museum and Art Gallery.

over *April Love* in his *Academy Notes*, praising its sweetness and use of colour. The girl at the centre of both pictures conforms to the angelic stereotype – blue eyes and a tremulous, child-like face framed by fine gold hair. Both wear vivid violet blue (a colour we will see on Lucy Audley, and very fashionable at the time), both are set against a sharp green backdrop. The violent colouring runs oddly counter to the otherwise ideally angelic

appearance of the women, and in both cases their vividness almost oblit-
erates the background males. Although never exhibited, Hughes's *Aurora
Leigh* of 1860, takes the image further: blonde Aurora in her acid-green
dress overwhelms her dim suitor. Ellen Heaton, who commissioned the
work, wanted a more traditional white dress, but Hughes held out for
green – another attempt perhaps to escape the stereotype, as Aurora
Leigh was an avowedly feminist figure. Ruskin, urging Heaton to com-
mission a work from Hughes, assured her that he was 'quite safe – *everybody* will like what he does'.[13]

These popular images have nevertheless none of the hell-fire Braddon
hints at in Lady Audley's portrait. The essence of Braddon's plot,
however, is the success with which Helen Maldon inhabits her successive
roles. Jan Schipper argues that Braddon's women 'mimicked and mocked
the male's assumptions about the proper female',[14] but Lucy Audley is
not simply an actress, putting her costumes on and off, she *becomes* her
other personae, and Braddon never uses her earlier, 'real' name as she
moves from one identity to another. As a not very successful actress
herself, Braddon would have been familiar with the dangers of inauthentic mimicry. There is no suggestion that her heroine is anything
other than a model governess to the Dawsons, and a loving and attentive
wife to Sir Michael. Alicia Audley's dislike of Lucy is based not on any perceived threat, but contempt for her childishness and china-doll looks.
Lucy's sunny kindness is welcomed by her husband's tenants and no
demons are visible until she feels threatened by the boorish Luke Marks
and misogynistic Robert Audley. I would suggest, then, that it is part of
Braddon's scheme to remind the reader of actual Pre-Raphaelite icons of
blue-eyed, golden-haired blameless girlhood, an ideal to which Lucy
Audley, in life, seems to conform, while at the same time colouring the *fictional* portrait in sinister lights. Her surface must remain fixed as the
Victorian ideal – whatever other identities may develop beneath. To be
really dangerous Lady Audley must look utterly innocent.

The strength of a novel, as opposed to that of a painting, lies in the fact
that several images can be held by the mind at one time, denying a single
viewpoint on which to rest. As Lyn Pykett has emphasized in *The
Improper Feminine*, her book on the Sensation Novel, *Lady Audley* 'is
staged as a spectacle, just as within the narrative the character is staging
herself' – and, furthermore, to add to the instabilities of the text's surface,
being *re*-staged as a painting. The heroine becomes the object of our gaze,
but as Pykett points out, there is 'no single ideological perspective' nor
even 'a coherent range of perspectives', but a series of conflicting views –
'if the sensation heroine embodies anything, it is an uncertainty about

the definition of the feminine'.[15] Nina Auerbach, in her study of nine-teenth-century iconography, *Woman and the Demon*, describes strategies for maintaining angelic faces in mid-nineteenth-century fiction: among Dickens's pure angels, Little Nell dies young to stay intact; Sheridan LeFanu's Carmilla, while a cat-vampire at night, keeps a daytime angel face; Thackeray's demonic Beatrix Castlewood lives side by side with the ageless angel, Rachel. Auerbach notes that Braddon 'employs with schol-arly precision angelic iconography for demonic purposes … it requires only the fire of an altered palette to bring out the contours of the one latent in the face of the other'.[16]

Indeed the novel's Pre-Raphaelite colouring pales the morning after the viewing of the portrait, when Lady Audley, after a sleepless night tor-mented by the knowledge of the proximity of her first husband, appears in pink muslin, seen within the classic Victorian frame for a domestic 'Queen' – in the garden, gathering roses and innocently singing. The men-acing suggestions of the night before are overlaid and confused by this very different style of female imagery. Robert Audley is half-attracted to her, but her request for Russian sables – dark, ultimate luxury – give him pause; and 'her pretty fingers … this one glittering with a ruby heart; that encoiled by an emerald serpent; and about them all a starry glitter of dia-monds' (87), if they seem seductive, are also sinister: the jewellery, Robert notices, is worn to conceal the marks of some violent struggle.

Pre-Raphaelite colouring seeps back into the picture when she gives Luke Marks fifty pounds on his marriage to her maid Phoebe: 'Lady Audley sat in the glow of firelight … the amber damask cushions of the sofa contrasting with her dark violet velvet dress, and her rippling hair falling about her neck in a golden haze'. When Marks insolently demands more, she realizes he knows something of her secrets, and confronts him 'her clear blue eyes flashing with indignation' (108–9). Shortly after, when Robert Audley menacingly confronts her with his suspicions of her role in George Talboys' disappearance, she faints against the amber cushions, and 'shadows of green and crimson [fall] upon my lady's face from the painted escutcheons in the mullioned windows' (120). The colours are lurid rather than demonic, and recall John Millais' popular painting *Mariana*, of 1851, in which Tennyson's long-suffering heroine – in violet blue velvet – stands at her window of stained glass; as in the painting, colour seems to suffuse Lucy from without rather than from within.

Robert is dismissed from Audley Court for his suspicions and takes up lodgings in the local inn. Braddon returns here to the figure of Phoebe here, who after her marriage, is running the inn. We have already heard of her dull wedding on a foggy morning in a grey cast-off dress of Lucy's;

now Robert assesses her pale hair, her 'light grey dress [which] fitted as precisely as of old. The same neutral tints pervaded her person and her dress; no showy rose-coloured ribbons or rustling silk gowns ... Phoebe Marks was a person who never lost her individuality. Silent and self-contained, she seemed to hold herself within herself, and take no colour from the outside world ... "That ... is a woman who could keep a secret."' (131) If we are to take Lucy's beautiful, richly-coloured appearance as evidence of hidden depravity and crime, is Phoebe's restraint and secretiveness a sign of innate decency and virtue? Or is she like her mistress playing a part? Phoebe is an ambivalent figure, partly because Robert Audley, our 'reflecting consciousness', is, as hero, an unsympathetic misogynist. Phoebe's 'individuality' is for him a question of suppressing colour and decoration. The contrast of Phoebe with Lucy is not in Phoebe's favour: her dull neutrality signals treachery not decorum. And Lucy's worldly colouring is, for the reader, a more seductive experience.

Robert Audley makes an ally of Phoebe in his pursuit of Lucy, but Phoebe cannot really represent for Robert a balance or contrast to Lucy – she is the wrong class and already married. His early flutter of attraction to Lucy is short-lived; the emotion that really galvanizes him is his feeling for George Talboys: 'Who would have thought that I could have grown so fond of the fellow ... or feel so lonely without him?' (161) Braddon's subversiveness has its limits, however, and so she introduces Clara Tallboys, George's sister, to provide Robert with the 'proper feminine' love interest.

Robert first sees Clara together with her father, stereotypically employed 'with some needlework, the kind generally called plain work, and with a large wicker basket, filled with calicoes and flannels standing by her' (187) – an image Braddon's readers would have immediately recognized as that of the Domestic Angel working on serviceable clothing for the deserving poor. She is initially silent and undescribed, but on their second meeting she is passionate in her love for her brother and her wish to avenge his death. Robert is 'awe-stricken' with admiration: 'Her beauty was elevated into sublimity... his uncle's wife was lovely, but Clara Talboys was beautiful. Niobe's face ... could scarcely have been more purely classical than hers. Even her dress, puritan in its grey simplicity, became her beauty better than a more beautiful dress would have become a less beautiful woman.' (200) The distinction between Phoebe's grey and Clara's is simply a matter of language and association – classical white statuary and puritanism place Clara on a pedestal, as a religious and cultural icon, for 'awe-struck' gentlemanly worship. (We might look both backward here to Defoe and Roxana's deceptive use of puritan dress, and forward to George Eliot's

Middlemarch, where classical statuary and puritan-grey lend their virtuous associations to Dorothea.) Having been put in place as Robert's
eventual 'reward', Clara disappears from the text, emerging briefly, 'very
plainly dressed in a black silk gown and a large grey shawl' (257), to
spur him on, and finally, to claim him. As with Laura Fairlie, her supposed attractions remain wisely unexplored.

Hard on the heels of Clara's sublimated severities comes the novel's
most worldly and sumptuous account of Lady Audley. It is always a risky
and potentially reductive exercise nailing a factual detail to a fictional
account; Mary Braddon was not a notebook novelist nor even as meticu-
lous about train timetables as Wilkie Collins. She wrote at speed, which
sometimes led to slips. (In a later novel she calls the Italian police 'car-
bonari' – a nice confusion of cuisine with law-enforcement.) She does,
however, refer specifically to one painter, Holman Hunt, in a scene in the
novel, after Lady Audley has left the bedside of the sick Sir Michael and
returned to her boudoir – the boudoir whose inner recess contains her
Pre-Raphaelite portrait. These two descriptions – the portrait of Lady
Audley and Lady Audley in the boudoir – occasioned James's criticism of
the novel. The second description of the boudoir runs to over a page and
is so overloaded with accounts of *objets d'art*, furniture, rich colours – as
well as references to notorious French queens and courtesans – the whole
bathed in firelight, with a storm howling outside, that Braddon might reasonably be accused of overkill. I have elsewhere criticized Braddon for
using descriptive detail indiscriminately,[17] but it might well be suggested
in defence of her style that this particular description has its equivalent
in Holman Hunt's *The Awakening Conscience*, a work which had a sen-
sational reception at the Royal Academy exhibition of 1854 and with
which readers of the novel would be familiar.

Virginia Morris rightly notes in her study of murderous Victorian heroines, *Double Jeopardy*, that 'there is no Hunt work as evocative of the
sense of feminine evil that Braddon is trying to create'.[18] She suggests
alternatives: either Rossetti's *Lucrezia Borgia* or Burne-Jones's *Sidonia
von Bork*, both of 1860, as sources for Lady Audley's 'portrait'. There
seems to be some confusion here between two very different parts of the
novel: on the one hand there is the Pre-Raphaelite portrait of Lady
Audley, and on the other there is a description of Lady Audley in her
boudoir (which happens to contain a reference to Holman Hunt).

Chris Willis on her 'Braddon Website' page points to the same Burne-
Jones work as possibly 'the original of Lady Audley's Pre-Raphaelite portrait'[19] relating it to the first description of Lady Audley, though she
acknowledges the colour is wrong. *Sidonia von Bork* is indeed gorgeous

Plate 5 Holman Hunt, *The Awakening Conscience*. 1854. Tate Britain, London.

and sinister, but as Pykett says, Braddon's image of Lucy Audley is always ambiguous, and the image of Sidonia could never have been described at the end of the novel as 'the pretty fair-haired woman' of the portrait. Moreover, Burne-Jones was almost unknown at this time; his apprentice watercolour was bought by a Newcastle magnate, James Leatheart, and not exhibited until 1892.[20] As for Rossetti, he exhibited only once, privately, in the 1850s, – though his work at this time has a significance to which I will return.

In turning, then, to a consideration of *The Awakening Conscience*, we need to be clear that the woman at the centre of Hunt's work bears no resemblance to Lucy Audley. Hunt's Fallen Woman, detaching herself from her lover's embrace, is suffused by a repentance that has been stirred by memories of lost innocence. This innocence is embodied in the sunlit natural world seen through the window of her luxurious 'love-nest'. Lucy Audley, in contrast, is alone and unrepentant to the last. Hunt's brunette wears a loose, ivory gown in the Aesthetic style, but Braddon describes Lucy only briefly, and in sensual rather than in sartorially fashionable terms – 'the rich folds of drapery [fell] in long undulating lines from the exquisite outline of her figure'. She is beautiful, 'but made bewilderingly beautiful by the gorgeous surroundings' (295). As is clear from Ruskin's letter to *The Times*, defending *The Awakening Conscience*, it is the fevered, magnified focus on the details of the *setting* in this painting that draws the eye, not the rather vacuous central figure: 'nothing is more notable', Ruskin wrote, 'than the way in which even the most trivial objects force themselves upon the attention'. He felt there was something especially sinister in 'the terrible lustre ... the fatal newness of the furniture',[21] most evident in the piano at which the girl sits. Her sheet music lies on the piano and on the floor; beside the piano is an embroidery frame, whose coloured silks also tumble to the floor. Behind her is a gilt-framed mirror that reflects her figure within a window-frame, against a garden view.

In Lady Audley's 'elegant chamber' the piano is open, 'covered with scattered sheets of music ... my lady's fairy-like embroideries of lace and muslin, rainbow-hued silks and delicately-tinted wools littered the luxurious apartment; while the looking-glasses, cunningly placed at angles and opposite corners, multiplied my lady's image'. She embroiders for herself in silks, we might note – no calicoes for the underclasses here. The reference to Holman Hunt follows, after which Braddon intensifies the account of the room by listing china, gold, ivories, cabinets, figurines, Indian filigree, pictures, mirrors and drapery. The image concludes with Lady Audley looking not at a redemptive garden, but 'into the red chasms in the burning coals' (294–5). This account of her background reverses the *découpage* of the portrait description; Lucy Audley's figure is now placed within a surrounding mass of luxury objects, which are recorded in one sweeping, panoramic gaze, a bonfire of the vanities – almost an English version of Delacroix's spectacle of sex, death and consumerism in *The Death of Sardanapulus*.

As she had reversed the male/female situations of Collins's *The Woman in White*, Braddon now takes Hunt's modern moral subject of a Kept Woman, saved from the 'wages of sin' (all those shiny new things) by a vision of Eden, and reverses it. Contained in this reversal is a protest at the implausibility of Hunt's hopeful vision. Lady Audley is fixed and defined by the 'wages' of her respectable marriage, by even more shiny new things. The notion of giving it all up for an epiphany of grass and trees, trusting to the mercies of the patriarchal world of Robert Audley, is mocked by the sound of the wind in the leafless branches outside Lady Audley's window. Her figure, left unrealized and indistinct amid the intensely realized welter of rich objects, is neither evil nor sympathetic, but more simply, disturbing.

The Garden of Earthly Delights in which Lucy Audley now finds herself has become a nightmare. She has seen no reason why a determined and competent woman should not survive by her wits and also have the right to amass the trophies of success and respectability, the paintings and *objets d'art* of a Victorian consumerist world.[22] Denied legitimate masculine paths to material and social rewards, she has worked through the means available to beautiful women: men. She has arrived at her goal, her connoisseur's boudoir, which is now also her trap. To keep it she has to 'wade in blood' much further, for repentance is not really an option, and so she attempts to do away with the growing number of men in her path who threaten her reputation and thus her material gains. Faced with the evidence of her 'crimes' (though we might note that only the semi-criminal Luke Marks is actually harmed), she claims hereditary insanity is to blame for her actions. In the novel's most astonishingly subversive statement, however, Dr Musgrave, having examined her, diagnoses that 'there is no evidence of madness in anything she has done. ... When she found herself in a desperate position, she did not grow desperate. She employed intelligent means, and she carried out a conspiracy which required coolness and deliberation ... She has the cunning of madness with the prudence of intelligence ... She is dangerous.' (379) – an uncertifiable and more alarming condition.

Holman Hunt's repentant Magdalene is not Lucy Audley, although the material luxuries of Hunt's picture, that led to 'sin', are avowedly there in Braddon's text. To uncover the image of Lady Audley herself, we might return to Rossetti, whose gallery of female beauty has so frequently been evoked in relation to Braddon's heroines. Indeed, Jennifer Carnell records that Braddon's favourite stage version of *Lady Audley's Secret* was that of 1863 with Ruth Herbert, who had also modelled for Rossetti.[23] I have said earlier, Rossetti did not exhibit during the 1850s. It cannot, then, be a question of Rossetti influencing Braddon, but rather that of an idea – the idea of the Dangerous Woman – which begins to replace that of the Woman in White, an idea which Braddon and Rossetti had begun to explore simultaneously. What Arthur Hughes's blonde angels lacked were 'the strange-coloured fires' (71) of Braddon's first 'portrait'. In the unrealized figure of Lady Audley in the second description 'it requires only the fire of an altered palette', the slumbering volcano of a Rossetti woman to emerge from behind Hunt's pale girl, to reveal the true colours of Braddon's heroine.

By the1850s the original Pre-Raphaelite group had disbanded; Rossetti had withdrawn, the movement had acquired new members and could now be seen as moving toward Aestheticism, or, as has recently been suggested, a British version of Symbolism.[24] Rossetti had begun to experiment with Italian Renaissance subjects and a simplified colour range. And among a series of watercolours featuring the Borgias we find *Rossavestita* of 1851, a single female figure against a plain background, in voluminous crimson dress, with the mass of gold hair that would become Rossetti's signature. There can be no actual connection between this sketch and that first Pre-Raphaelite description of Lady Audley, but there they both are – startlingly crimson and gold heralds of things to come.

Rossetti moved back into oils in the late 1850s, and, phasing out his anorexic maidens, decided to 'exploit the more voluptuous style of Titian and Venetian art in general'.[25] Big, blonde Fanny Cornforth also entered Rossetti's life at this time and displaced ailing Elizabeth Siddal as model and mistress. The pivotal work in his new style was *Bocca Baciata*, painted in 1859 and exhibited in 1860 at the Hogarth Club. This innocent/seductive half-length figure of Fanny, trapped between a parapet and a dark floral background, richly dressed and jewelled and with flowing red-gold hair, marks the emergence of the distinctive Rossetti Woman. Placed in 'hieratic scenes of various kinds' these pictures 'arrange themselves in a dialectic of "Madonna and Whore" figures'.[26] There followed a succession of increasingly dangerous, beautiful females– *Fazio's Mistress*, 1863; *Morning Music* and *Venus Verticordia*, 1864; *The Blue Bower* and *Il Ramoscello*, 1865; *Monna Vanna* of 1866; *Lady Lilith*, started in 1864 and finished in 1868. They don't stop there, of course: like Mary Braddon's women they have many years of life ahead, but these sirens of the 1860s, who 'turn traditional portraiture on its head',[27] share enough characteristics with Lucy Audley – who turned traditional heroines on their heads – to make my point.

Perhaps the first thing to note is that the paintings are without attendant males – as are the two central descriptions of Lady Audley. What drives Lucy Audley is not sexual desire, after all – the man is only her means to an end, which is the possession and enjoyment of luxury. 'Luxury', as Lyn Pykett puts it, 'is erotic to Lady Audley.'[28] Rossetti's women are most frequently shown at dressing tables, usually alone,

Plate 6 D. G. Rossetti, *Lady Lilith*. 1864. Delaware Art Gallery, USA.

gazing into mirrors, or abstractedly out at the spectator – or, as Andrew Wilton suggests, 'into their own soul'.[29] Rossetti said of the first of these self-caressing women, *Fazio's Mistress* of 1863, that the picture 'was chiefly a piece of colour ... done at a time when I had a mania for buying bricabrac, and used to stick it into my pictures'.[30] With their vibrant colour, nets of golden hair and 'bricabrac', *Fazio's Mistress, Lady Lilith* or *Monna Vanna* might sit at the vacant centre of Braddon's version of *The Awakening Conscience* – and reverse Hunt's intentions. Hunt called Rossetti's new style 'remarkable for gross sensuality of a revolting kind',[31] and there is indeed nothing redeemed or redeemable about these big, brooding women, who threaten unnameable things if once allowed out.

Rossetti's women have not abdicated their positions as Queens in Gardens or Angels in Houses, but the fiction of power attached to such empty titles now threatens to become real. His Liliths, Pandoras and Proserpines do not exactly suggest wrongdoing or malevolence, but they are far too big for their spaces, and they push up against and out of parapets, windows, curtains and high hedges. Rossetti's rendering of dress has moved from an archaeological approach to a much less specific treatment, in which voluptuously draped figures can inhabit Titian's Venice, Winterhalter's mid-nineteenth-century Europe or the medievalizing modes of late nineteenth-century British Aestheticism. Shown in half-length and close to the picture surface, demanding the spectator's attention, Rossetti's women display symbols of the World, the Flesh and quite possibly the Devil: jewels, bottles, mirrors, brushes, textiles, and, above all, hair.

Mary Braddon's concluding account of Lucy Audley is similarly selective: the dreary room in the mad-house has a 'faded splendour of shabby velvet and tarnished gilding'; what appear to be mirrors turn out to be 'wretched mockeries of burnished tin' (389) – and a mockery of her luxurious boudoir. The light of a single candle illumines her figure, which rises out of the darkness in a defiant blaze of diamonds and golden hair; while her dress, undescribed but presumably dark, merges with the gloom. Confronting her adversary, Robert Audley, she plucks 'at the feathery golden curls as if she would have torn them from her head. It had served her so little after all, that gloriously glittering hair; that beautiful nimbus of yellow light.' (391–2) I resist defining Lady Audley by a single image, because I believe Braddon uses multiple images to confuse rather than define, but Rossetti's *Lady Lilith* contains enough suppressed violence, moral ambivalence, self-caressing sensuality – and hair everywhere – to make one wonder if Rossetti had not recently read *Lady Audley's Secret*. The companion poem he wrote for the painting speaks of Lilith winding round Adam's heart 'one strangling golden hair'.[32]

Like Lilith of pre-Christian legend, Lady Audley is a capable and intelligent woman, who sees herself the equal of the male, who refuses to lie down under a series of early reverses and then, bent on self-improvement like David Copperfield or Julien Sorel, sets out, like them, to secure much more than bare survival. Those are her transgressive secrets. For a woman in mid-nineteenth-century Britain the means to respectability and prosperity is a man, and, as she says, the means to a man are her golden-haired, blue-eyed, prettily-dressed good looks and the meanings society attaches to these looks. Angelic virtue only becomes tricky when things go wrong. Her angel self is still a workable pretence until Sir Michael consents to her incarceration, after which she confesses to hereditary madness as her 'secret'.

Braddon, as I have indicated, uses a montage of conflicting images to convey ambivalence. The portrait within Lady Audley's boudoir contains the artist/creator's insight – the prototype Rossetti woman in blazing red and gold – but other images drawn from the art of her time, and *beyond* her time, coexist and often conflict with that portrait. Images late in the novel are left unrealized, inviting the reader to colour them according to the way he or she has read the woman within her surroundings: there is, as Lyn Pykett says 'an uncertainty about the definition of the feminine'. If Derrida is right in believing that ethics begin with uncertainty, then Braddon's final blurring of Lucy Audley's image – in motivation as well as dress – is a move toward formulating an ethic in opposition to the ruling one. I have said that both Rossetti and Braddon continue to explore the Femme Fatale; this I should perhaps qualify by adding that Braddon's Lucy Audley is – as far as I have read in her immense oeuvre – the only consistently ambivalent and therefore memorably dangerous woman: the rest conform to the Victorian ethic or die. Although Braddon mentions that Lucy Audley's death takes place years later, our last image is of her blazing defiance, and of a 'pretty, fair-haired woman' (390) in a portrait, in the novel's final pages.

The ambivalence is then not only Lucy Audley's but Braddon's own ambivalence over her creation – she didn't do it again, though she had dealt a fatal blow to the old Woman in White. The precarious trajectory of Braddon's own career – from poverty to bare subsistence as an actress, to mistress then wife of an improvident man, and then hard-won security in respectable Richmond – did not invite further risks. It needed, in fact, a Rossetti – a man, most importantly – but also an outsider, a self-styled hedonist, who both shocked and seduced Victorian England with his images of women, to write tenderly and frankly of his mistress while she slept,

> I lay among your golden hair
> Perhaps the subject of your dreams,
> These golden coins. (D. G. Rossetti, *Jenny*, 1860)

–6–

'Mind and Millinery': George Eliot's *Middlemarch*

For Henry James, George Eliot represented the furthest end of the literary spectrum from Mrs Braddon – 'If she is not George Eliot', he said of the novelist Mrs Craik, 'neither is she Mrs Braddon.'[1] Eliot might have categorized Braddon's *Lady Audley's Secret* as yet another 'Silly Novel' by a 'Lady Novelist', one of the 'mind-and-millinery species' that she attacked in her essay of 1856. Braddon's unmasking of blonde, blue-eyed Lady Audley – superficially the Lady Novelist's 'ideal woman in feelings, faculties and flounces'[2] – would, however, have found favour with Maggie Tulliver, in Eliot's *Mill on the Floss* of 1860, who had had enough of books 'where the blonde-haired women carry away all the happiness'.[3] But Lady Audley's hidden face is, as we have seen, simply the demonic reverse of the 'angel' obverse and a sensationalist shock-tactic, at most a protest, rather than a considered reflection of the reality of women's lives.

There is no happy outcome for Maggie Tulliver; but at the end of *Middlemarch*, of 1871, both brunette Dorothea Brooke and blonde Rosamond Vincy marry again, with the traditional complement of prosperity and babies; the equation of marriage with 'happiness', however, is left unclear. The representation of Rosamond and Dorothea, in their search for fulfilment, does dwell on the seductive blonde hair of Rosamond but more crucially involves ideals of womanhood current in the early 1830s – a period of political reform. Their appearances, in particular their dresses, are ways in which they attempt to articulate these ideals, markers on the road to fulfilment.

Middlemarch is a historical novel; not quite what Richard Altick calls the Victorian 'distanced' novel, since, though it is set in a rememberable past, it does not end in the writer's present – it does, however, like the distanced novel, imply an affinity with it. Altick singles out *Middlemarch* as exceptional among distanced novels in its attempt to recreate 'the particular mental atmosphere, the basic attitudes and assumptions that prevailed in that earlier day'.[4] Those ideals of womanhood, formulating in the years before Victoria's accession in 1837, and descending like an iron curtain thereafter, had a bearing on the situation of women, and on the debates about women's education, rights and employment in the latter part of the century. Gillian Beer has pointed out how fully *Middlemarch* was 'in touch with the issues being debated in the women's movement of the 1850s and 1860s, and how thoroughly it entered the debates'.[5] The aim, therefore, of Eliot's deployment of dress will be to convey the period's 'attitudes and assumptions', as well as to represent the material world of 1831; but in neither case will it be so obtrusive that we lose the novel's relevance to the issues of 1870.

James had criticized Braddon for overloading her narrative with meaningless realistic detail. For Eliot 'the faithful representing of commonplace things'[6] was an article of faith; and true realism, as G. H. Lewes pointed out, was not '*detailism*' – 'coat-and-waistcoat realism' – but the kind of realism that harmonized rather than conflicted with the idealism of the preceding generation of writers. Realism, he believed was 'the basis of all Art, and its antithesis is not Idealism but *Falsism* … either paint no drapery at all, or paint it with the utmost fidelity'.[7] We tend – unthinkingly perhaps – to equate particularity with authenticity, and Eliot attacked the Lady Novelist for the way she 'chooses to conduct you to true ideas of the invisible … [by] a totally false picture of the visible'.[8] There is an echo here of Carlyle's *Sartor Resartus* of 1831, the *fons et origo* of all dress theory, and a work which influenced Eliot's early writing.[9] Carlyle insists on the 'unspeakable significance' of dress as a spiritual symbol: 'the thing visible, nay the thing imagined, the thing in any way conceived as visible, what is it but a garment, a clothing of the higher, celestial invisible?'[10] An honest representation of the everyday world was an almost religious duty, therefore, and a means whereby to trace the inward movements of the soul.

Fidelity, however, brought its own problems. When Eliot turned in 1861 to the composition of the historical novel *Romola*, she rejected the generalized sartorial shorthand of 'cloaks', 'veils' and 'robes' etc. which like an all-purpose theatre wardrobe, served to clothe almost any period described in romantic fiction. But James considered that with *Romola* Eliot's equilibrium 'was lost … and reflection began to weigh down the scale'.[11] She and Lewes spent months in Florence researching the book, and when they returned to London she 'applied for a ticket to the British Museum, trudging up to Bloomsbury to check the last details on Florentine dress'.[12] She herself later regretted her 'tendency to excess in this effort after artistic vision',[13] and James, for all his admiration, was unsparing: 'a twentieth part of the erudition would have sufficed, would have given us the feeling and colour of the time'.[14]

Braddon had drawn on the Pre-Raphaelites to describe Lady Audley but had focused on effects rather than minutiae. Eliot, however could be said to be more Pre-Raphaelite than Braddon in her rendering of Renaissance dress in *Romola*: the detailing of Monna Brigida's dress in Italian terms, for example, is analogous to the archaeological rendering of the costume and setting of John Millais' *Isabella*, a painting inspired by Keats's poem, *Isabella: or the Pot of Basil*.

> Three rows of pearls and a lower necklace of gold reposed on the horizontal cushion of her neck; the embroidered border of her trailing black velvet gown and her embroidered long-drooping sleeves of rose-coloured damask were slightly faded, but they conveyed to the initiated eye the satisfactory assurance that they were the splendid result of six months labour by a skilled workman. ... A handsome coral rosary hung from one side of an inferential belt, which emerged into certainty with a clasp of silver wrought in *niello*; and on the other side, where the belt again became inferential, hung a scarsella, or large purse, of crimson velvet, stitched with pearls.[15]

The description is assuredly accurate. Each detail is recorded, the wearer's intentions noted, and the reader guided to a response; but to a degree that the image becomes a confused blur. We might even miss the fact that the lady is fat. The photo-realistic phase of Pre-Raphaelitism was over, in fact, by 1860; the group had reformed, and as I suggested in Chapter 5, their work was moving in a Symbolist direction. Kathryn Hughes records in her biography of Eliot that she also consulted the encyclopaedic knowledge of Renaissance Florence of the painter Frederic Leighton – though Leighton's correctly draped Roman and Renaissance ladies are invincibly Victorian. Deference to Leighton added an over-upholstered air to *Romola*, rather than the innovativeness she sought.

Eliot's fiction after *Romola* displays fewer 'tendencies to excess' of this kind, but prosperity had afforded opportunities for a little domestic consumerism. Lewes and she bought a new house in Regent's Park in 1863, and Owen Jones (author of *The Grammar of Ornament*) was put in charge of the décor. Jones also took it upon himself to give Eliot 'a stern lecture on her general neglect of personal adornment ... [and] bossed her into a silver-grey dress'.[16] If she now appreciated the virtues of economy in narrative description, she had herself become aware of the pleasure of indulgence in clothes. Her sharpened appreciation of dress must have come into play when she began writing *Middlemarch* in 1869. Anne Hollander notes that Eliot takes pains to be precise, 'not just about details of costume, which indicate date, but about the phenomenon of personal perception and aspects of self-awareness that are felt in terms of dress'.[17]

If there are no descriptions in *Middlemarch* comparable to that of Monna Brigida's costume in *Romola*, something powerful in Eliot's perception of dress led Ellen Moers to declare, in her *Literary Women*, that Dorothea Brooke has 'what must be the most stunning wardrobe in Victorian fiction'.[18]

The novel, however, famously opens with an account of Dorothea and Celia Brooke's 'plain dressing'.[19] Dorothea's beauty is enhanced by 'poor dress' and her sleeves are no more stylish than those of Renaissance Madonnas; her bearing, nevertheless 'seemed to gain the more dignity from her plain garments, which by the side of provincial fashion gave her the impressiveness of a fine quotation from the Bible, – or from one of our elder poets, – in a paragraph of today's newspaper'. Celia, said to have common sense as opposed to Dorothea's cleverness, wears 'scarcely more trimmings', though there is 'a shade of coquetry in its arrangements'. Dorothea's taste in dress, Eliot explains, 'was due to mixed conditions, in most of which her sister shared'. As Karen Chase points out, 'a principle of *explanation*'[20] has been established to answer the implicit question of why both girls – especially Dorothea – dress so plainly. The 'pride of being ladies', their 'unquestionably good', Puritan ancestry, and that 'well-bred economy' which frowned on show and 'regarded frippery as the ambition of a huckster's daughter. ... Such reasons would have been enough to account for plain dress, quite apart from religious feeling, but in Miss Brooke's case, religion alone would have determined it.' (5)

In the opening passage's subordination of description to explanation, the narrator's perspective is generalized, situated in no particular time or place. Chase, however, mistakes Celia for the huckster's daughter of provincial tastes, with whose 'frippery' Dorothea's 'poor' dress is contrasted. It is not Celia but Rosamond Vincy who is the huckster's daughter, and the 'yard-measuring and parcel-tying' (5) days of Mr Vincy, the provincial silk merchant, lie not so very far back in the past. These apparently generalized references, used to throw the sisters' style into relief, become significant when we meet Rosamond, 'a maiden apparently beguiled by attractive merchandise ... the reverse of Miss Brooke' (61), words that recall the earlier references to shopkeeping and frippery, and suggest that the question of dress at this stage is not, as Chase says, 'a somewhat factitious puzzle'[21] but intended as a pattern of images worth our attention.

Although Dorothea's wardrobe is as yet scarcely 'stunning', Eliot does convey its strikingly dissident effect. A reviewer of 1872 hoped that young girls would not, like Dorothea, 'vow to dress differently from other women and ... regulate their conduct on the system of general disapproval',[22] and what we learn of Dorothea's dress is what it *isn't*, rather than what it is. Sleeves are mentioned in the novel's second line, and a glance at the fashions of the early 1830s confirms the period's fixation on sleeves. Known as *gigot* (leg-of-mutton) – or, with some justice, *imbecile* sleeves – the sleeve of the 1830s ballooned to the elbow, then narrowed tightly to the wrist: for sheer volume and elaboration the sleeve of the 1830s has never been surpassed.[23] Indeed, the upper half of women's bodies at this period carried a demanding load of collars, ruffs, ribbons, capes, scarves, lace, flora and fauna. Dorothea's choice is therefore a clear statement of dissent – her plain sleeves are conspicuously different, an intentional reference, perhaps, to Aesthetic or 'reformed' dress of Eliot's own time. Dorothea's image is neither in nor out of fashion: acceptable to a reader of 1871, it is also comparable to a timeless Bible verse or poem set gravely amid the day's trivia.

'In literature', Hollander observes, 'devotedly modish women could never be shown to be devotedly virtuous, and truly virtuous women usually dressed unfashionably'.[24] But there is an ironic colouring to Eliot's initial account of Dorothea and her pursuit of the virtuous life which suggests a rejection of the stereotype, as it retails her enthusiastic schemes, her tendency to 'seek martyrdom, to make retractions', to kneel down suddenly on brick floors to pray. Local opinion – which one is inclined to share – prefers Celia, finding Dorothea altogether 'too unusual and striking' (7). The irony sharpens as the kaleidoscope of impressions settles into a specific time-and-place perspective when we see the sisters at a table trying on their late mother's jewellery. Once again the *découpage* – the narrator's selection of a descriptive focus – is on the upper half of the body. Dorothea 'shudders' at the idea of wearing a jewelled cross, and pushes all the jewels onto Celia, until Celia finds some emeralds that catch Dorothea's attention: '"They are lovely," said Dorothea … while her thought was trying to justify her delight in the colours by merging them in her mystic religious joy'. She decides to take them, though Celia worries that she might suddenly 'renounce the ornaments, as in consistency she ought to do' (9). These inconsistencies are gently mocked, but Dorothea's delight in the gems also suggests an aesthetic need, and a half-conscious sense of how they might enhance her looks.

There is something confused and disproportionate about Dorothea's enthusiasms, renunciations and reforming ardours, an indication perhaps of a mind frustrated by social limitations and a narrow education, but as W. J. Harvey suggests 'there is an element of playacting about her schemes',[25] even a certain egoism. Laurence Lerner, however, insists

that while there are absurdities in Dorothea's behaviour, she is, nevertheless, 'being – quite simply – compared to all that is fine'.[26] These views
are not mutually exclusive. Dorothea's reading among poets, theologians
and reformers leaves her with a sense of intellectual excitement and
potential, a desire to make a difference to her world, but with no way of
channelling her energies. Mrs Craik – if neither as good as Eliot nor as
bad as Braddon – put her finger on the problem in 1858 in her advice
book: 'looking around upon the middle-classes ... it appears to me that
the chief canker at the root of women's lives is the want of something to
do'.[27] Dressing is one activity Dorothea can control. Unwilling to conform
to gender codes that correlate femininity to external ornament, her
appearance can be read as a dissenting experiment in self-representation
and therefore arguably egoistic playacting: playacting mitigated, however,
by a desire to submit to some ideal task or person, and inspired by idealism, by 'all that is fine'.

Dorothea's education has been 'at once narrow and promiscuous' (8).
We learn of her admiration for poets and philosophers, but she would
also have been familiar with the advice manuals beginning to appear in
the early part of the century, and in a torrent by the 1840s. Many of these
advice books, from Mrs Chapone's *Letters* of c.1790 to those contemporary with *Middlemarch*, had a heavily religiose tone.[28] Eliot wrote excit-
edly in 1840 to her former teacher about the most influential of these,
Woman's Mission, by Sarah Lewis: 'Do recommend to all your married
friends ... the most philosophical and masterly on the subject I ever read
or glanced over'.[29] After reading the French source for *Woman's Mission*,
Eliot's enthusiasm waned; at around the same time she began to question her own religious faith. T. R. Wright points to 'the absence of God' in
the novel, and suggests – as had early reviewers – that this is anachronistic: 'Dorothea in 1830 would have turned to God for comfort in her
sorrows and disenchantments',[30] as indeed the young George Eliot did
when initially enthused by *Woman's Mission*, a book uncompromisingly
rooted in the Christian faith.

Although *Middlemarch* 'never for a moment suggests God might exist',
it deals nonetheless with 'religious need', the search for meaning and
purpose in life. Sarah Lewis asserted the centrality of women's role in the
life of the nation; on the other hand, she was opposed to women's political rights, or indeed to any active role outside the home, even a philanthropic one. Instead she celebrates what she sees as woman's new,
spiritually exalted, domestic position, a contrast to her past role as ornament and sex object: her 'mission' is that of 'instrument[s] (under God)
for the regeneration of the world'[31] – no less. As Helsinger, Sheets and

Veeder suggest, in their survey of *The Woman Question*, Lewis 'helped define [the terms] 'mission', 'sphere', 'influence'... invoked throughout the period to awaken women's aspirations *and* to curtail their activities'.[32] The pattern woman exhibits 'devotion to an ideal good, self-sacrifice, sub-jugation of selfish and sensual feelings', and above all that quality 'on which a woman's value and influence depend ... the renunciation of self'. She does not seek publicity; she is educated 'not only to please, to adorn, but to influence, and by influencing to regenerate'.[33] Lewis locates this regenerative mission within the home and dissipates some of its lofty vagueness by relating it to the upbringing of children. Vagueness returns, however, when the question of the childless woman's mission is addressed: a single paragraph assigns to her 'the establishment of peace and love, and unselfishness, to be achieved by any means ... The poor, the ignorant, the domestic servant, are [her] children.'[34]

All very stirring, but where to begin? Dorothea's disappointment is understandable then, when, on a visit to her future home, Casaubon's house and parish of Lowick, she finds no deprivation – 'there was nothing for her to do in Lowick' (72). If Casaubon's parish has no need of her zeal, his intellectual ambitions, centred on his projected Key to all Mythologies, will instead, she decides, be her 'mission'. Renouncing self and subju-gating her aspirations to his, 'she was going to have room for the energies which stirred uneasily under the dimness and pressure of her own igno-rance and the petty peremptoriness of the world's habits' (28). Dorothea's choice of the 'ugly and learned' (30) Casaubon, however, is met with a chorus of dismay as a perverse denial of normal, 'sensual feelings' – 'a shadow of a man. Look at his legs!' (44), Sir James Chetham protests – reactions that only add to her sense of aloofness from the world's 'petty' concerns.

Most advice manuals had a chapter on dress, but the precepts of *Woman's Mission* soared above the quotidian, and, beyond suggesting that an interest in adornment was part of woman's degenerate past, little guidance was offered on the personal appearance of the woman on her mission other than self-renunciation and repression of the senses. Dorothea, with all the time and money in the world, and given nothing to do by Casaubon, has little other than her trousseau to occupy her. How does she choose to present herself now to the world as amanuensis, muse and bride to Casaubon? It is during Dorothea's honeymoon in Rome that Ellen Moers first spots the 'stunning' wardrobe.

Moers, in her discussion of Madame de Staël's 'performing heroine' Corinne, dismisses Gérard's portrait of de Staël as a guide to Corinne's appearance – 'too depressing' – and tells us to look instead 'at Dorothea

Brooke in *Middlemarch*, as posed by George Eliot in a museum in Rome'.[35] Corinne, applauded by adoring Roman crowds, is compared by de Staël to a Greek statue, robed in white like a sibyl, but 'not so far out of fashion as to be liable to a charge of affectation'.[36] De Staël is here trying to solve the problem with which portrait painters such as Reynolds had wrestled in the previous century – how to convey a sitter's universal qualities while retaining their contemporary individuality, of which dress was a key aspect. Reynolds invented a vaguely classical wardrobe, with mixed results – we shall be looking at an example in Chapter 8. His rival, Thomas Gainsborough, rejected 'fancied dress' as being detrimental to true likeness, and Reynolds acknowledged that Gainsborough's 'undetermined manner' succeeded in conveying a general effect, while being specific enough to remind the spectator of the original. Similarly, the closer a fictional character's qualities approach the universal the better the work is judged to be, but, as Hollander points out, a character's 'inner awareness of physical and spiritual selfhood is simultaneous, and physical selfhood must include clothes ... the way things look, and are felt to look, is essential to *them*'.[37] There may be universal emotions but there are no universal clothes.

It was central to Eliot's project that Dorothea's qualities should both transcend and be *of* her time: there must be sufficient detail to place her without incongruity in her context, but enough of an 'undetermined manner' to contain the universal. Observed by Casaubon's nephew Will Ladislaw and his artist friend Naumann, Dorothea is posed in front of a statue of Ariadne, in the Vatican: 'a breathing, blooming girl, whose form, not shamed by the Ariadne, was clad in Quakerish grey drapery; her long cloak, fastened at the neck, was thrown backward from her arms, and one beautiful ungloved hand pillowed her cheek, pushing somewhat backward the white beaver bonnet which made a sort of halo to her face around the simple braided dark-brown hair' (121). Moers points out that de Staël's image of a publicly acclaimed female genius was a politically motivated fantasy rather than an early feminist rallying cry – but a fantasy that, all the same, continued to inspire feminists. Dorothea's ambitions are now domestically directed, governed by self-renunciation, and so her admirers are quietly appreciative individuals, not cheering thousands. But Eliot's distanced view of Dorothea, through the admiring eyes of a stranger, framed by Christianity's central edifice and set against a famous image of pagan female beauty, does nonetheless invoke the timelessness and celebrity that justifies Moers' analogy with Corinne. Eliot's now sparing use of dress detail allows real and ideal images to coexist in the mind's eye – Lewes' realism harmonized with idealism – and evokes not Dorothea's articulated or even realizable ideals but those which, in other times, might be hers.

For the moment, however, Dorothea's honeymoon is not going well. James considered that Eliot's treatment of human relations had left the banalities of Braddon behind, but the marriage, he felt, 'is treated with too much refinement'.[38] On the question of physical relationships Eliot is mute. Dorothea's ardours have so far been expressed in religious terms, but in Rome she is confronted by pagan as well as Christian art. She has already had problems 'with severe classical nudities and smirking Renaissance Correggiosities ... painfully inexplicable, staring into the midst of her Puritan conceptions' (47); the implications of Rome 'first jarred her as with an electric shock and then urged themselves on her with that ache that belonged to a glut of confused ideas' (124). Dorothea's ideals may be intellectual and philanthropic, but, as a young bride, surely also those of romantic love. She has chosen to dress soberly and simply, but the style also happens to suit her. When she inadvertently places herself, enveloped in grey and white, in front of a nude Ariadne, Eliot is therefore not simply contrasting a clothed with an unclothed form, Puritan with Pagan, ideal with real, but also drawing attention to the 'breathing, blooming girl' whose body is as desirable as Ariadne's. The puritan grey cloak does not conceal this fact.

Dorothea's preference for grey has been established earlier at a dinner party, when she enters the room 'in her silver-grey dress' (56) – the colour, we might remember, chosen by Owen Jones for Eliot. Grey, as John Harvey points out in his *Men in Black*, was a colour valued by the Victorians as 'a virtuous colour, associated in Christian use with the faithful conjugality of doves'. Like Moers, he sees Dorothea here as 'dressed exceptionally finely'.[39] In Rome her grey cloak is matched with a bonnet of white beaver, a felted fur fabric used mainly for winter head-gear. 'Nothing [in nineteenth-century dress]' Willett Cunnington says, 'changes so markedly as the popular taste in colour.' According to Cunnington, the late 1820s favoured primary colours – azure blue, pink, jonquil, scarlet, yellow,[40] for example – but also grey. *Middlemarch* lies within the period of dress defined by Cunnington as Romantic (1822–1839); this period marks the end of the Vertical Epoch (1800–1822) with its taste for primary colours, and the start of the Gothic Epoch (1822–1899) which favoured secondary tones, patterns and mixtures and, after 1850, fierce artificial shades. Dorothea's grey might be unusual for a young woman, even avant-garde, but not unfashionable.

The season is late autumn, and Dorothea's outfit, against the white marble and stone walls of the Vatican, creates a subtly monochrome image of wintry tones, but also as Naumann says, 'a fine bit of antithesis' – the voluptuous Ariadne is cold marble, the Quakerish Dorothea is a living, breathing beauty, 'the most perfect young Madonna I ever saw'(121). Naumann is one of the German school of Nazarenes, a group of painters whose aims were comparable to but more avowedly religious than those of the Pre-Raphaelites. William Dyce, active in mid-century, and associated with the PRB, is close in style and subject matter to the Nazarenes, painting austere but passionate madonnas and saints: images which find an echo in Dorothea's self-presentation.

Plate 7 William Dyce, *Madonna*. 1832. Tate Britain, London.

Eliot has already compared Dorothea with the virgin Saints Theresa
and Barbara; Naumann adds maternal aspects. Dorothea's cloak is recognizably a fashion garment – the wide sleeves and collars of the 1830s
needed capacious outerwear – but it has also generic, 'olden-days' connotations, useful in historical fiction, and here, of course, recalling the
blue cloak of the Madonna. Hats were at their widest around 1830, and
the circling brim of Dorothea's white bonnet, pushed to the back of her
head, translates into a halo. Her outfit is therefore fashionable if severe;
but also – when removed from time and place – translatable into attributes of the Virgin Mother. Naumann, expanding his view of Dorothea,
says he would like to dress her as a nun, divining in her appearance
renunciation and idealism. He wants to universalize Dorothea's nature
through art, but, all the same, the idealism he perceives is of her time,
compatible with Cunnington's view of the early 1830s as 'the first step in
the romantic career of the Perfect Lady'.[41]

Perfection, however, takes many shapes. Dorothea's is a spiritual
search, but there were other, more material ways of being 'perfect'.
Dorothea is not, after all, to everyone's taste; Tertius Lydgate,
Middlemarch's new, young doctor, finds it 'troublesome to talk to such
women. They are always wanting reasons.' (60) Lydgate may be an
advanced man of science, but he is unthinkingly reactionary about
women. The concept of the 'rational woman' as man's companion and
intellectual equal, promoted by Jane Austen and Mary Wollestonecraft at
the end of the previous century, in opposition to the ornamental child-
woman, has not disturbed Lydgate's prejudices. Between Dorothea's two
appearances in grey, however, he meets the more amenable Rosamund
Vincy, in azure blue. It is at the tea-table, that classic *locus* for romantic
encounters in the English novel, that he first sees her, and marvels 'how
lovely this creature was, her garment seeming to be made out of the
faintest blue sky, herself so immaculately blond, as if the petals of some
gigantic flower had just opened and disclosed her; and yet with this
infantine blondness showing so much ready, self-possessed grace' (102).

The fatal meeting of these two – submerged iceberg and scientific man
– has been carefully prepared. The novel's opening dismissal of 'frippery'
is recalled when we meet Rosamund, 'who had excellent taste in costume
with that nymph-like figure [which gives] the largest range to choice in
the flow and colour of drapery'. Her education, in Mrs Lemon's school
'included all that was demanded of the *accomplished female* – even to
extras, such as the getting in and out of a carriage' (62). To achieve lady-
like perfection, the key word, Cunnington says, is 'accomplishments': 'the
ambitious young female was cultivating her sensibilities; helped by those

invaluable little books of etiquette, she was constructing ... an idealized world of refinement as she moved away from the realm of fact'.[42] One of the most popular 'little books' was Dr Gregory's *A Father's Legacy to his Daughters*, first published in 1774, but still selling in the nineteenth-century.

Gregory is strong on 'refinements and delicacies'[43] – the words appear on almost every page. 'Elegance', often coupled with 'refinement and delicacy', is 'the high polish' of all other qualities, the 'perfection of taste in life and manners'.[44] 'The love of dress', he declares, 'is natural ... and therefore proper and reasonable.'[45] a proposition demolished by Mary Wollstonecraft in 1792.

> I am unable to comprehend what either he or Rousseau mean when they frequently use this indefinite term. If they told us that in a pre-existent state the soul was fond of dress, and brought this inclination with it into a new body, I should listen with a half-smile, as I often do when I hear a rant about innate elegance ... It is not natural; but arises, like false ambition in men, from a love of power.[46]

Despite Wollestonecraft, the notion gained strength in the nineteenth century, when, in the sharpening divergence of styles between male and female clothing, women's dress became highly expressive and decorative, and modishness came to be considered a natural feminine weakness, aligned to fickleness – but as Wollestoncraft suggests, and Eliot demonstrates, this 'natural weakness' can be manipulative. Casaubon's ambitions for his Key to all Mythologies lead him to try to bully Dorothea, from beyond the grave, into sacrificing herself to his useless project. Is there, in Rosamund's 'power-dressing', a comparable threat to Lydgate? – at the end of the novel Eliot concludes that Rosamund's effect on Lydgate has been a 'torpedo contact' (408).

Lydgate's 'spots of commonness', the unreflecting egoism which governs 'his feeling and judgement about furniture or women', leave him easily beguiled by the fashionable refinements and delicacies peddled by Dr Gregory and embodied by Rosamond. He has stereotyped gender expectations, and he finds a stereotype. As for Rosamond, it was part of her cleverness, Eliot tells us, 'to discern very subtly the faintest aroma of rank' (106): much of Lydgate's attraction is his careless superiority, his elitist assumption 'that there would be an incompatibility in his furniture [his clothes and his women] not being of the best' (96). There is much of Thackeray's dandy in Lydgate. Despite their plain dressing, Rosamond envies the Miss Brookes's good breeding; and 'she could hardly have mentioned a deficiency' (169) in Lydgate's appearance. If we think it improbable that passion can be aroused by a style of dress, Eliot asks us to consider 'whether red cloth and epaulets have never had an influence of that sort. Our passions do not live apart in locked chambers, but dressed in their small wardrobe of notions, bring their provisions to the common table and mess together' (107) – we might recall Pen's adolescent desire, in Thackeray's *Pendennis*, to join the army for the uniform, or Fanny Bolton falling in love with him in his white trousers and hat.

In contrast, Dorothea's self-fashioning, if inconsistent and theatrical, is directed less at the beautification of herself but looks outward – 'I should like to make life beautiful – I mean *everybody's* life' (140): fulfilment lies in what she can do for others. Rosamond, on the other hand, is 'from morning to night her own standard of a perfect lady' (107). She rarely considers beauty other than in relation to herself – 'what is the use of being exquisite', she wonders, 'if you are not seen by the best judges' (268). Perfection of behaviour is to be measured by the etiquette manuals, and perfection of appearance by magazine fashion-plates. Rosamond is the candle in Eliot's celebrated 'pier-glass' analogy, to whom, it seems, all the little lines on the world's surface lead; even at the last she sees herself as the 'graceful creature with blond plaits … [who] had always acted for the best – the best naturally being what she best liked' (411). Mrs Lemon's pattern pupil exhibits finish 'in all the delicacies of life' (105) and is 'adorned with accomplishments for the refined amusement of man' (170). Her principal talent is the perfect imitation of her piano teacher's playing; similarly, she emulates current ideals of female gentility. Her pattern-books are not poets or theologians, nor even the pieties of Mrs Chapone, but the softer slopes of Lady Blessington's *Keepsake Annual*, a forerunner of the woman's magazine and repository of tearful verses, romantic tales, mildly educational essays, garnished with engravings of well-bred beauties, sweet children and modest peasants.[47]

Blanche Amory in *Pendennis* is the Keepsake Beauty in full flower, Rosamond is an early bloom. *The Keepsake* flourished during the 1830s and 1840s, but Altick has found *Middlemarch's Keepsake* number to be in fact an anachronism – the *Keepsake* scene in Chapter 27 is set in 1830, the volume in question is from 1831.[48] Rosamond, at any rate, has spotted the latest publishing fad; *The Keepsake's* red and gold binding, gilt-edged pages and tissue-papered engravings make it a genuinely pleasurable object to handle – its contents, as Lydgate immediately sees, are another matter. 'Did you ever see such a "sugared invention"?' (171) he asks derisively of an engraving. Having already identified Lydgate as a more eligible prospect than the average Middlemarch swain, Rosamond adroitly switches from admiration of *The Keepsake* to polite amusement.

Figure 13 A Keepsake Beauty. *The Keepsake*, ed. Lady Blessington, 1845, London: Longman, Brown, Green and Longman.

She is intuitively fashioning herself according to Lydgate's taste, while her imagination leaps ahead, furnishing a marital home and visiting his grand relatives. Eliot assures us there is nothing 'sordid or mercenary' in her previsions, but Rosamond's ideas have 'a shaping activity'. Lydgate may not intend to marry, but he is like 'a jellyfish which gets melted without knowing it' (172). How does she 'shape' herself in order to shape her world, and particularly Lydgate, to her own liking?

Like the first image of Dorothea, our initial impression of Rosamond, through Lydgate's eyes, is generalized – a dazzling figure in blue, crowned by 'wondrous' blonde plaits. It takes a woman's eye, her Aunt Bulstrode's, to get down to specifics. Engraved 'Keepsake Beauties' were half-length as a rule, and it is the upper body, the erogenous zone of the 1830s, that interests Mrs Bulstrode and Rosamond. J. C. Flügel, in his study *The Psychology of Clothes*, suggests that erotic focus in dress history shifts from one area of the body to another:[49] breasts were interesting in the 1690s, for example, in the 1920s it was legs – the head and shoulders certainly had it in the 1830s. Mrs Bulstrode, on a visit to the Vincy's, is 'handsomely dressed, but she noticed with a little more regret than usual that Rosamond ...[was] expensively equipped ... the quilling inside Rosamond's bonnet was *so charming* that it was impossible not to desire the same kind of thing for Kate ... Rosamond's eyes also were roaming over her aunt's large embroidered collar.' This silent exchange is followed by sharp words on Rosamond's relationship with Lydgate who, though well-connected, has no money: 'My dear Rosamond,' Mrs Bulstrode pronounces, '*you* must not think of living in high style.' Rosamond silently vows 'to live as she pleased' (186) – intending, no doubt, not only to maintain standards in bonnets, but to have large embroidered collars as well.

Lydgate, we have been told, is imperceptive about women and furniture; he simply assumes he is entitled to the best article available. He proposes and is accepted, wedding plans go ahead and he takes a house 'much as he gave orders to his tailor for every requisite of perfect dress' (217). Rosamond's decision therefore to invest her father's money and her own efforts in an expensive wardrobe is calculated to appeal to just that 'spot of commonness' in Lydgate – he looks no further than her costly

Figure 14 An embroidered collar. *Gracefulness*, ed. Arthur Freeling, *c*.1835. London: George Routledge.

finish, and will not balk at further expenditure on the same principle. We may therefore expect embroidered collars.

Eliot now brings the two young married women together under the eyes of Ladislaw, who is flirting with Rosamond but in love with Dorothea, lending the occasion an extra piquancy:

> Let those who know, tell us exactly what stuff it was that Dorothea wore in those days of mild autumn – that thin white woollen stuff soft to the touch and soft to the eye. It always seemed to have been lately washed, and to smell of the sweet hedges – was always in the shape of a pelisse with sleeves hanging all out of fashion. Yet if she had entered ... as Imogene or Cato's daughter, the dress might have seemed right enough: the grace and dignity were in her limbs and neck; and about her simply-parted hair and candid eyes the large round poke [bonnet] which was then the fate of women, seemed no more odd than the golden trencher we call a halo. (268)

The earlier image of Dorothea, which fused real and ideal, Christian with Classical, is developed further. The soft white that replaces her puritan grey has already been noted by Ladislaw when he sees Dorothea in 'some thin woollen-white material, without a single ornament ... as if she were under a vow to be different from all other women' (226). This next description adds not concrete but sensuous details of touch, sight and smell, giving the image actuality without fixing it in time: the fabric may be challis, a new, fine wool and silk mix from France, particularly adapted to soft, draped lines. The pelisse was a coat-dress popular in the early 1800s, and suited to the period's vertical styles; still worn in 1829, it was gone by 1835, replaced by mantles and cloaks. The 'out-of-fashion' hanging sleeves recall the pelisse's over-sleeve of circa 1810, falling open from the elbow; or possibly the 1860s loose 'pagoda sleeve': both, at any rate, conspicuously different from the fashionably bloated norm. The poke-bonnet absolves Dorothea from a complete disregard for fashion, operating again as a halo.

The perspective now shifts to that of a 'calm observer', Ladislaw being too agitated by Dorothea's entrance to reflect on the contrast between the two women. Eliot, however, as Gillian Beer points out, shatters sexual stereotypes, '[s]he refused to oppose "Madonna" and "fallen woman"'.[50] Rosamond is happy to see Dorothea, as someone grand to impress; Dorothea looks 'admiringly at Lydgate's lovely bride', and puts out her hand. They are caught at a moment of eye-contact, and with Dorothea's image already established we are asked to consider Rosamond's 'infantine blondness and wondrous crown of hair-plaits, with her pale-blue dress of a fit and fashion so perfect that no dressmaker could look at it without emotion, a large embroidered collar which it was to be hoped all beholders would know the price of, her small hands duly set off with rings, and that controlled self-consciousness of manner which the expensive substitute for simplicity' (268).

If initial descriptions of Dorothea were tinged with irony, the novel's ironic zone has now shifted to Rosamond. Her style is not mocked as vulgar or coquettish, but Eliot makes it damagingly clear that she has fashioned her image with a view to exciting envy for a modish wardrobe and large bank account. She wants the power that accrues to the appearance of material and social superiority – though paradoxically the current ideal of femininity is one of sweet simplicity: *Woman's Mission,* indeed, harps a good deal on 'simplicity' as central to woman's influence:[51] and Rosamond has her 'madonna' aspects, too – angelic in celestial blue and crowned with gold. It is the 'large embroidered collar' that betrays the movements of her soul. Dorothea's ideal is spiritual, an altruistic desire for good. Her appearance therefore aspires to the abstract and sculptural, it is colourless, undecorated, classically simple, as though she cared little for prettiness and fashion. It is rather hard on Rosamond to be given the role of the day's trivia to the timeless poetry of Dorothea's stunning wardrobe.

This scene is placed at the exact mid-point of the novel, and we might say of it, as Gillian Beer says of a landscape description in *Adam Bede*, that 'it works first as a picture, framed and composed. But it works also as a narrative, restless with unseen consequences.'[52] Dorothea has come to consult Lydgate about Casaubon's illness, but is already conscious of the attraction between herself and Ladislaw; Rosamond, though newly wed, is prepared to consider flirtatious diversions, and Ladislaw, unable to pursue Dorothea, is happy to oblige. At Dorothea's entrance Ladislaw is mortified to be found with Rosamond, Dorothea disconcerted to find him there and Rosamond's nose put out of joint by Ladislaw's subsequent praise of Dorothea: 'When one sees a perfect woman', he says loftily, 'one never thinks of her attributes.' (270) For Rosamond, who sees herself as Middlemarch's benchmark of perfection, and who will not have missed the *démodé* aspects of Dorothea's costume, this remark is peculiarly galling. From this point the novel's concern with the four characters is to show Dorothea freed from the dead hand of Casaubon and united with Ladislaw, and to chart the demoralisation and final paralysis of Lydgate in Rosamond's grip.

When we next see Rosamond on a cold spring day, she is pregnant, 'in a cherry-coloured dress with swansdown trimming about the throat' (288), her appearance seems soft and warmly promising, but she loses the child, and apart from a moment when her infantine beauty in 'transparent, faintly-tinted muslin' (367) moves Lydgate to guilty pity for the sacrifices his financial ruin must impose on her, we hear little more of her clothes – their work is done. This last dress is colourless compared to her earlier primary brilliance. Dorothea's clothes, however, continue to play their part in her narrative. Casaubon's dead hand not only operates through his testamentary threat to disinherit her if she marries Ladislaw, but through her exaggerated mourning. Casaubon's death has fortuitously delivered her from having to devote herself to the Key to all Mythologies. Nothing in their life together had produced happiness or fulfilment, and nothing after his death suggests heartbreak. It could be said that her heavy mourning operates as a cover, even penance, for an absence of grief. Our first glimpse of her after Casaubon's death is with Celia and her baby. Celia, 'all in white and lavender like a bunch of mixed violets' (302), is an image of light and life that overrides the widow's weeds.

When left to herself, Dorothea's gloom returns, not for lack of Casaubon but for lack of purpose. Back at Lowick, looking down the avenue of limes, which seemed 'to represent the prospect of her life, full of motiveless ease', she stands in her 'widow's cap ... [which] made an oval frame for the face, and had a crown standing up; the dress was an experiment in the utmost laying on of crape; but this heavy solemnity of clothing made her face look all the younger, with its recovered bloom' (335). There is general critical agreement that irony disappears from the depiction of Dorothea in the latter part of the novel; I would suggest, however, that it returns with Dorothea's strivings after ultimate widowhood. Mrs Cadwallader, one of the novel's sharply commonsensical characters, tries to restore Dorothea's sense of proportion: 'think what a bore you might become yourself to your fellow-creatures if you were always playing tragedy queen and taking things sublimely' (332). Dorothea is again playacting – in another role, another costume, but the part of inconsolable widow is an inauthentic dead end.

According to Lou Taylor's book *Mourning Dress*, by the 1850s 'mourning outfitters were enjoying a booming trade. Women's magazines were full of anxious inquiries into the minutiae of mourning etiquette.'[53] Eliot's readers would be familiar with Queen Victoria's protracted mourning after Albert's death in 1861, but by 1870 her reclusive gloom was viewed less sympathetically. Celia's white and lavender in fact also defers to her brother-in-law's demise – though not terribly seriously. 'It is mourning crape', Taylor says, 'that above all epitomises the middle-class Victorian widow. It was a lightweight, semi-transparent, black silk ...

every hint of the beautiful sheen and softness of silk was carefully removed ... giving the fabric an extraordinarily lugubrious and hard finish. Crape was used as a trimming on dresses, cloaks and bonnets worn for the first two stages of mourning. During the first period of a widow's mourning the entire bodice and skirt of her weeds were completely covered with crape.'[54] Crape was expensive, difficult to handle and to maintain, and thoroughly unattractive – just the thing for Dorothea at her most self-denying. Will Ladislaw, wondering later how it was 'that he saved himself from falling down at her feet ... used to say that the horrible hue and surface of her crape dress was most likely the sufficient controlling force' (336).

Dorothea's 'tragedy queen' appearance temporarily quenches Will's ardour, and demonstrates her desire to achieve the 'utmost laying on of crape'. But as her physical beauty was enhanced rather than dimmed by silver-grey, her love for Ladislaw is as much expressed as repressed by the excess of crape. Dorothea's mourning 'protests too much'; why should she need such a weighty reminder of Casaubon? The laying aside of so much crape will be proportionately dramatic. We might look ahead thirty years to the incongruous mourning of Milly Theale, in Henry James's *Wings of the Dove*; it sets her apart but also throws into relief her strange beauty. When she finally changes her black garments for white, her altered image undermines Merton Densher's love for Kate Croy – until then so much more elegant than Milly. In James's novel we see how the black dress shifts in Merton's imagination from Milly to Kate.[55] In *Middlemarch* a similar metaphoric shift occurs when Dorothea's overblown mourning-rhetoric is transformed by Mrs Bulstrode, in the novel's most poignant moment, into a timeless ritual, a statement of grief at the humiliation of a loved husband.

Headgear is the pivot of this shift. If sleeves in 1830 were *imbecile*, hats and bonnets were even more so. 'Bonnets were inadequate to express the exuberance of feeling', Cunnington comments of the period's attitude to headgear, 'and hats became the mode: huge hats, enormous hats, of Leghorn or silk, with towering crowns and immense brims trimmed with up to a hundred and twenty feet of parti-coloured ribbons or with feathers or masses of flowers, together with wide streaming ribbon strings. At the spectacle horses shied and dogs in the street barked at them'.[56] Even Dorothea's widow's cap has 'a crown standing up'. In the summer following Casaubon's death, this cap, so resolutely at variance with the summer heat and the ebullience of fashionable millinery, begins to annoy Celia. She begs Dorothea to throw it off: 'I am so used to the cap – it has become a sort of shell', Dorothea replies defensively. Taking matters into her own hands, Celia removes it, freeing the braids of dark-brown hair, and declaring that 'Dodo need not make such a slavery of her mourning' (339). Dorothea then has a sharp difference of opinion with Mrs Cadwallader, which causes Celia to comment that 'taking your cap off made you look more like yourself in more ways than one. You spoke just as you used to when anything was said to displease you' (340), perceiving that Dorothea's intellect, as well as her hair, has now been freed.

When the pious pillar of society, Mr Bulstrode, is revealed as a whited sepulchre, the ladies of Middlemarch gather to discuss the situation, homing in on the headgear of Mrs Bulstrode and her girls as barometers of their social awareness: 'she was with her girls at church yesterday and they had Tuscan bonnets', Mrs Toller observes, adding that '[h]er own had a feather in it. I have never seen that her religion made any difference to her dress.' Mrs Plymdale retorts that Mrs Bulstrode 'wears neat patterns always, and that feather I know she got dyed a pale lavender on purpose to be consistent. I must say it of Harriet that she wishes to do right.' (460) In her confused way Mrs Plymdale is defending Mrs Bulstrode against the stereotyped notion that sincere religious observance is incompatible with elegance. Clothes, Mrs Plymdale feels, must be 'right' for the occasion, and a smart bonnet is 'right' for church. In fact, the reference to Tuscan bonnets, 'of English straw with low slanting crowns, the brims rather square and wide',[57] is the novel's most precise fashion detail: Cunnington records the 'Tuscan' as *the* bonnet style of 1831. And as we have already seen, Mrs Bulstrode's taste in collars has been ahead even of Rosamond's. But Mrs Plymdale is right – an interest in dress does not signal an irreligious heart or a trivial mind. A good mind and heart can coexist with any amount of millinery.

Mrs Bulstrode's instinct for appropriateness in dress moves beyond questions of fashion when she finally learns of her husband's fall: 'She took off all her ornaments and put on a plain black gown, and instead of wearing her much-adorned cap and large bows of hair, she brushed her hair down and put on a plain bonnet-cap which made her look suddenly like an early Methodist.' (463) Dorothea's anti-fashion gestures, renunciations of ornament, exaggerations of mourning, have been attempts to create an authentic self; she has asked Carlyle's central question in *Sartor Resartus*: 'Who am I: what is this ME? A Voice, a Motion, an Appearance?'[58] But her answers have at times been at variance with emotional, aesthetic and physical aspects of herself. She has no truck with the calculating coquetry and meretricious style touted by *The Keepsake*'s 'sugared inventions'; nevertheless, she has an instinct for beauty, attracts and is attracted by the opposite sex, facts that she

damagingly tries to ignore. Mrs Bulstrode, on the other hand, has not
lost her sense of self to 'an idealized world of refinement', as Cunnington
accuses the Perfect Lady of doing, and as Dorothea and Rosamond, in
their different ways, might be said to have done. She understands 'the
realm of fact' and that she must now dress in acknowledgement of
change. When her husband raises his eyes to her, from the depths of his
misery, the meaning of her dress is instantly apparent – 'her pale face,
her changed mourning dress, the trembling about her mouth, all said,
"I know"'. Her mourning does not repel the man she loves, but instead,
taking his hand, 'they cried together, she sitting at his side' (464). Here,
Dorothea's widow's cap and mourning black have found their place –
though only a reputation has died.

Mrs Bulstrode's assumption of mourning coincides with the laying
aside of Dorothea's. Bulstrode's disgrace has involved Lydgate, and
Dorothea hurries to comfort Rosamond – only to find Ladislaw once again
with Rosamond. She leaves quickly and spends a tormented, sleepless
night. At dawn she opens her curtains and sees, in the fields beyond, a
man with a bundle, a woman with a baby and a shepherd with his dog –
'the manifold wakings of men to labour and endurance'. She is, she
decides, 'a part of that involuntary, palpitating life'. Her decision to rejoin
the world, to endure reality, expresses itself in a change of dress. As T. R.
Wright perceives, 'the significance of Rosamond's affection for mirrors in
contrast with Dorothea's penchant for views through windows … reinforces the notion that progress in perception is marked by decreasing
self-centredness'.[59] The universal scene of common humanity, framed by
the window, is Dorothea's 'mirror', a scene in which she must find
herself. She tells her maid 'to bring my new dress; and most likely I shall
want my new bonnet today'. Dorothea's decision is prompted by a wish
'to acknowledge that she had not the less an active life before her because
she had buried a private joy; and the tradition that fresh garments
belonged to all initiation … made her grasp after even that slight outward
help toward calm resolve' (487). As with Mrs Bulstrode, her change of
dress signals a change of direction – the lightness and freshness, the
rightness of her dress, is as much the discovery of an authentic self as it
is a communication to the world. 'A sense of being perfectly well-dressed,'
a lady is reported as saying to Emerson, 'gives a feeling of inward tranquillity which religion is powerless to bestow.'[60] This otherwise comic
remark comes close to solemn truth in *Middlemarch*. In both Rosamond's
sense of her 'perfect', therefore unchangeable, dressed self, and in Mrs
Bulstrode's equally fashion-conscious imperative for change, Eliot draws
us into their self-awareness, mediated in terms of a particular period in

dress. Dorothea's self-awareness and need for change of dress – as acute as Mrs Bulstrode's – is not tied to specific fashions, we do not learn the particulars of Dorothea's new outfit; she sees herself within a timeless world, part of 'that involuntary, palpitating life', real but also ideal.

Ironically, the 'reality' she decides she must endure – Ladislaw's love for Rosamond – has no reality at all. Ladislaw rather cruelly spurns Rosamond, hurries to Dorothea at Lowick and after a few more misunderstandings, they finally embrace. The words that bring this about are typically Dorothea: 'I don't mind about poverty – I hate my wealth. ... We could live quite well on my own fortune – ... seven hundred a year – I want so little – no new clothes – and I will learn what everything costs.' (500) We might spare a thought for Rosamond, who also ignores cost but who hasn't the income to ignore poverty; like Becky Sharp, she might be a 'good woman' (or at any rate a better) on five hundred a year – Dorothea has seven hundred. If we are to conclude that Dorothea is the more admirable pattern of womanhood, Eliot is too honest not to record the naivety of Dorothea's definition of 'poverty', and her disingenuousness in renouncing 'new clothes' within a few hours of putting them on.

It would be pleasant to report that, having found True Love and left off mourning, Dorothea then indulges in some of Mrs Bulstrode's festive millinery. However, if there is now a Methodist governing Mrs Bulstrode's appearance, there has always been a Puritan behind Dorothea, whose austerity is as powerful an influence as her awakened aesthetic sense. Dorothea will enjoy a little penitential economy in the regulation of her wardrobe – and, besides, the Puritan style suits her.

It is, as Barbara Hardy says, 'attitudes to clothes, rather than the actual clothes, which are important'[61] – although we should not ignore the pin-point accuracy of detail that testifies to Eliot's faithful – if now unobtrusive – representation 'of commonplace things'. Dorothea's impatience with conventions, which has at times seemed playacting, is nevertheless a consistent expression of her personality, though it is not heedlessness. Hardy examines Chapter 30, in which Dorothea, entering the house from a walk, implores Lydgate for the truth about Casaubon's condition. First she 'throws off' bonnet and gloves, and then, when Lydgate has made plain the seriousness of the situation, she 'unclasps her cloak, throwing it off as if it stifled her' (182). Hardy feels that these gestures are in keeping with 'her neglect of appearances, conventions, propriety and vanity', and with her frank relationship with Lydgate at this moment of crisis 'when polite formality is too slow and too fussy'. The urgent removal of her outerwear expresses her 'desire to break out and breathe or do something'. Hardy sees this moment as part of the novel's continuum, and, once we connect image to image, we see how this scene relates to that first rejection of ornament, those *démodé* sleeves and the final removal of widow's cap and weeds As Hardy says, 'Dorothea's attitude to her clothes belongs to the whole presentation of her person and personality and character in this place at this time.'[62]

Hardy's is a convincing perception, but I return to the need to acknowledge Eliot's care for detail – neither she nor Dorothea 'neglect appearances': Dorothea after all chooses a modish bonnet, the silver-grey colour popular with the Victorians and the cloak that was to replace the pelisse. She is alert to fashion but not a slave to it. And there is even something contemporary about the way she creates a style to suit her developing individuality, a style that transcends time and place, and is wholly her own – a woman both of and beyond her time, who reminds Naumann of female archetypes of pagan sensuality as well as of saintly renunciation, and is also one to whom he feels attracted. Middlemarch society registers her 'difference', but no one finds her absurd – Rosamond, we remember, admires her. Dorothea's style only partly anticipates the dress-reform movement, in which, as Hollander says 'the desired way of looking at the moment had to be flouted'[63] and which always begins by looking ugly. Her appearance is striking, unconventional but evidently seductive: it convinces in 1831 and 1870 and still seems 'stunning'. Satire traditionally ridicules *non*-conformity in dress – Charlotte Lennox's accounts of Arabella's bizarre outfits in *The Female Quixote*, for example – but Eliot derides Rosamond's *conformity*, finding Dorothea's dissent finally admirable.

Rosamond's enslavement to fashionable, media-manufactured stereotypes fixes her within her solipsistic mirror, moulds her into that immovable force, the iceberg that wrecks Lydgate. She is inflexibly *of* her time, her choice of primary colours and embroidered collars fix her to the late 1820s; she cannot imagine circumstances in which the purchase of the last fashion is not a given right, for her physical self-image is inescapably linked to it. Her 'torpedo contact', a ruthless exercise of pure ego, first demoralizes Lydgate, shapes him into a fashionable doctor and then kills him. She survives unscathed into another more prosperous marriage, making 'a very pretty show with her daughters' (512), and if happiness is a 'good' marriage and a secure income, the blonde has carried it away again. Commentators generally agree that the resolution of Dorothea's story in marriage with Ladislaw is something of an anti-climax. But Eliot is anticipating both Henry James and Thomas Hardy in questioning the Victorian domestic ideal of home as the ultimate sanctuary and the marriage-relation as the conclusive narrative reward. Domestic violence, associated in Dickens, for example, with the underclass, shades off in the second half of the century into middle-class domestic terror, intellectual or aesthetic power replacing brute force as instruments of domination.[64] If Ladislaw seems a tame sort of husband for Dorothea, Casaubon was an intellectual bully. '[T]hose determining acts of her life', Eliot admits of Dorothea, 'were not ideally beautiful. They were the mixed result of young and noble impulse struggling amidst the conditions of an imperfect social state.' It is cold comfort to be assured that 'the growing good of the world is partly dependent on unhistoric acts' (515).

Henry James felt that Dorothea 'plays a narrower part than the imagination of the reader demands', and his novel of 1881, *The Portrait of a Lady*, is, like Eliot's, a critique of the late nineteenth-century's redundant attitudes and assumptions about women and marriage. Isabel Archer wonders rather crossly why 'marriage' is always the conclusion to speculations on what she might 'do'. She finds no answer herself and her marriage is an inescapable catastrophe – a more pessimistic conclusion than Eliot's. Isabel, with her New England heritage, also affects a Puritan wardrobe, of black and white, rather than grey: colours that are no colour, though grey offers more shades of possibility. If, in 1831, Dorothea's destiny seems unachieved, Eliot sees a 'growing good' for other Dorotheas in other times. Twenty years later, however, James felt things were not going her way. In truth, neither James nor Eliot found much in the 'imperfect social state' of their world that would acknowledge the potential of such women. Eliot's representation of Dorothea reflects her belief that 'absolute definitions of woman's nature and ... woman's mission'[65] were foolish, but such definitions had, if anything, hardened by 1870.

Dorothea wears identifiably 1831 fashions, but her appearance can be read within Classical, Biblical and Romantic contexts; as W. J. Harvey says, Eliot sets into motion 'those forces and pressures which we feel to be the sinew and bloodstream not just of Middlemarch but of *any* reasonably sophisticated society'.[66] Framed by, and looking out of windows, Dorothea looks for a place within a timeless world; Rosamond, looking into mirrors, measures herself against fashionable templates – both seek the Perfect Lady. Dorothea's search is directed by moral and intellectual longings for some significant social role, a role that in fact scarcely existed for middling-badly educated, middle-class girls in mid-century, middle England. Her dress is therefore chronologically, even geographically unstable, eluding the attitudes and assumptions of Middlemarch. Eliot offers Dorothea as a model not of achieved ambition but of admirable aspirations wasted by a society in which, as Eliot wrote in the novel's first version, the rules of conduct 'are in flat contradiction with its own loudly-asserted beliefs' (514). The novel, as V. S. Pritchett concludes, 'offers neither hope nor despair but simply the necessity of fashioning the moral life',[67] and this Dorothea does.

Rosamond's ideals are defined by dominant codes of dress and manners, and they are therefore achievable – and achieved – as long as she is solvent. She succeeds by what was to become standard Victorian practice, the exploitation of the male; and as Mary Braddon implied, the male, once exploited, is disposable. We might remember Lydgate's terrifyingly prescient story of Madame Laure, who murdered the husband who stood in the way of success. 'I do not like husbands', she warns, 'I will never have another' (98). Our last dress image of Rosamond is of her wrapping a soft white shawl around herself, but 'inwardly wrapping her soul in cold reserve' (488). While her image is similar to that of Dorothea in 'thin white woollen stuff, soft to the touch', Rosamond's white shawl becomes a carapace of ice against Lydgate, a refusal to open her heart to him, or to deviate from her materialist ideals. We might recall that earlier scene of Dorothea and Lydgate, when Dorothea flings off coat and bonnet and emotionally lays herself bare, appealing to a shared humanity that lies beyond transitory codes of gender relations or of dress etiquette. The dress of the two women has been different in detail, though in the end, apparently similar: what finally matters, however, is a difference of attitude and of aspiration. 'The central tenet of the elegant life,' according to Balzac, 'is an elevated sense of order and harmony which makes poetry out of everyday things.'[68] Eliot, like Baudelaire's ideal artist, has extracted from fashion 'whatever element it may contain of poetry within history, and distilled the eternal from the transitory':[69] she has made poetry of cloaks and bonnets, to give Dorothea Brooke the most stunning wardrobe in Victorian fiction.

–7–

Shades of White: Henry James's 'The Siege of London' and 'The Author of *Beltraffio*'

If Henry James acknowledged Honoré de Balzac to be his master, he might perhaps have admitted George Eliot – fictionally speaking, of course – as his mistress. James wrote on Balzac and Eliot all his life, and his critical writings are central to his oeuvre; if he had never written a novel he would still be read as a key, early modern, literary critic. Written in the mid-1880s, at the same time as 'The Siege of London' and 'The Author of *Beltraffio*', James's essay, 'The Art of Fiction' criticized the English novel for being 'addressed in a large degree to "young people"' and therefore 'rather shy'[1] of addressing serious moral issues. He must have felt, however, that *Middlemarch* was – as Virginia Woolf later said – 'one of the few English novels written for grown up people',[2] for in his Preface to *The Portrait of a Lady*, of 1881, he acknowledges his debt to Eliot and, in particular, to *Middlemarch*.

As well as attacking the Anglo-American novel for its timidity, James also accused it of being a 'shapeless, diffuse piece of machinery, padded to within an inch of its life'[3] – and Eliot's work, as we have seen, was not exempt. James's reviews complain of her rusty plots and over-detailing – 'so much drawing and so little composition'.[4] Eliot might have felt that with friends like this who needs enemies. By the time she wrote *Middlemarch*, however, Eliot had learnt from *Romola* the lesson she gives Casaubon, that labour and erudition do not guarantee success.

James's own views on realism, after *The Portrait of a Lady*, were changing. Throughout his career he wrote on art, and his exhibition reviews of the 1880s reflect a growing conviction that photographic realism was aesthetically and intellectually trite. At the same time, in 'The Art of Fiction', he demanded 'solidity of specification'[5] from the fiction writer, and continued to admire Balzac's ability to make vivid 'the machinery of life, its furniture and fittings'. He admits, however, that Balzac's 'things' 'are at once our delight and our despair'.[6] Commenting on a long description of clothes in Balzac's *Eugénie Grandet,* James concludes that 'these things are described *only in so far as they have a bearing upon the action* ... If you resolve to describe a thing, you cannot describe it too carefully. But as the soul of a novel is its action, you should only describe those things which are accessory to action.'[7]

James continued to worry at the question, and if, in relation to art, he was never easy with Impressionism, he came to appreciate the work of Whistler and enthusiastically promoted John Singer Sargent, whose art owed more to a European than an Anglo-American tradition. Similarly, in relation to literature, we find James turning from the English novel's 'loose baggy monsters'[8] to the more elliptical style of European writers such as Flaubert and Turgenev: a style which strove for the *'mot juste'*, where, as James said, 'every touch must count'.[9]

I propose to focus on two of James's stories: 'The Siege of London' of 1883 and 'The Author of *Beltraffio*' of 1884, works from a period that marks his shift into his more symbolist style. Within a short story, where character and plot must swiftly be established, dress is a 'touch' that carries extra symbolic weight: the modern short story was indeed said, by Turgenev and others, to have emerged from Gogol's 'The Overcoat'. Dress is part of the 'seen' from which we may 'guess the unseen', where we may 'trace the implication of things.'[10] 'Is *she* respectable?'[11] an observer asks of the heroine at the start of 'The Siege of London'; and this might equally be asked of the wife of 'The Author of *Beltraffio*'. Neither woman is young; one trails a colourful past, the other is an icon of virtue; both, however, significantly wear white. What might the choice of white, this 'touch', suggest?

As has been obvious from the start of this study, white dress on a woman has many resonances. It was a sign of youth, innocence and purity, and had become almost mandatory formal wear for the Victorian *jeune fille*; white was also correct summer-wear in the nineteenth-century for most ages. White, as we have seen, can also be negative, cold and colourless; it is associated with shrouds and ghosts; touched with black, it marks a stage in nineteenth-century mourning dress. And – it goes without saying – represented dress has moral implications. As James half-jokingly said of a collection of seventeenth-century portraits: 'It is nothing that you be great or good, it is everything that you be dressed'.[12] Whistler's 'Little White Girls', often portraits of his mistress, teasingly subvert Victorianism's *idées fixes* of female purity. Dress brings into question the status of cultivated appearances: how far are the images we fashion to produce certain effects inauthentic? Being dressed is, after all, never natural. Tony Tanner, in his study of James, places this problematic relationship between aesthetic and ethical values 'close to the heart of James's work'.[13]

Mrs Headway, the heroine of 'The Siege of London', has no illusions about herself – aged 37, she has been married and divorced 'so much, and so easily' (SL 599). The Europeanized American, Littlemore, who observes her progress in London, first knew her as Nancy Beck, '[o]n the back piazza in San Diego' (SL 569) – a location he continues to see as her 'proper setting' (SL 585). There was little that was 'proper' about San Diego in 1880,[14] however, despite its early identity as a mission-town. Ceded to the United States by Mexico in 1848, it had a booming, volatile population, and was home to every kind of lawless adventurer or speculator. Littlemore even suggests that Mrs Headway is no stranger to the use of firearms.[15] With the proceeds of her marital 'speculations', Mrs Headway has headed for New York society, but New York, she says, 'decided I was improper ... not a decent woman came to see me' (SL 603). London society, however, was more receptive to upwardly mobile rich Americans. 'Comparisons were often made by social leaders in New York with English society', according to Eric Homberger, New Yorkers 'felt that their society had to be even more exclusive':[16] as Waterville, a young American diplomat and Littlemore's friend, smugly reflects, New York 'was quite capable of taking a higher stand in such a matter than London' (SL 604).

Since Littlemore's account of Mrs Headway colours Waterville's view of her, as well as that of the reader, we might consider just what *he* was up to in San Diego. James is in fact careful to sketch his antecedents before launching into the story proper. Educated at Harvard, Littlemore swiftly dissipated a fortune and went West to replenish his pockets. With a taste for horses and cards, and having 'mastered none of the useful arts' except 'the great art of indifference' (SL 577), he had the good fortune to invest the proceeds of a poker game in a successful silver mine upon whose profits he now lives, 'doing nothing ... with a sort of artistic perfection' (SL 578). By the 1880s America had entered the Gilded Age of the Robber Barons – Gould, Carnegie and Vanderbilt – and the xenophobic Waterville might well reflect on the foundations of New York's 'high' moral stance – and on whether Littlemore's speculations have been any more respectable than Mrs Headway's.

The two men first see her at a theatre in Paris. Looking around for pretty women, Waterville spots Mrs Headway –'the one in white, with the red flowers' (SL 566). (Red flowers, as readers of *La Dame aux Camélias* will recall, have rather dubious connotations.) Confused by Mrs Headway's dress-signs, Waterville appeals to Littlemore to settle whether or not she is 'respectable'. Recently arrived in Europe, and used to the

Figure 15 Dinner Dress. Fashion Plate, *Sylvia's Home Journal*, London: Ward Lock & Co., 1879.

moral clarities of New England, Waterville has already mistaken *demi-mondaines* for 'nice' women, and vice versa. 'No, she's not respectable' (SL 567), Littlemore firmly replies. We next meet Mrs Headway, 'dressed in white, including a white bonnet', accompanied by Sir Arthur Demesne, a young English aristocrat. She is 'even prettier than at a distance ... [with] the bloom of a white flower' (SL 569, 572). Describing her to Waterville, Littlemore betrays his own confusion – she is intelligent, ignorant, spirited, audacious, always attractive and 'very nearly as well-dressed as they had just beheld her'. But he is sure that she has never exactly sold herself: 'she didn't accept money' (SL 575).

Littlemore, interested in 'this new incarnation of Nancy Beck' (SL 579), renews his acquaintance with her, and she tells him bluntly 'I want to get into society' (SL 583). She finds Sir Arthur's devotion rather boring, but marriage to him will give her social position and victory in New York – according to Homberger, '[t]o achieve social success in New York, it occasionally became necessary to kick-start the process in London'.[17] She no longer wants to attract vulgar attention, she says; she wants to emulate Sir Arthur's modesty and good taste. However, she admits he is puzzled by her past, and asks Littlemore to vouch for her. As he does not believe in 'women's rising again. He believed in their not going down' (SL 580), he prevaricates. 'Snobbery', as Lionel Trilling says, 'is the peculiar vice not of aristocratic societies ... but of bourgeois democratic societies',[18] and Littlemore is more in thrall to class prejudice and double standards than is Sir Arthur. Mrs Headway turns away, 'drawing her far-trailing skirts' (SL 589) – an embodiment of her complicated past and lingering seductiveness.

Peggy McCormack sees feminist themes and sympathies in the resistance of James's middle-period protagonists to 'an antipathetic, masculine-dominated exchange economy'.[19] Mrs Headway neither seeks wealth in London nor is sought for her wealth – unlike less happy Jamesian women. Her 'siege' is conducted more seductively: wealth buys 'weapons' – dresses, for example – but as means to an end. 'If I'm all right here, I can snap my fingers at New York' (SL 605), she says – acceptance in London will banish shades of San Diego. According to Milton Rugoff's study of sexuality in Victorian America, if an 'improper' performance 'could be given a morally or socially acceptable name or setting, it might well be approved'.[20]

Her performance is tested at a weekend at Sir Arthur's country house, where she is scrutinized not only by Sir Arthur's mother, but also by London society. Waterville has also been invited, and Lady Demesne tells him, on arrival, that Mrs Headway has been dressing for two hours (later exaggerated to three). At last Mrs Headway appears, taking three minutes to descend the staircase. (Skirts at this period not only had long trains but were skin-tight.) Waterville holds his breath, but 'Mrs Headway entered English society very well ... with the trophies of the Rue de la Paix trailing behind her' (SL 614). James's big 'dress-moments' are often questions of effect rather than description – here, all eyes turn toward her as she rustles forward, and conversation comes to a stop. Waterville first worries that she seems 'alone amongst many', but, as the evening proceeds, decides 'she looked foreign, exaggerated; she had too much expression'. Although he dismisses her finally as 'a very vulgar woman', he is chagrined to see that 'she was not in the least neglected. On the contrary, in the part of the room where she sat the crowd was denser, and ... agitated by unanimous laughter. If she should amuse them, he said to himself, she would succeed, and evidently she was amusing them.' (SL 615–6)

The next morning finds her in the garden with Sir Arthur, 'adorably fresh, in a toilet which Waterville ... felt sure would not be regarded as the proper thing for a Sunday morning in an English country-house: a *négligé* of white flounces and frills, interspersed with yellow ribbons – a garment which Madame de Pompadour might have worn when she received a visit from Louis XV'; he feels she looks 'dreadfully un-British and un-Protestant' (SL 619). The dress, in its summery garden setting, sets off Mrs Headway's beauty, suggests youth, pleasure and *fêtes champêtres*, but it also highlights Waterville's prejudices in associating seductive styles with France, immorality and Catholicism. However, when Lady Demesne calls Mrs Headway 'horrible' and appeals for evidence of scandal against her, Waterville declines –'I have seen nothing of her that is not perfectly correct.' She was 'extremely open to criticism', he reflects, 'yet she was not horrible' (SL 628).

Interestingly, Mrs Headway's dress has been worn before in James's 'wardrobe'. It first appeared in his review of a work by the Anglo-French painter James Tissot, 'The Deck of the H.M.S. Calcutta', of 1877, in which he attacked Tissot's 'vulgar and banal' realism – a longer acquaintance with the lady's 'stylish back and yellow ribbons', he wrote, would be 'intolerably wearisome'.[21] The similarities between this description

Plate 8 James Tissot, *The Deck of the HMS Calcutta*. 1877. Tate Britain, London.

and Daisy Miller's 1878 dress of 'white muslin, with a hundred frills and flounces, and knots of pale-coloured ribbon'[22] has already been noted by myself and other commentators,[23] and Tissot, who actually owned the dress, used it again at least three times. We might wonder why James – disliking Tissot's work – returned to it himself? In his review, James makes clear that his criticism is not of the dress's modishness, but of the hard finish of Tissot's painting that denied the viewer an imaginative response: 'its figures become mannequins, drained of potential life'. As I have indicated elsewhere, '[I]t is tempting to suggest that James wanted to show what could be done with such material in more talented hands'.[24] As we see, the dress sets off complicated responses in Waterville, revealing more about his narrow New England prejudices than about Mrs Headway. But, for all his disapproval, Waterville, as Littlemore observes, falls a little love with her.

Littlemore, too, betrays some warmth in his defence of Mrs Headway against his sister Mrs Dolphin's attack: 'It seems to me that she's quite as good as the little baronet ... he's a nonentity, and she at least is somebody' (SL 639). The two men are in truth confused and fascinated by Mrs Headway. She is not, as John Kimmey points out in his study of Henry

Figure 16 American Belle. *c*.1880. George Du Maurier, *English Society*, London: Osgood McIlvaine, 1897.

James and London, 'exactly typical of American women in search of husbands in London'.[25] In response to her often brutal candour (and insistently white appearance, perhaps), Littlemore complains she has 'no
shading'; Waterville, on the other hand believes 'she was several women
at once' (SL 589–90). Their confusion may spring from an element of role-
reversal in the relations between Mrs Headway and Sir Arthur.

In contrast to the powerful impact of Mrs Headway's appearances, we
hear that Sir Arthur is modest, with 'the prettiest, silkiest hair', delicate
complexion, and that 'his round blue eye' has a 'childlike candour' (SL
593) – a very model of Victorian womanhood, in fact. Mrs Headway's siege
of London succeeds not only through the feminine seductions of dress but
also by her entertainment value – her quite masculine 'clubability': 'It's a
settled thing that I'm an American humorist: if I say the simplest things
they begin to roar.' (SL 631) Not being at all clever, Sir Arthur is neither
talkative nor entertaining. But he *is* romantic, drawn to Mrs Headway 'precisely [for] her foreignness ... she made the time pass as it passed in no
other pursuit' (SL 595). There is something of James's Catherine Sloper[26]
about his mild, worshipful passivity; and like Catherine, when pushed, he
proves stubbornly loyal. At the last, when Littlemore invites questions
about Mrs Headway's past, Sir Arthur declines, himself resisting the
sexual/economic exchange system, in which 'purity' is a coin of worth,
discerning in Mrs Headway more durable and interesting values.

For Mrs Headway, the past becomes material for her comedy-act; she
knows that 'as a product of fashionable circles she was nowhere, but she
might have a great success as a child of nature' (SL 596). Kimmey finds
a good deal of Thackeray's Becky Sharp in her, as well as of George Du
Maurier's cartoon society-women – large ladies who bear down purpose-
fully on rather wispy men. Both types of women exert covert domestic and
social control, while appearing conventionally artless and submissive;
like them, Mrs Headway, playing the 'child of nature'[27] in white frills,
'pretends to be less complicated than she is'.[28]

Lady Demesne, with her own 'carefully-preserved purity' (SL 624), is
unimpressed. She makes a last frantic appeal to Littlemore for the truth.
Knowing the couple to be engaged, Littlemore allows that Mrs Headway
is 'not respectable'. But it is too late: they have been 'privately, and it was
to be hoped, ... indissolubly, united' (SL 649). And all in all, the English
aristocracy has benefited. Dull Sir Arthur has chosen a wife for her very
difference to his own kind, because she is amusing and refreshing, her
chic and wit a credit to him.

Mrs Headway's white dresses are not offered, then, as false testimony
to a 'pure' life, but are – like Daisy Miller's dresses – evidence of innate

good taste; tokens of wealth, certainly, but not of immoral earnings. White presents a clean slate, that American determination to pick oneself up, dust oneself down and start all over again. As Littlemore reflects, 'people don't change their nature; but they change their desires, their ideal, their effort' (SL 643). Mrs Headway's white dresses are central to her effort, an expression of fresh ideals. Although not exactly young, she has a kind of unquenchable innocence that transcends sexual experience. If, in refashioning herself, she glosses over her past, she does not quite lie. When pushed, neither man can say anything worse than that she has married and divorced immoderately. She is not respectable but she is, broadly speaking, a good thing.

Figuring four times in paint and at least twice in literature – as Mrs Headway's dress does – gives a dress a certain éclat. Another dress of 1884, whose representation set Paris and London buzzing, and to which a book has been devoted,[29] may be worth a detour. James was at the time enthusiastically promoting John Singer Sargent, the painter of the dress, as worn by Amélie Gautreau in her portrait, *Madame X.* Amélie Avegno, like Nancy Beck, had come from the American South, and had laid 'siege' to Paris in the late 1870s, capturing a banker, Pedro Gautreau. Amélie was strikingly beautiful, with white skin, auburn hair, dark eyes and an impossibly long, tip-tilted nose. 'Slender, yet full-bosomed and with her singular face, nineteen-year-old Amélie Avegno Gautreau was the bold new era's bold new ideal of feminine beauty'[30] – and she did not hide her light under the matrimonial bushel.

Like James, Sargent was an expatriate American, educated in Europe, who with talent and charm, was also conquering Paris in the early 1880s. Together, John Singer Sargent and Amélie Gautreau were 'two of the most visible imports of the day ... Amélie Paris's greatest American beauty and Sargent the city's brilliant young American painter'.[31] Sargent met Amélie in 1883, and, as 'a fellow upstart American who shared her goal of fame in Paris'[32] he identified with her. A successful portrait of Amélie at the next Salon would establish him. He started work on preliminary sketches in 1883, and entered the portrait for the Salon of summer 1884. James met Sargent early in 1884, and saw the portrait when it was taking its final, daring shape. In a letter he admits he 'only half-liked it',[33] but in an essay of 1887 on Sargent, calls it 'superb ... [t]he author has never gone further in being boldly and consistently himself', but also recalls that the portrait occasioned 'unreasoned scandal'[34] – something of an understatement.

James in his letter describes Madame Gautreau as 'half-stripped' and in the later essay, as wearing 'an entirely sleeveless dress of black satin'[35]

– but it was not the exposure of flesh that scandalized spectators. As Deborah Davis says, 'Salon attendees were used to seeing artistic renderings of naked women'.[36] It was the shape, colour and one single detail that caused outrage. To us the sleek black dress seems the essence of elegance; its very simplicity, however, was not only eccentric – Mrs Headway, remember, was a froth of frills – but it drew attention to Amélie's superb figure and an apparent absence of petticoat. The final devastating straw was the fallen shoulder strap – what indecencies did this not imply? The portrait became the Salon's storm-centre, and if Sargent was dismayed, his dismay paled before the fury of Amélie's mother, who, in a terrible scene in his studio, declared her daughter ruined, and demanded the withdrawal of the portrait. Sargent refused, but the picture returned, unsold, to his studio, where he adjusted the errant strap.[37] It was true, however, that Amélie's career never recovered – unlike Sargent's. No one accused her of anything, but she never escaped the portrait's erotic undertones. As James would have appreciated, the very vagueness of the suggestions lent them power. In the dress, people 'traced the implications of things', they guessed the 'unseen' from the 'seen' – alas.

The Gautreau affair, and James's meeting with Sargent, took place between the publication of 'The Siege of London' in 1883, and 'The Author of *Beltraffio*' of July, 1884. His appreciation of Sargent's work was immediate and it is tempting to see something of Sargent's influence in James's spare, metaphorical treatment of dress in 'Beltraffio'. The details of Mrs Headway's dress, despite James's dislike of Tissot's super-realism, are recognizably those of Tissot's favourite frock. Mrs Ambient, the woman at the centre of 'Beltraffio', is always in white – a more deliberate choice even than Mrs Headway's – but her appearance is as economically rendered as the svelte column of black, so unjustly fatal to Amélie Gautreau's reputation. Mrs Headway, with her murky reputation, finally emerges as 'good', vindicating her white wardrobe, but Mrs Ambient, impeccable in white, is bad. Critical comment generally damns her. Is her white dress therefore deceiving? James's reticent use of dress comes, as Anne Hollander says in her study of art and dress, from his 'very deep acknowledgement of the power of clothing',[38] and the Gautreau scandal would have confirmed his instincts. Dress 'has a flowery head', Elizabeth Bowen writes, 'but deep roots in the passions'.[39]

Beatrice Ambient is at first glance a virtuous wife and devoted mother. In an English garden, 'delicate and quiet in a white dress', her image is 'worthy of the author of a work so distinguished as *Beltraffio*' – according to the young American writer, who has made his journey to pay homage to the novelist. She does, however, kill her child – which on a scale of respectable behaviour, must rank very much lower than Mrs Headway's flexible approach to marriage. While the two stories are close in date, we have moved from a comedy of manners in 'The Siege of London' to a darker stage of James's work in '*Beltraffio*', a stage containing *The Turn of the Screw*. Mrs Ambient's white dress does not hide a black soul, any more than the Governess's dark dress in *The Turn of the Screw* clothes a guiltless one, but she does significantly wear a miniature of her child on a black ribbon against the dress – James's single detail, his 'fallen shoulder strap'.

The relation between ethical and aesthetic values, so close, as Tanner says, to the heart of James's work, is the focus of the fatal conflict of husband and wife over their small son, Dolcino. In 'The Art of Fiction' James attacks 'the deep-seated Philistinism'[40] of Victorian Britain and its 'evangelical hostility to the novel' and argues for the writer's freedom of subject. That a novel might be 'a source of corruption' is to James a meaningless notion: 'the deepest quality of a work of art', he says, 'will always be the quality of the mind of the producer'.[41] But for Mrs Ambient the 'quality' of her husband's mind is precisely the problem. It is the spectre that haunts her being, as the ghosts haunt the Governess.

Mark Ambient's *Beltraffio*, a novel set in Renaissance Italy, has, according to the narrator, provoked a scandal – 'it was a kind of aesthetic war-cry'.[42] The narrator is a devotee of Ambient and of 'the other great man, the one in America' (AB 867), clearly Walt Whitman. On the publication of James's story, Ambient was at once identified by readers as J. A. Symonds, whose books on Italian and Greek culture, according to one outraged contemporary critic, were 'too fond of alluding to the unmentionable'.[43] Symonds' life and work were indeed dedicated to making mentionable the 'unmentionable' fact of homosexual desire. James denied the identification of Ambient with Symonds,[44] but his notebook of March, 1884 records a letter from Edmund Gosse about Symonds: 'poor S.'s wife was in no sort of sympathy with what he wrote; disapproving of its tone, thinking his books immoral, pagan, hyper-aesthetic'. James immediately saw a story in it: 'the opposition between the narrow, cold, Calvinistic wife, a rigid moralist; and the husband, impregnated even to morbidness ... with the aesthetic way of life ... the dénouement to be the fate of the child',[45] What were to become *fin de siècle* code-words for homoeroticism – 'aesthetic', 'artistic' and 'pagan' – pepper the story. Mrs Ambient thinks her husband 'no better than an ancient Greek' (AB 892) – and we may assume she is not thinking of sculpture.

James's relation to British Aestheticism is a vexed topic, as Jonathan Freedman's book on the subject makes clear. The associations of

Figure 17 Aesthetic Dress. Cartoon by George Du Maurier, London: *Punch*, c.1880.

aestheticism with homo-eroticism – anachronistically reading back from the Wilde trials of 1895 – have muddied the whole issue, and defences of James's 'moralism, his realism and his Americanism', mounted against such associations, leave his 'rich and subtle response'[46] to the Aesthetic movement unaccounted for. James's portraits of artists and writers, and his essay, 'The Art of Fiction', show clear allegiance to the Aesthetic project, its radical empiricism and its rejection of a 'moral mission' for art. But James, as we shall see in *'Beltraffio'*, also interrogates Aestheticism, distancing himself from its 'affectation, its hypocrisy, its fraudulence, its moral and aesthetic failures'.[47] It was from Aestheticism's vapid posturing, its associations with effeminacy, that James wished to dissociate himself.

Alan Sinfield points out that 'the idea of the aesthetic as effeminate is grounded in the fact that literature ... [has] been in a state of conflict around imputations that there is something intrinsically feminine in its constitution'; James therefore felt he had to insist that fiction 'be accorded all the seriousness of history',[48] a traditionally male province. Mark Ambient is not a proto-Gabriel Nash, of James's novel *The Tragic Muse*, of 1890, an aesthete who takes himself so un-seriously that he dematerializes. *The Tragic Muse* and '*Beltraffio*', as Eric Haralson points out, 'antedate decisive events [the Wilde trials], but participate in the conversion'[49] – that is, James in neither case merges the aesthete with the homosexual but, reading backward from those trials, Ambient and Nash appear to be part of a climate that led to that decisive shift which defined the homosexual personality-type, and from which it is now difficult to escape.

The place of Aestheticism in art has been re-examined by Andrew Wilton, who suggests – as I mentioned in Chapter 5 – that the work of Burne-Jones, G. F. Watts and the later Rossetti should be relocated within European Symbolism, with the work of Puvis de Chavannes, Moreau and Böcklin.[50] Aestheticism had its roots in France (the phrase 'Art for Art's sake' was originally Gautier's) but Wilde's outrages against Victorian 'earnestness' and the lampooning of aesthetes by Du Maurier in *Punch*, gave British Aestheticism 'a somewhat frivolous reputation, but it was a serious development which must be assimilated into any full account of Symbolism'. Wilton sees in Burne-Jones's allusive art – admired by James – 'a principal channel for the dissemination of a distinctive and highly influential, British Symbolism'.[51] I would suggest that placing James within this re-reading of Aestheticism as an aspect of European Symbolism makes sense of developments toward a metaphoric style in his own work, as well as reflecting his changing preferences in art.

Mrs Ambient's rigid, Calvinistic attitude to the aesthetic novel in '*Beltraffio*', carries the burden of accountability for the story's catastrophe, though the tale substitutes for the Calvinism of James's preliminary notes less definable, more visceral beliefs. Ambient's aestheticism is not left unscathed, but its superficial, 'over-the-top' aspects, its effeminacy and posturing, are transferred to his sister, target of the narrator's mockery, with her 'Michel-Angelesque attitudes and mystical robes' (AB 878). Miss Ambient, however, is irritating, not dangerous. Societal antagonism to art, as embodied in the conflict between husband and wife, is a more serious and, here, fatal matter. According to her sister-in-law, Mrs Ambient believes that her husband's influence on Dolcino is 'a subtle poison'. 'If she could,' Miss Ambient tells the narrator, 'she would prevent Mark from ever touching him.' (AB 887)

The battle over Dolcino, as recorded by the narrator, is not an intellectual one – there is no discussion – it is physical. Its violence among the teacups, in an English summer garden, is as shocking as the spectres' irruption into the garden at Bly in *The Turn of the Screw*. Dolcino is first forcibly held by his mother though he wants his father. He escapes and Ambient immediately seizes and kisses him. She then requests the child's return, but Ambient refuses to let him go, cruelly asking the child to decide between them. Dolcino chooses his father, and they move off. Mrs Ambient is left to explain to the narrator, with brutal candour, her dislike of her husband's work, his admirers and his 'tone': 'I am very different from my husband. If you like him, you won't like me.' (AB 875) Dolcino soon after falls ill. Meanwhile the narrator is given the manuscript of Ambient's new novel to read and, in a misguided attempt to reconcile husband and wife, he urges Mrs Ambient to read it. The next morning he sees her in a white dressing gown, 'at the front gate in colloquy with the physician' (AB 905). She sends the doctor away, and – as he later learns from Miss Ambient – though Dolcino worsens, she gives him no medicine, does nothing the doctor orders, and watches her child die.

Given James's distaste for 'the hypocrisy and pharisaism of English life',[52] and the story's dark conclusion, we might read into Mrs Ambient's 'cold, lady-like candour and well-starched muslin dress' (AB 880), the life-denying bigotry of Anglo-Saxon attitudes to the novel. The notebooks certainly suggest this. But James, in the process of creation, does not withdraw sympathy from his characters nor impose narrow meanings. In 'The Siege of London' the image of Mrs Headway is conveyed by Littlemore and Waterville, whose prejudices the reader takes into account. The narration of 'The Author of *Beltraffio*', however, is controlled by an easily overlooked, nameless narrator.[53] He tells us that Mrs Ambient thinks him 'an intrusive and even depraved young man' who flatters her husband's worst tendencies. He repeatedly speaks of her as cold and detached; he differs from her, he says, 'inexpressibly' (AB 898). We never 'go behind' Mrs Ambient, but we might consider her perspective: a young American has arrived with an introductory letter from Walt Whitman, and is staying apparently indefinitely, at the invitation of her husband, with whom he is closeted every evening. With her child ill in bed, the young man thrusts a manuscript on her, whose contents take even further the – to her – vile subject matter of *Beltraffio*. She decides her son is better dead. Ambient is more accurate than the narrator, when he describes his wife as 'a very nice woman, upright, clever [but] there's a hatred of art – there's a hatred of literature!' (AB 893) We may find her values and her actions reprehensible, but she is no more cold or detached than the Governess at Bly, in her passionate battle against the threat that she believes menaces the innocence of childhood.

If the narrator's account of Mrs Ambient is then unreliable, how does he see Aesthetic Miss Ambient – a likely ally in that she detests her sister-in-law, admires her brother and is alarmed for Dolcino? Miss Ambient does little more, in fact, than relay tittle-tattle about the family, and, despite their apparent common 'aesthetic' cause, the narrator finds her first comic and then repellent. '[C]rumpled and dishevelled', she droops about the house, in contrast to her 'smooth-haired, thin-lipped and perpetually fresh' (AB 880) sister-in-law, efficient hostess and nurse, in simple, starched white. James, through the narrator's perspective, lavishes an almost *Romola*–like attention on the details of Miss Ambient's appearance: 'medieval … pale and angular with … black hair intertwined with golden fillets and curious chains. She wore a faded velvet robe, which clung to her when she moved, fashioned as to neck and sleeves, like the garments of old Venetians and Florentines … She was a singular, self-conscious, artificial creature, and I never more than half penetrated her motives and mysteries. I am sure, however, they were less extraordinary than her appearance announced.' She has, he concludes, 'little real intelligence …[she is] a restless yearning spinster … she wished to be looked at, she wished to be married' (AB 878–9). The over-loaded account (running to two pages) has, as with Eliot's description of Monna Brigida's dress, a weakening effect – in this case, I suggest, deliberate. And, as with Waterville's description of Mrs Headway's frilly frock, it reveals as much of the describer as the described. Miss Ambient is not likeable, and, though she gushes embarrassingly about 'Art', her Aestheticism is all clothes and no content. But we might note how the narrator's hostility shifts from her unattractive appearance to contempt for her intellect, to his suspicion that she is after his virtue. His hostility sharpens when she tells him that Mrs Ambient's decision to allow Dolcino to die followed *his* insistence that she read her husband's new novel. We would do well reflect on this narrator a little – with, I suggest, the famously unreliable narrator of *The Aspern Papers* in mind.

To Mrs Ambient, the real threat – however she sees it – lies in this young American, who has laid 'siege' to her English fastness. Aestheticism is not the problem; it is its unmentionable associations, which torment her imagination as the Governess at Bly is tormented. Ambient himself has never forced his wife's hand over questions of his work or his beliefs. He is 'perfectly decent in life',[54] a conventional Victorian paterfamilias, if 'addicted to velvet jackets … and loose shirt collars' (AB 867). The narrator, on the other hand, is subject to the 'hyper-aestheticism' and 'morbidity', assigned to Ambient in James's notebook. He sees his trip to England as a 'little game of new sensations' (AB 865) and, as Haralson says, persists in 'seeing everything – but especially the 'languid and angelic' Dolcino – in a precious Pre-Raphaelite frame'.[55] There is a profound divide between the narrator's attitude to art and James's. What the narrator admires in Ambient's work is his 'effort to arrive at a [perfect] surface' (AB 891), the very basis of James's attacks on Tissot and Braddon. Ambient causes the narrator's heart to 'beat very fast' (AB 867), but his strongest, most 'morbid', effusions are for the beauty of Dolcino: 'There was something touching, almost alarming in his beauty, which seemed to be composed of elements too fine and pure for the breath of the world ... he was too charming to live' (AB 870–1). When Mrs Ambient refuses his offer to carry indoors the visibly ailing Dolcino, he regrets that 'I never touched Dolcino' (AB 902) – strengthened in the New York Edition to 'I never laid a longing hand on Dolcino'.[56] How much of his 'longing' is apparent to Mrs Ambient and how it feeds her already heightened alarm is worth considering.

We might also consider Peggy McCormack's observation that there is a feminist side to James's middle-period protagonists. Miss Ambient, despite her 'Reformed' dress, is no militant: she is as decorative and dependent as any Victorian 'Angel' and finally disappears into a convent. But Mrs Ambient resists male dominance and the male values that she perceives as a threat to her child. As Alan Sinfield and Eve Kosofsky Sedgwick have made clear, 'the paths of male entitlement, especially in nineteenth-century [Britain], required certain intense male bonds that were not readily distinguishable from the most reprobated bonds'.[57] Politics, the Army, business, service to the Empire, club and intellectual life, all central sources of power, depended on close male relations, where effeminacy, as Sinfield says, is not banished by Victorian ideals of 'man-liness', but is its forbidden if 'necessary corollary'.[58] Mrs Ambient's 'feminism' is not characterized by a desire to share or abrogate male power, nor to encourage feminine aspects in the male, but to insist on the autonomy of her domestic sphere. Feminism was not (is not) a consistent, monolithic entity. Articulate, independent women, such as novelists Eliza Lyn Linton, Mrs Humphrey Ward and George Eliot were anti-suffragist, but feminist to the extent that they insisted on the importance of women's education and the centrality of female values to the nation's welfare. The woman-controlled, matriarchal world of the Victorians was in fact making its last stand before succumbing to the twentieth-century world of male technology, financial and imperialist institutions. Mrs Ambient, like the heroines of Linton's, Ward's and Eliot's novels, is profoundly serious about the significance of her traditional female role, and her appearance is consonant with this view of herself.

I have suggested elsewhere that Isabel Archer's decision, in James's *Portrait of a Lady*, to reject New Woman freedoms and return to her

corrupt husband, actually accords with John Ruskin's ideal of womanhood, set out in his essay 'Of Queens' Gardens'. Isabel's is an act of deliberate self-renunciation, but also an assertion of moral and spiritual
superiority.[59] Ruskin argued that the moral and philanthropic powers of
the female sphere counterbalanced the political and financial powers of
men. It was in truth an ersatz power, with no real base: but if the imaginative leap from the welfare of the domestic hearth to that of the nation
was a logic-defying one, for the anti-suffragists it represented an attractive and authoritative basis for their argument, which was not an anti-
feminist one. The moral health of the home became the woman's *raison
d'être*, and we can see, therefore, how '"purity" [became] in part a feminist cause ... attacks on the immorality and decadence of aristocratic
culture were the staple of purity tracts'.[60] The very vagueness of the
terms used, allowed for a kind of unfocused public hysteria about imagined but necessarily unspoken threats. Hilary Fraser, writing on gender
and the Victorian periodical, describes how 'sentiment and sensation-
alism became the staples of domestic journalism',[61] and the effects of this
climate of obfuscation, sentimentality and hysteria on immature minds
can be traced in the Governess's narrative in *The Turn of the Screw* – or
in the reactions to the Wilde trial of 1895.

Mrs Ambient, in her battle to protect the sanctity of her home and
child, puts on 'the armour of light'. Her white dress is not detailed: its
cold rectitude operates as metaphor rather than as fashion. But in trying
to visualize its material form within the styles of the period, the heavily
boned, tightly laced 'cuirass' bodice offers the requisite repressiveness
and impregnability. As the period's defining garment, the 'cuirass' had,
according to the dress-historian, Penelope Byrde, 'the appearance of a
piece of armour'.[62] This is a very different fashion-statement from Mrs
Headway's soft seductions, though of the same colour and date. Du
Maurier's formidable cartoon women often sport this bodice; the starched
shirt-front of the New Woman is another version. Mrs Ambient's steely
surface repels, but it also conceals and constricts the maternal breast
beneath, and the emotions within. Her one gesture of unease, noted by
the narrator at the dining-table, is to her breast; 'she attended to her
dinner, watched the servants, arranged the puckers in her dress' (AB
880). Elizabeth Wilson, in her study of fashion and modernity, points to
the ambiguity of dress, which 'links [the] body to the social world, but
also more clearly separates the two. Dress is the frontier between the self
and the not-self'.[63] This 'frontier', for Beatrice Ambient, is a battlefield
between the purity she must defend and the 'degeneracy' of the homo-
social world (the 'not-self') – sitting there across the dinner-table – that

Figure 18 'Cuirass' bodice; House Dress. Fashion Plate, *Sylvia's Home Journal*, London: Ward Lock & Co., 1879.

threatens her domestic citadel. Arranging what is most visible and vulnerable – her bodice – she reinforces her defences.

White is, of course, a symbol of innocence, a *tabula rasa*, but blank sheets are also ignorant ones, and one of James's most persistent themes is the necessary distinction between ignorance and innocence. Mrs Ambient's rejection of her husband's work is a consequence of her deliberate and defensive ignorance of it – 'I don't read what he writes.' (AB 876) We can only speculate – as she herself has speculated – at what she finds or thinks she finds, when she does finally read his novel. The Governess in *The Turn of the Screw* – an ideally ignorant/innocent Victorian girl – raises spectres from the 'hideous obscure'[64] by imagining 'horrors' she should neither know nor speak of. Sidgwick has outlined in *Epistemology of the Closet* the way that the marginality of terms, found throughout James's work, such as 'horrors', 'monstrosities', 'dreadful things', allow for a creative secrecy: as Peter Rawlings puts it, this cultivated secrecy about secrets 'releases a fiction-enabling discourse predicated on … a world of appearances for which there is no corresponding reality'.[65] James has not only made us 'think the evil'[66] that is released into the minds of these two women, but drawn us into the catastrophic outcome of ignorant obsessive speculation (obsessive *because* it is ignorant) – the death of innocents. The Governess, for an appalled moment before Miles's death, looks into the abyss: 'if he *were* innocent what then on earth was I?'[67] – a question that Mrs Ambient might ask of her blind hatred of her husband's work.

Purity is an idea lightly, even self-mockingly played on in Mrs Headway's dress, but purity to Mrs Ambient is an ideal for which she is prepared to kill – it is not difficult to point to later greater atrocities based on such fanaticisms. 'We prefer' Tony Tanner says, 'not to envisage the possibility of hidden atrocity under the smooth social surface, but for James it was a perpetual possibility.'[68] Amélie Gautreau's shoulder strap might be explained by faulty dressmaking; to us it is a witty touch to an elegantly minimalist image, and sympathetic to the twenty-first-century eye. But in the mind of *fin de siècle* Paris society, unspeakable sexual depravities surged up from prurient depths at the sight of it, an effect Sargent may have calculated but, in charity, not the social death it signalled for Amélie. The atrocity lay not in Amélie but in the minds of the beholders – she hoped, surely, for no more than a celebration of her beauty. Atrocities, however, do take place beneath the respectable surface of English society, beneath Mrs Ambient's smooth white armour, in the name of a misguided virtue as dangerous as any evil; an atrocity to her child, herself and Ambient, all dead within a few years of each other.

Why have both women – such very different women – chosen to wear white? Though respectability concerns both, the effects they produce are polarized: high comedy on the one hand, dark tragedy on the other. Looking out of the 'house of fiction', James says in the preface to *Portrait of a Lady*, some see black and some white – although they may be seeing the same thing. Anticipating Roland Barthes, James perceives dress as a language whose meanings are always over-determined, shifting, capable of infinite deferral. The represented garment is one thing, the 'real' garment, another. The 'real' garment can be represented – translated into language or paint – in any number of ways, communicating almost an infinity of meanings, depending on observer or representer. Barthes' comment that 'clothes are a meaning within a specific group, as well as shaped physical mass',[69] is dramatically – to us absurdly – corroborated by the Amélie Gautreau scandal. And, as James surely noted, the less physical detail offered, the more meaning is possible.

Dress 'reflects' nothing, Barthes says, but may react to external disturbances. The social disturbances under the surface of *fin de siècle* London (or Paris) provide fissures for an energetic newcomer to flourish, for a white flower to 'bloom'. Mrs Headway in her life-enhancing wardrobe is the confident, stylish, amusing American Woman whose time has come. But dress can ward off as well as attract; and Mrs Ambient, encased in her icy armour, subject to a reactionary climate of moral hysteria, reacts tragically both to external disturbance and to her own emotional conflicts. She wears stiff stark white with a touch of black – in effect, mourning-white. No other detail is offered: white becomes all that we see, an engulfing, isolating purity – broken only by the portrait of Dolcino on a black ribbon. (James may even have remembered Lucy Audley's ring on a black velvet ribbon that ties her to a husband she believes dead, and whom she then 'murders'.) Detail, as James said of Balzac's descriptions, must be 'accessory to the action'; the action of 'The Author of *Beltraffio*' in fact takes place 'off-stage', in the mind of Mrs Ambient, to whose movements we have no access, other than in those few 'touches' that 'count'. As the story progresses the detail of the black-ribboned portrait evolves from a simple sign of mother love, to a dark portent, then finally to a memorial to a child, dead in the name of 'purity' – a detail far darker in its implications than Mrs Headway's Pompadour-frills, or Amélie Gautreau's slipping strap. Dress in this fiction is shown to be socially central, but it is also a symbolic system: these garments, so close to the body, also, as James has shown us, articulate the soul – in triumph or torment and, oddly enough, in white.

–8–

Consuming Clothes:
Edith Wharton's *The House of Mirth*

Among Edith Wharton's recollections of Henry James, in *A Backward Glance*, is an anecdote that characteristically could be read against herself, in which James – just as characteristically – is mischievously ambiguous. 'What was your idea in suspending the four principal characters in "The Golden Bowl" in the void?' she asked. 'Why have you stripped them of all the *human fringes* we necessarily trail after us through life?' ... after a pause of reflection he answered in a disturbed voice: '"My dear – I didn't know I had"'[1] – either he was modestly admitting a fault, or suggesting that Wharton was a careless reader. The characters in question are in fact furnished with all the accoutrements of the Gilded Age super-rich, not least their clothes[2] – sparingly detailed but very much to the point. James's development of a symbolist treatment of dress was fully realized in *The Golden Bowl* published in 1904, the year before Wharton's *House of Mirth*, and read by her, one guesses, while she was working on her novel. She never overcame her dislike of James's late style, but her fictional treatment of dress has, all the same, much in common with his.

The conversation between James and Wharton took place some years after the publication of *The House of Mirth*, in 1905, and after her own mock-indignant reply to W. R. Thayer's letter, praising her novel: 'I must protest, & emphatically, against the suggestion that I have "stripped" New York society. New York society is still amply clad.'[3] She was of course playing on the word 'stripped', Thayer had intended only to compliment her on an unsparing satire of a society described later by Robert Heilbroner as one of 'staggering dishonesty ... that we are accustomed to look back upon with a blush, ... grotesque in its trappings'.[4] Wharton, within that society, anatomizes its deceits and trappings and if, by the end of the story, one could say that she had conveyed its material excesses – its 'human fringes' – she had also 'stripped' it to its venal soul. But she did so with little hope of converting it to more humanity, more taste and less extravagance: as she said, it remained (remains) in every sense, 'amply clad'.

The novel's incipit is a characteristic New York scene – a crowd in front of Grand Central Station – in which the figure of the central character Lily Bart, catches the attention of the novel's main 'focalizor', Lawrence Selden, whose description introduces her to the reader. His perspective is at first distant and the découpage panoramic, placing Lily's still figure, 'wearing an air of irresolution ... which might be the mask of a very definite purpose',[5] against the moving crowd, ascribing to Lily an equivocation which is actually his own. Continuing to dither, he observes there was 'nothing new about her' (3), but adds that she always interests him. He moves into view to see if she will try to evade him, and when she instead comes eagerly to greet him, his hedging and dodging seem to have been needlessly circuitous.

Once they meet, Selden's view of Lily is close and detailed; he remarks on her 'radiance', then focuses on her head and hair, level with his eyes, as they walk:

> Her vivid head, relieved against the dull tints of the crowd, made her more conspicuous than in a ball-room, and under her dark hat and veil she regained the girlish smoothness, the purity of tint, that she was beginning to lose after eleven years of late hours and indefatigable dancing ... [He] was conscious of ... the crisp upward wave of her hair – was it ever so slightly brightened by art? ... Everything about her was at once vigorous and exquisite, at once strong and fine. He had a confused sense that she must have cost a great deal to make, that a great many dull and ugly people must... have been sacrificed to produce her. (4, 5)

Read carefully; Selden's description reflects as much of himself as of Lily. We see Lily from several viewpoints, notably her own, but Selden is the Jamesian 'centre of consciousness', and in giving him the traditional nineteenth-century narrative authority of the lawyer – middle-class, male and 'expert'[6] – Wharton is preparing for the final 'stripping' away of narrative complacencies and assumptions – 'My last page' she warned, 'is always latent in my first.'[7] Again, Selden qualifies his admiration of Lily with gossipy criticism and contradictions: she is 'girlish' but shows the wear of a decade of late nights: her waving hair is 'crisp', but is it dyed? She is a beautiful 'Art' object, but at what cost?

Because they are walking and talking together, it is Lily's hat and hair that Selden notices. Hats would indeed have been hard to miss in the early years of the century: expanding both outwards and upwards, the hats of the period were immense confections, involving entire birds, or sporting '18 roses on top, 18 under the brim at the back and sides, and 36 rose-leaves'.[8] Michael Carter interprets this explosion of millinery, 'at all the canonic sites of modernity – the street, the café, the brothel and the race-track' (and the railway station), as 'ubiquitous witness to the birth of modernity ... The modernist new, before it encased itself in the ideology and style of functionalism, poured itself into that which was about to disappear.'[9] These hats were often worn asymmetrically, anchored precariously by pins: 'Movement', according to Fiona Clark, 'was the key to the style.' They seemed to float upon the head, and 'had never before been less securely located in relation to the head, and the actual shape of the hat had never been less apparent'.[10] In 1903 large lacy veils added to the confusion, revived after some years out of fashion by the new craze for motoring. Veils were often dark and heavy, and embroidery added to both decorative and defensive functions. Lily's hat is fashionable, as one would expect, but also concealing, unstable and blurred, the last extravagant gasp of a vanishing order.

A contemporary review of the novel conceded that Wharton has a 'fine manner, but it is like the fine gowns of her heroines, a fashion of the times ... What she says will not last.'[11] More interesting than the critic's error of judgement is his impression of the novel's 'fine gowns'. The impression is understandable, but in fact there is essentially only one *described* dress in the novel, one that relies for its substance on an analogous painted dress in Joshua Reynold's portrait *Mrs Lloyd*, and is the focus of the novel's climax. At the station Selden tells us only of the arresting effect of Lily's appearance, which against the 'dinginess, the crudity of the average section of womanhood' looks 'highly specialized' (5). After an indiscreet tea in Selden's flat, Lily, on the train to a country-house weekend at Bellomont, spots Percy Gryce, shy bachelor heir to millions and fellow-guest. In contrast to the distance and ambivalence of Selden's view of Lily, we are now made intimately aware of her physicality, when, walking up the train, she 'accidentally' sways against Gryce, enveloping him 'in the scent of her dress' (18). A decorous, calculatedly seductive tea-scene with Gryce follows, interrupted by a third guest, Bertha Dorset, who joins the pair and maliciously sabotages Lily's tête-à-tête.

Given the near-absence of concrete detail, the *impression* of fashionable excess is worth considering, particularly in view of the highly particularized accounts of dress that Wharton had given in *The Age of Innocence*, a novel often associated with *The House of Mirth*. *The Age of Innocence*, published in 1920, is in fact a historical novel – like *Middlemarch*, it covers a period within the memory of its readers – one whose continuity with the present Wharton wanted to maintain. Dress references in *The Age of Innocence* are therefore specific to that period, since the 1920 reader's consciousness of the dressed-image had to be adjusted – though they are not so distanced as to turn the novel into a costume-drama. Wharton's fiction immediately after *The House of Mirth* and like it set in 'present time', is, on the other hand sparing of dress references: the dress of the eponymous Madame de Treymes, for example, is characterized by its effect of making everyone else look dull: Anna Leath in *The Reef* hardly seems dressed at all, while her rival, the anti-ingénue Sophy Viner, is nailed by one recurring, very seductive black dress and pink cloak.

Anne Hollander, noting the frequent imprecision of fictional representations of dress, accounts for this in several ways, the most usual being the assumption that reader and author have in common a mental image of the way people look. In representing important human qualities, however, literature shares with painting a general prejudice that the closer these qualities are felt 'to approach the universal the better the fiction.... Consequently, the style of their dress, their historically determined ... way of looking, is assumed to be irrelevant.'[12] This aim no doubt lies partly behind Lily's decision in the novel to wear a 'timeless' dress for the *tableau vivant*. But awareness of the mental self is not separable from the physical; the way things look and the way they are *felt* to look is intrinsic to identity – a truth central to the reading of Lily Bart. As Hollander points out, the sense of clothes, 'which always varies according to the look of clothes, must actually vary through history much more than the feeling of love or vengefulness or embarrassment or triumph'.[13]

In her own life, Wharton had an acute awareness of the power of dress: her autobiography opens with her infant self being 'put into her warmest coat and very pretty bonnet, which she had surveyed in the glass with considerable satisfaction',[14] and she recalls that her earliest ambition was to be the best-dressed woman in New York, like her mother. Wharton's first encounter with James is self-mockingly characterized by her failure to attract his attention with a beautiful new hat.[15] Those hats of her youth, with veils 'as thick as curtains', were to her dramas: 'the effect was dazzling when the curtain was drawn'. If we think, Wharton says, that those incognito heavily-veiled heroines of the Victorian novel are all improbable clichés, 'the novelistic formula was based on what was a reality'.[16] And, as we see, the veils of 1870 had usefully returned around 1903 to conceal and reveal Lily Bart.

How does Lily see herself? She is the product of both old and new New York, but Lily Bart's only lessons have been in good manners and the upkeep of appearances: after the ruin and death of her parents, Lily considers her beauty her single usable asset. Cash and looks are thus inseparable and the social dictats of the period reinforced the lesson. Mrs Haweis, doyenne of taste in *fin de siècle* Britain, opened her advice book *The Art of Beauty* by affirming that the culture of personal beauty 'especially of female beauty, is of the first interest and importance ... its cultivation may even become a duty';[17] though her notion of 'beauty', as one can see from her frontispiece, is vague and mystical. In 1901, Ella Fletcher's beauty manual hailed the American Beauty's path in life as 'a rose-bordered one, a royal progress; for to Beauty the world ... pays homage ... every experience in life teaches her that her share of its successes and pleasures will be in proportion to her own ability to please ... the first and most important influence is physical beauty'.[18]

Wharton avoids particularizing Lily's appearance *because* of its central importance. Concrete detail risked fashion-plate jargon, and to use the 'literary style' (216) with which the novel's despised journalist 'little

Figure 19 Ideal 'Beauty'. *Frontispiece* to Mrs Haweis, *The Art of Beauty*, London: Chatto and Windus, 1883.

Dabham' treats Bertha Dorset's frocks would have defined and banalized the presentation of Lily. Wharton writes in her autobiography of going through her early prose on an 'adjective hunt', to achieve 'concision and austerity',[19] and like James, she saw in George Eliot's *Romola* the perils of lavish description: 'for all its carefully studied detail', she wrote, '[it] remains a pasteboard performance'.[20] But neither is her indeterminate treatment of dress simply a reliance on a general memory-bank. Wharton wants Lily's image to exist beyond time and yet to be historically determined: her stated aim was 'to give dramatic significance' to a frivolous society 'through what its frivolity can destroy':[21] this depiction of destructiveness was both particular and far-reaching in intention. If the novel were simply a corrective social satire, details of extravagant costuming would be an obvious target, and Lily, 'stripped' down in Swiftian style to a cadaver, would be a butt for laughter or a *memento mori*: but Lily is a member *and* a victim of her society. Uncertain and tragicomic, she is in thrall to society's imperatives of money and appearance, part of its decadence, yet apprehending values beyond time, something finer but too frail to survive the savagery of New York's leisure-class barbarians. 'Business in this age of barony,' Heibroner says, 'was a brutal business and the price of morality was apt to be defeat.'[22] Lily's death is not exemplary, nor cathartic, but is instead an uneasy scene that implicates the reader. Her appearance will therefore be suggestive and elusive, inwardly and outwardly sensed, open to interpretation, misinterpretation and re-interpretation.

The House of Mirth can be read, however, as a companion volume to Theodore Veblen's satire of 1899, *The Theory of the Leisure Class.* Conspicuous waste of goods finds its perfect expression in dress, Veblen says: 'our apparel is always in evidence', and expense is critical – 'what is inexpensive is unworthy'.[23] To survive in New York's Gilded Age, with its post-bellum standards of conspicuous consumption and waste, and its inheritance of an increasingly hypocritical moral code, Lily must maintain a protean ability to accord with her surroundings. Starting from Grand Central Station, she is on the move: she lives in the houses of others and to earn her keep she must be a credit to her hosts in appearance and manners. One of Veblen's parasitic 'vicarious consumers', Lily is a member of the 'spurious leisure class – abjectly poor ... but morally unable to stoop to gainful pursuits';[24] she consumes on behalf of others, which demands a well-stocked wardrobe. This in its turn consumes and wastes her: the central point of my argument here.

The acquisition, upkeep and performance of dress eats away at Lily, ages, starves and demoralizes her, and threatens to make of her Carlyle's nightmare figure – a 'mere hollow shape', fit for the dust-heap. Fashions in Wharton's novels, as Martha Banta perceives, 'do more than confuse the onlooker; they erase the unique personalities of their wearers'.[25] As Lily wearily says to Gerty Farish, 'You think we live *on* the rich ... it's a privilege we have to pay for ... by going to the best dress-makers and having just the right dress for every occasion, and always [being] fresh and exquisite and amusing' (266). This is an accurate representation of the upper classes of the time. In Edwardian England '[l]adies on a four-day visit to a country house could not wear the same dress twice and so would have required at least twelve to sixteen complete ensembles';[26] a New York woman of fashion, around 1900, according to Caroline Milbank, might change her clothes as often as six times a day.[27] Wharton, without itemizing such a superfluity of goods, nevertheless conveys the instability of Lily's persona, the improvisation and fragility of her social act and, most importantly, the relentless erosion of her being, 'rootless, blown hither and thither on every wind of fashion' (319). 'Until *The House of Mirth*', Cynthia Griffin Wolff says, 'no one had troubled to detail what it would be like to be the woman thus exalted and objectified.'[28]

Lily lives according to ideals of femininity comparable to those of George Eliot's Rosamond Vincy; worse perhaps, in that the ostensible moral code of New York society had no longer any relevance to lived standards, something Lily never quite grasps: Rosamond could at least rely on Middlemarch's family decencies. Like Rosamond, Lily cannot conceive of a life *not* lived in luxury – luxury is the air she breathes. But Rosamond's requirements pale before Lily's, whose standards of wealth are those of Wall Street's robber-barons, now making Europe's monarchs look shabby.[29] Her shopping is indeed so consuming an occupation that she has a maid to help. Lily has, like Rosamond, been taught to be useless, and after fifty years of improving education for girls, she has not even benefited from a Mrs Lemon.

The Trenor's house at Bellomont provides the first and most sympathetic setting for Lily's performance, and like a star-actress, she has sent her maid and trunks on ahead. Selden's judgement of Lily as always conscious of her effect is accurate – she is constantly assessing her audience, dressing herself for another role. He is wrong, however, to assume that her plots are prepared: as Sartre's Roquentin says, 'contingence is the essence of existence'[30] – for Lily it is all improvisation, a re-arranging of properties to hand to achieve the next effect. Before going to Bellomont Lily confides to Selden her sense of the precarious artifice of her situation, the brute realities that underlie the glamour of a *femme disponible*, and her need of a wealth-creating male: 'Your coat's a little shabby – but who cares?... If I were shabby no one would have me; a woman is asked out as much for her clothes as for herself ... Who wants a dingy woman? We are expected to be pretty and well-dressed till we drop – and if we can't keep it up alone, we have to go into partnership.' (12) But Lily's analysis merely entertains Selden, indicating his untroubled acceptance of the status quo.

We share her contentment, then, when she enters the bedroom at Bellomont, 'with its softly-shaded lights, her lace dressing-gown lying across the silken bedspread, her little embroidered slippers before the fire, a vase of carnations filling the air with scent ... her whole being dilated in an atmosphere of luxury. ... But it was not the luxury of others that she wanted.' (26) The setting suggests indulgence and sensuality: discreet servants have provided light, warmth and scent; luxury versions of ordinary objects – slippers, dressing-gown, bedspread – display their silken seductions. It is a 'bedroom-scene' of a woman 'ravished' by pleasures she knows to be short-lived but which she longs to be able to stabilize. Wharton focuses on lingerie, not only because these garments allow us a voyeuristic intimacy with Lily, and suggest the extra luxury of hidden consumption, but also because fashion at this period, with its lavish use of lace, aspired to the condition of underwear, underwear itself having become more important: 'there is something very attractive', a commentator of 1900 finds, 'about the elaborate petticoat with its frou-frouing mysteries'.[31] These garments are not to be too closely and indecorously described; they remain as yet mysterious and detached from Lily, waiting to be worn and enjoyed in a solitude the reader may not share.

In the first representations of Lily then, we have moved from a publicly viewed, high-fashion item of outerwear – the hat – to the effect of a dress on one individual in a closer, quasi-public context, to the intimacy of a bedroom where we share the rapturous expansion of Lily's being among beautiful materials, objects and sensations. Here she is her own spectator, and because these things are so near to Lily's physical and spiritual self – they are her personal 'shell', to use James's term – we begin to relish what James called the sense 'of another explored, assumed, assimilated identity'[32] through the medium of dress.

Ostensibly, Lily is at Bellomont as a valued friend of the Trenors. Judy sees Lily's role as that of a creditable guest and handy secretary; but with Percy Gryce unexpectedly available, the weekend's central purpose for Lily herself becomes marriage – at 29, time is short. What does she choose from her trunks to dress the roles she has to play? When Judy grasps that Lily's hopes are on Gryce, eager 'to smooth the course of true love', she advises her against wearing her 'scarlet *crêpe de chine* for dinner' (45). 'Soft and sinuous' crêpe de chine was one of *the* fashion fabrics of the early 1900s,[33] appropriate to an evening of conspicuous waste with cards and cigarettes. But scarlet, the colour associated with the Whore of Babylon, will hardly accord with Gryce's conservatism. He has been ruled by an Old New York mother, and now is not the time, as Judy implies, to play the chic twentieth-century vamp. Instead, Lily appears in Judy's dress of the previous year, giving a sufficiently good impression at dinner to arrive at an understanding with Gryce that she will join him for church next morning. In preparation she lays out 'a grey gown of devotional cut' (53). But Lily's tailoring of her identity along carefully chosen unfashionable lines is sabotaged by the unexpected arrival of Selden, who for Lily represents another world and other values from either Trenor's Wall Street or Gryce's dull 'Americana'. Selden's values, she feels, are somehow more interesting and admirable than her own.

Lily, Wharton tells us, 'for all the hard glaze of her exterior ... was like a water-plant in the flux of the tides' (53). Next morning 'the sight of her grey dress and borrowed prayer-book flashed a long light down the years ... [A] great bulk of boredom ... loomed across her path. And who would consent to be bored on such a morning?' (57) The summer day invites her 'to happiness' – and to Selden. Yielding to inward 'tides', she unrepentantly watches from the window, Gryce's 'crestfallen face' as he sets off without her; she puts on 'a dress somewhat more rustic and summerlike in style than the garment she had first selected, and rustling downstairs, sunshade in hand' (58), seeks out Selden. She finds him with Bertha Dorset, 'whose lace-clad figure ... detached itself with exaggerated slimness against the dusky leather of the upholstery' (59).

Dress, Hollander says, 'has not only no social but also no significant aesthetic existence unless it is actually worn'[34] – though a decision not to wear something may also be significant. We have several unworn dresses here, the scarlet sheath of a Belle Époque siren and the puritan, conservative grey – not to mention the lacy negligée worn 'off-stage'. Then there are the two dresses that Lily actually wears – Judy's cast-off and the 'rustic' summer dress, the latter set against the slinky lace of Bertha Dorset. The extremes of vamp and nun could be (have been) part of Lily's repertoire, but are now discarded; the lace negligée was worn but hidden. Judy's cast-off has been successful, but promises boredom to Lily. 'Old' New York matrons, anxious to avoid vulgar display, often kept their Paris dresses in wraps for a year; in 1903, however, the *New York Herald* noted that while in the past, 'no woman would have been ashamed to wear a dress a second year or last year's hat, nowadays, they won't wear them more than three or four times'.[35] The vista of Grycean boredom that is conjured up by the grey dress sends her back to her wardrobe for a change of role and direction, and a different man in view.

Lily adroitly contrives to meet Selden in the park, for which her rustling summery dress, a pastoral note under a parasol among trees, perfectly accords with his image of her, imbued with the 'wild-wood grace [of] ... a captured dryad' (13), The dress's 'message' is similar to that of James's Mrs Headway in her frilly *fête champêtre* dress – 'summer, sunshine and falling in love' – but how might it look, and how does it conform to the fashions of the time, to Bertha's serpentine lace and Lily's own scarlet crêpe de chine?

Lily is constantly poised between the old, exclusive New York of Mrs Astor's 'Four Hundred' – which ended with Mrs Astor's breakdown in 1906 – and the moral and financial free-for-all of Veblen's consumer capitalist society. Coincidentally perhaps, the concept of women's clothing began to change around 1904. 'There were signs that the S-bend was about to be replaced by a more vertical silhouette',[36] Jane Ashelford records, and she illustrates the earlier style with a portrait of 1902 of an English society matron, Mrs Julius Drewe, in a 'rustic', frothy summer frock against a studio 'landscape'.[37] The skirt, supported by a mass of lacy petticoats, flares out at mid-calf to produce the desired Art Nouveau curve – although Mrs Drewe does not have quite the bust for its upper reaches. The dress's artless girlishness is undercut by the evident expense of its quantities of fragile chiffon and lace and its coyly erotic 'lingerie' effect, an effect we can see multiplied in a *Punch* cartoon of a London evening party. These soft curves, however, were under threat by 1904, when Paul Poiret created his revolutionary 'Confucius' coat – a vertical top-to-toe sweep of lacquer-red silk. Lily's crêpe de chine and Bertha's lace sheath are in the Poiret mode, and the drama of the style is evident in Sargent's flamboyant portrait of the Wertheimer sisters.

The pared-back simplicity of the new style was to be the essence of twentieth-century modernity, an 'aesthetic of absent things'.[38] It conjured up an overt, sophisticated eroticism, worlds away from the frothy *faux* girlishness of Mrs Drewe or Lily's 'country maid' outfit. The Victorian female icons of angel and demon were by now played out: '[v]ice was no longer so rigidly separated from virtue ... there was a new 'half world' that began to dissolve moral barriers. Edwardian society, on both sides of the Atlantic, cared even more about money than about breeding.'[39] Lily's dress, in its parkland setting, is an intuitive appeal to Selden's nostalgia for the 'woman and garden' imagery of fifty years back, which had been promulgated by John Ruskin's *Sesame and Lilies*. His invitation to Lily to

Figure 20 Evening Dresses. Cartoon, London: *Punch*, 1904.

join his 'republic of the spirit' (68) requires her – like the Biblical lilies of the field – to be flawlessly but 'naturally' beautiful, to have a moral aspect to her beauty, free of all material concerns. But Selden's 'republic' is a fantasy, to which he does not in truth subscribe. Lily herself exposes its speciousness when she remarks that 'the only way not to think about money is to have a great deal of it' (69).

Bertha Dorset's lace sheath and her own scarlet crêpe de chine do not belong in Arcadia; they are not superior to curves and chiffon flounces, but they represent the resistless impulse of fashion and evolution – Bertha survives, Lily does not. As Martha Banta observes, 'Wharton viewed women's fashion as one of the markers by which she traced shifts in the social habitus occupied by her fictional characters. The clothes with which her female protagonists adorn themselves *speak to where they are.*'[40] Lily's shift in the 'wrong' direction is perilous in Veblen's merciless world. 'Dress', as he said, 'must not only be conspicuously expensive and inconvenient, it must at the same time be up to date'.[41]

To survive, Lily needs to marry, to maintain the calculated strategy she began in her pursuit of Gryce in which neither love nor respect had

Plate 9 J. S. Sargent, *Ena and Betty Wertheimer*. 1902. Tate Britain, London.

played a part. Seduction is work, marriage a business deal, dress crucial to fiscal confidence. Part of Lily knows this, part rejects it. Her declaration to Selden, at the close of their woodland tête-à-tête, that she will look 'hideous in dowdy clothes; but I can trim my own hats' (73), should have been recognized by him as one of love – an echo, surely, of Dorothea's similar declaration to Ladislaw in *Middlemarch*. It is a marriage proposal in which she renounces Veblenian imperatives for Selden's 'republic'. The twentieth-century sound of the automobile returning from church breaks the silence that follows her words, and the moment is lost. But in truth, Selden's republic is nowhere and nothing: as Lily herself remarks 'you spend a great deal of time in the element you disapprove of' (70). He is too fond of his book-lined bachelor flat and social round to exchange them for love-in-a-cottage and a 'dowdy' wife.

Despite brief, more cynical perceptions, Lily cannot shake off her own deeper idealisms. At the Van Osbrugh 'simple country wedding' – a gala of consumption with hired trains, tables of gifts and even an 'agent of cinematographic syndicate' hired to record it all – Lily, dreaming of herself as a bride some day, sees Grace van Osburgh as a 'mystically veiled figure' (87). Less agreeably, observing the guests and congratulating herself on her own perfection, she feels that 'other girls were plain and inferior from choice ... no one need have confessed such acquiescence in her lot as was revealed in the "useful" colour of Gerty Farish's gown and the subdued lines of her hat: it is almost as stupid to let your clothes betray that you know you are ugly as to have them proclaim that you think you are beautiful' (89). Because to Lily the bride is 'mystic', details of the wedding dress are relayed to her later by Aunt Peniston, with the painful rider that her informant thought Bertha Dorset the best-dressed woman at the wedding.[42] The day indeed ends badly, with news of Percy Gryce's engagement to the plain, inferior Evie Osburgh.

Lily not only thinks, she knows she is beautiful. But fashion demands novelty: people 'would welcome her in a new character ... as Miss Bart they knew her by heart. She knew herself by heart too, and was sick of the old story.' (100) Briefly solvent, thanks to Gus Trenor, Lily gives a donation to Gerty Farish's charity for needy young women; with the effect that 'Lily felt a new interest in herself as a person of charitable instincts' (112). Bolstered by a novel sense of virtue, her 'self-complacency recovered its lost outline' (113). Instead of passively waiting for another Gryce to come into her sights, for whom she must then invent a performance, Lily sets herself the problem – which, as Wolff says, Wharton set herself: 'Can a woman take an active role and *make* beauty, become the master craftsman; or are women fated to passivity ... objects that can be admired, collected and cared for – and deprived thereby of human dignity?'[43] Can she recover her lost outline, create a new moral aspect for her beauty, and fashion for herself an authentic identity that – and here is the real problem – will also find out true love and a husband?

It has seemed, sometimes, across this study of dress in fiction that the Little White Dress is the answer to every young, youngish and older maiden's prayer. It is, however, a treacherous option; like the Little Black Dress, it is a highly over-determined garment; it comprehends youth, virtue, summer, innocence, ignorance, ice, rigidity, death – and much else besides. Lily, inspired by her discovery of a 'better' self, worthy of 'the republic of the spirit', and searching for a fresh image, co-opts the painter, Paul Morpeth, to 'produce' a *tableau vivant* of herself as Joshua

Plate 10 Joshua Reynolds, *Mrs Lloyd inscribing a tree*, 1775–1776. Photographer unknown. Courtesy of Waddesdon, The Rothschild Collection (Rothschild Family Trust)

Reynolds's *Mrs Lloyd* – an eighteenth-century society woman, in a 'pure' white dress, on the point of marriage.

> Under Morpeth's guidance her vivid plastic sense, hitherto nurtured on no higher food than dress-making and upholstery, found eager expression in the disposal of draperies, the study of attitudes ... the gorgeous reproductions of historic dress ... But keenest of all was the exhilaration of displaying her own beauty under a new aspect: of showing that her loveliness was no mere fixed quality, but an element shaping all emotions to fresh forms of grace. (131)

Selden's 'vision-building faculty' (134) sees the scene with subtle differences.

It was as though she had stepped not out of, but into, Reynolds's canvas, banishing the phantom of his dead beauty by the beams of her living grace ... she had purposely chosen a picture without distracting accessories of dress or surroundings. Her pale draperies, and the background of foliage against which she stood, served only to relieve the long, dryad-like curves that swept upward from her poised foot to the lifted arm ... he seemed to see before him the real Lily Bart, divested of the trivialities of her little world, and catching for a moment a note of that eternal harmony of which her beauty was a part. (135)

Cynthia Griffin Wolff has outlined the way that *fin de siècle* art forms actually emphasized rather than counteracted society's reactionary demands for decorative passivity in women. Art Nouveau flattened and distorted the female form, turning it into something for consumers to purchase, in objects like lamps and vases, repeatedly associating it with floral forms – especially lilies. Fashionable portraiture, in the hands of J. S. Sargent and Giovanni Boldini, emphasized an attenuated elegance, 'a flattering but shallow likeness'.[44] One might argue for Sargent's depth as a portrait painter, but images like Boldini's, exaggeratedly long and slender, in a splashy bravura style, provided the art milieu that was familiar to Morpeth and to Lily's audience. Selden's reading of Lily is that of the connoisseur: dehumanized, focusing on her curving lines, insisting on her distance from everyday reality, and yet paradoxically declaring this to be the 'real' Lily. Lily herself takes pleasure in the drapery of her 'gorgeous' historic dress, which Selden dismisses as 'triviality'; Lily believes her new image expresses her individual, moral self – Selden sees only 'eternal harmony'.

Dressing, as Hollander says, 'is always picture-making, with reference to actual pictures that indicate how clothes are to be perceived'.[45] Wharton, rather than actually describing Lily's dress, draws on the reader's knowledge of a painting, recently purchased by the Rothschilds and therefore in the news. This is not, however, the kind of imagery on which early twentieth-century industrialized society modelled its material self: fashion was being shaped by another medium. Hollander's description of turn-of–the-century fashion as a 'blur of chic'[46] owes more to photography than painting, to the need for a garment to be seen in a single, 'snapshot' glance. Fashion had begun to tailor itself to a new way of recording its own quickening pace, and a symbiotic relationship was to be established between camera and clothes. Lily, rather than recreating herself on contemporary lines, however, deliberately locates the terms of reference for her new self in an eighteenth-century painting. Her new image is based on the lightly-clad nudes of classical antiquity, on a celebrated collector's item – but 'dead, dead, dead', as James's Milly Theale says of her counterpart in a Renaissance portrait. Lily has looked for a new self where Milly had perceived death.

Lily, in turning to the *tableau vivant* as a medium to present herself to the society audience at the Brys' party, was drawing on performance as well as painting for her new self. Mrs Lloyd was wearing a dress invented by Reynolds in her portrait, a neo-classical style different from the fashions of 1779 in which the portrait was painted: thus the image that Lily has chosen recedes further into the past. Classical fashion plates, according to Hollander, 'have perhaps been the most common of all in Western art ... what the well-dressed nymph is now wearing has been the subject of many pictures and ... a steady source of inspiration for the stage':[47] Poiret's vertical style of 1904 was in fact also a modernist interpretation of the classical, a forerunner of the abstract modes of the 1920s. Lily, however, has chosen to regress to an eighteenth-century painted and invented dress, there by making herself doubly unreal. She has chosen a style in which the lines of a nude body are clearly visible, set in a stagy landscape with as much substance as Selden's 'republic' – which is perhaps why he responds so enthusiastically to it.

Reynolds's Mrs Lloyd, in simple white in a 'natural' setting, writing her future husband's name on a pasteboard tree, was an idealized icon of female virtue: her image, as Wolff points out, coincides with a specifically new New York taste of around 1900 for murals and statuary featuring 'figures of chaste women and girls ... draped in white or the national colours ... variously labelled "Justice", "America", "The Law"'. These images were unrealistic, yet as Wolff says, 'the possible inference is not without significance: "Our women are pure" – so the public lesson could be read.'[48] *The American Girl's Home Book*, of 1883, instructs its readers in the preparation of scenery and costumes for parlour performance of *tableaux vivants* and 'living statuary', and suggests subjects such as 'Faith, Peace, and Glory'[49] – to be draped in much linen sheeting. But, on the other hand, less respectable versions of these symbolic posturings were to be found in the burlesque theatre of New York's sleazy underside, featuring women as 'classical' statues, their erotic content – and their persons – emphasized rather than disguised under the scanty, euphemistic drapes of 'Venus' or 'Psyche'.

So, although Lily has taken the initiative in presenting a new self to her society, her image is open to several interpretations, and might have very different associations, outside her control and determined by the viewer: the *tableau vivant* performer is herself silent. 'Deuced bold thing to show herself in that get-up;' Ned Alstyne leeringly remarks, 'but gad, there isn't a break in the lines anywhere, and I suppose she wanted us to know it'

(135), betraying a familiarity with 'burlesque' perhaps, but also – more tellingly and damagingly – the way Lily's appearance is likely to be interpreted by what a recent financial journalist described as 'the masters of the universe boys will be boys culture of Wall Street'.[50] Selden, overhearing the remark, is indignant: 'This was the world she lived in, these were the standards by which she was fated to be measured!' (135), but is silent, afraid to betray an interest, complicit in that world he so disdains. Gus Trenor's response to Alstyne's guffaws at what Lily's dress reveals – 'it's not her fault if everybody don't know it now ... Damned bad taste, I call it' (138) – is even coarser and more threatening for the anger it contains; Trenor feels he has paid for Lily's 'fal-bals' without yet getting a 'return'. That she is perceived as sexually marketing herself becomes clear when Jack Stepney describes Lily as 'standing there as if she was up at auction' (157).

Lily believes her audience's response 'had obviously been called forth by herself and not by the picture she impersonated ... the completeness of her triumph gave her an intoxicating sense of recovered power' (136). Unable to acknowledge the sexuality of her own female body, she has nevertheless exploited it to 'recover' her power: but the self that is seen, the power that is 'recovered' is sexual. Nudity as a symbol in art is one thing, the near-nudity of an acquaintance in the drawing-room is another. Maureen Howard's essay on the novel points to the way that Reynolds's portrait cuts off Mrs Lloyd's sculptural bust from her body, whose thighs 'are selected and illuminated by a bold triangular shaft of light. The focus is an erotic choice.'[51] It needs little imagination to see how startling Lily's exhibition of herself in transparent white muslin must seem, especially if Morpeth's lighting effects were unscrupulously accurate. Selden is silent, and Gerty Farish's loving admiration is irrelevant since she is a powerless woman. Interestingly it is Sim Rosedale who sees Lily as she wants to be seen: 'when I looked at you the other night at the Bry's, in that plain white dress, looking as if you had a crown, I said to myself: "By gad, if she had one she'd wear it as if it grew on her."' (176) Lily's marketing has in a sense been effective – her image has been changed and recharged. But it is not the image she imagines, of an Arcadia in which a beautiful Lady vanquishes a chivalrous Knight. And it is Rosedale, the self-made man whom Lily despises, that is the romantic, not Selden.

The 'Reynolds' moment that Lily sees as the triumphant acknowledgement of her beauty is in fact the start of her fall. The acquisitive desires she has stirred lead with crude logic to Gus Trenor's attempted violation of her the next evening; in flight from Trenor's house, she is seen, 'in a haze of evening draperies' (161), by Selden, who unhesitatingly leaps to the worst conclusion. He breaks his appointment with her next day, and leaves New York. Fleeing Trenor, Lily finds refuge with Gerty, and in the cold light of morning, in the dingy bedroom, she sees 'her evening dress and opera cloak lying in a tawdry heap on a chair. Finery laid off is as unappetizing as the remains of a feast.' (167) The hazy evening dress has turned into a cold, morning reality of soiled clothes: a sight she is usually spared by her maid, but which should now constitute a sharp reminder of how society, on which she depends, assesses her 'new' self, and of the financial and social abyss that now threatens. Her situation is deteriorating rapidly by the time Rosedale makes his proposal, at the end of Book I, 'to provide for the good time and do the settling'. But, as she had put on Reynolds's 'Grand Manner' with Mrs Lloyd's dress, careless of its real effect, so she maintains a Grand Manner with Rosedale, turning down his offer with disdain – 'whatever I enjoy I am prepared to settle for' (177) – an absurd self-deception, as she has nothing and owes everything.

In contrast to the gathering gloom at the close of Book I, the bright spring opening of Book II in Europe is an unexpected shift. It is in some ways a replay of the novel's incipit: a crowd scene – in Monte Carlo – on which Selden comments and from which figures emerge. He sees it as a *tableau* 'staged regardless of expense' (184), and it is the same satiated New York socialites of Book I who detach themselves, though without Lily. Lily is instead 'talked about' as being 'a tremendous success' (187); but Carrie Fisher, a successful social parasite and alert to the hard reality below luxury surfaces, confides to Selden that Lily has been dangerously flighty and disdainful of opportunities. Her present position on the Dorset's yacht as a distraction for George while Bertha pursues a new *affaire*, looks particularly tricky.

The clothes of Book II are less individually distinguishable than those of Book I, and function more metaphorically. Events of Book I seemed to build up to the triumphant *tableau* scene, then tumble into catastrophe; in Book II Lily's flights and drops accelerate, until her career becomes a dizzy downward spiral through New York's social layers. Wharton allows only brief glimpses of Lily's appearance, her sense of the worlds she passes through and which then pass her by, until in a final rendering of accounts, we pause for a last look at the Reynolds dress.

Lily's apparent restoration to the circles of the wealthy, on a yacht at the start of Book II, makes that fall the more vertiginous. The *New York Herald* listed American yachts in the Mediterranean in 1900 – the Leland's Egyptian yacht, for example, crewed by picturesque Turks, and the Widener's *Josephine*, with 'ceiling and walls of carved French walnut except for a grand boudoir, which was white and all in Louis XV style'.[52]

The fashion for sport 'marked the eclipse of the boudoir' and yachting, according to Hebe Dorsey, 'was becoming more and more the fashion, causing another change in lifestyle'.[53] This life, free from the constraints of 'old' New York, was more flagrantly libertine in behaviour, more openly competitive in consumption. The special outfits needed for such a life did not need to be itemized – journals such as the Herald were full of accounts of the 'trappings' of the super-rich. Selden, from among the hangers-on, observes Lily's effect rather than the detail of her costume, among the yachting crowd in a Monte Carlo restaurant. Her contrast to Bertha Dorset, begun at Bellomont, is now sharply highlighted.

Watching her at dinner, Selden admires 'the way in which she detached herself, by a hundred indefinable shades from the persons who most abounded in her own style ... the differences came out with special poignancy, her grace cheapening the other women's smartness ... Yes, she was matchless.' In contrast to Lily's command of effects, Selden observes that Bertha seems at first over-concerned with her gown: it has 'surprises and subtleties' that Selden feels will challenge Mr Dabham's journalese, but, as the evening goes on, she achieves 'full command of it, and ... [produces] her effects with unwonted freedom. Was she not indeed, too free?' (215–6) What might we guess of their dresses from the effects they produce?

What Selden implies is that Bertha is uncorseted. Poiret, establishing his fashion house in 1903, set out 'to dispense with the basic structured fashion of bodice and skirt, replacing it with a simple, high-waisted garment ... devoid of fussy decoration or rigid corsetry'.[54] This new dress may to some degree approximate the style of Lily's neo-classical *tableau* dress, but it has the cachet and authority of a Paris fashion, worn at an upper-class social occasion, not at an entertainment with dubious connotations. For Lily now to make everyone else look cheap (by a trick of style that is not explained) is a miscalculation, a little pragmatic dinginess would have been more appropriate – she is, after all, a beggar at the Dorset's table, and furthermore, 'for a young woman, especially one who wasn't married, to appear to be trying to lure men by her rich dresses'[55] was considered unseemly. Bertha Dorset is her patron, and her rival with Selden. Bertha's reputation is protected by her married status, and her 'social credit [by] an impregnable bank-account' (264). Lily has no family, fiancé, husband, nor much of a bank account. So when she turns prior to leaving, 'with a smile and a graceful slant of the shoulders to receive her cloak from Dorset', that cloak – her trappings, her cover, her human fringe – is suddenly no cover at all. At Bertha's public declaration that 'Miss Bart is not going back to the yacht' (218), Lily is shockingly 'stripped' – Selden's silence removes the last shred of social cover. Thrust out into the night, in a cloak, friendless and moneyless, Lily becomes that Victorian cliché, the Fallen Woman. She has been thrown out into the cold for her sins – the very antithesis of Virtue on a Monument, the image she believed she had embodied.

Lily tries to pass the moment off with a show of good manners, still believing in the unassailability of her innocence. Similarly she passes off the humiliating scene of her subsequent disinheritance by Mrs Peniston with graceful dignity, 'tall and noble in her black dress' (221), giving weight to Veblen's otherwise eccentric definition of manners as just another example of conspicuous waste. It is only now that Lily begins to realize how, despite a beautiful appearance and perfect behaviour, she cannot control the way she is seen; her 'story' is in other hands: 'What is truth? Where a woman is concerned it's the story that's easiest to believe ... once she is talked about she's done for' (226). Helplessly observing the erosion of her own identity, she reflects that 'society did not turn away from her, it simply drifted by ... letting her feel ... how completely she had been the creature of its favour' (262). She turns for sympathy to Gerty and, 'settled ... in Gerty's easy chair' (264), she loosens her furs, ruefully reflecting on her poverty. But her furs against Gerty's meagre furniture are an astringent pointer to Lily's continuing self-indulgence, a reminder of other, poorer lives and a guard against sentimentality.

Drifting next through the 'vast gilded void' of the hotel world, as Mrs Hatch's secretary, Lily lives in an 'atmosphere of torrid splendour [in which] moved wan beings as richly upholstered as the furniture' (274). She recognizes its tawdriness but is driven by need and a hunger for luxury, however fugitive. Her life becomes 'a jumble of futile activities' (175), which she registers as from a great distance, and her own appearance seems no longer to interest her. When Selden re-enters her world, what he sees of her is withheld, we hear only of the 'wilderness' of vulgarity in which he finds her and her fierce resentment of his disapproval. The drop from here to the grim realities of a milliner's workroom is abyssal and yet only reveals another side of the consuming, wasting, leisure-class world – the side of the 'dull and ugly people [who] had been sacrificed to produce her' (5).

To grasp at the shreds of respectability associated with millinery is to reach for another cliché whose day is done. Trained in nothing but 'fancy-work', Victorian middle-class womanhood, when poverty threatened, turned to the work of the milliner and the sempstress as jobs of last resort – some way behind governessing. Lily fantasizes about 'a shop, all white panels ... where her finished creations, hats, wreaths, aigrettes and the rest, perched on their stands, like birds'. Reality is the stale air of a workroom peopled by 'dull and unhealthy girls', and her 'inability to sew spangles on a hat frame' (284–5). This failure recalls her declaration to Selden that whatever happened, she could always trim a hat – she can't. Good taste in hats is not synonymous with skill in millinery, which at this period was admittedly demanding. Millinery magazines for the years 1900–1910, according to Fiona Clark, 'illustrate the evolution of the hat from basic shape to final trimmed form, but it would be almost impossible to infer the former from the latter',[56] so laden was it with trimmings. We first saw Lily in a hat, distant, fascinatingly enigmatic, her beauty marking her out from the crowd. The last fashion item we see her with is a hat, not alluringly on her head but close-to, unworn and ugly, in her hand – a skeleton hat, stripped, waiting to be turned into a work of art. As she has failed to create a viable self, so she fails to create this ephemeral object of beauty: hats are not only the most mutable item in a fashionable outfit, but – with hindsight – this is their last great moment in the history of Western fashion. Lily's failure with the hat ends her attempt at independent survival and she is sacked – defeated, consumed by a hat.

In the workroom, manual skill and financial success are all that matter. Lily realizes that though she is 'a star fallen from the sky' of the glamorous life to which her fellow-workers contribute, she herself is of no interest: 'they were awed only by the gross tangible image of material achievement' (286). We might guess, then, that furs, veils and luxury have fallen away and that Lily has found that 'useful' colours and 'subdued' hats are not an 'acquiescence in dinginess' as she once thought, but an acceptance of reality. Even so, the realization can make little difference, for 'she had neither the aptitude nor the moral constancy to remake her life on new lines'. Walking home, after her dismissal from the millinery workshop, she catches glimpses of women she has known, a hallucinatory procession of splendour out of her past; the future, on the other hand, 'stretched out before her grey interminable and desolate' (301). On impulse, she calls on Selden, in what becomes a farewell. When she tells him that the things he has said to her have kept her 'from really becoming what many people have thought me' (307) her 'impeccable naivety' is ironic. Selden is always wrong about Lily, and his behaviour usually in bad faith: he feeds her illusions, while doing nothing to help; rather than distance himself from her enemies, he continues to enjoy their hospitality. It is Lily's idealism that gives substance to his empty rhetoric.

Lily, now alone, opens her trunk and reviews her life through the 'few handsome dresses left … An association lurked in every fold: each fall of lace and gleam of embroidery was like a letter in the record of her past.'

(317) Candace Waid sees the theme of women and writing as central to the novel, and these dresses 'seem to carry the power of letters', records of the past that 'envelop'[57] Lily. There have been alternative 'writings': to save her reputation she could have used Bertha's incriminating letters to Selden. But not only would this have implicated Selden, it would also have reduced her to Bertha's moral level – a surrender of self-respect when little else remains to keep out the cold. Selden himself views the possible break-up of the Dorset ménage as 'a vast unpacking of accumulated moral rags' (209). In contrast to the merciless destruction of Lily's life and reputation, the Dorsets' respectability is pieced together again, their 'dirty rags' (their letters) self-servingly ignored by Selden, and, ironically, destroyed by Lily herself.

I would like to return at this point, briefly, to Roxana's Turkish Dress, which, as we saw in Chapter 2, she wears in a quasi-public solo performance, to great applause. Afterwards she keeps it in a trunk, but the memory of the dress, with its immoral associations, threatens to sabotage her future – and probably does so, to judge from the novel's abrupt catastrophe. If Wharton knew Defoe's novel, she has played an ironic variant on its theme of hidden vice. Lily too keeps her triumphal dress in a trunk, to the bitter end, but it is 'virtue' that lies hidden in its white, transparent folds – vice, in the eyes and minds of the beholders, is what is publicly voiced and, uncontested, becomes fatal to the reputation on which her life depends. When Pandora unpacked her box of disasters she found Hope at the bottom. What Lily, however, draws from the bottom of her trunk is 'a heap of white drapery, which fell shapelessly across her arm' – the Reynolds dress, a dead hope. 'It had been impossible for her to give it away, but she had never seen it since that night' – the night 'where she had stood with Lawrence Selden and disowned her fate' (317).

Lily's Veblenian pursuit of material goods, the fate she 'disowned' for love, had called up no answering response in Selden, and since she has accepted his imagined standards, his rejection of her love destroys her sense of worth. The society to which he belongs sees neither profit nor utility in those moral intuitions that continue to gleam, like her beautiful dresses, from the 'real' Lily. The Reynolds dress is shapeless and white, a shroud waiting for a body. A dress not worn has, as Hollander says, no social or aesthetic meaning, but a dress that has been worn acquires meaning retrospectively: as a shroud it will be a memorial to Lily's virtue, and hollow testimony to the leisure-class consumption that consumed her. The Dorset rags of adultery, though purged from Lily's trunk, remain 'amply' to clothe a frivolous and unregenerate society. In Selden's posturings over Lily's death-bed it is, however, 'stripped' one last time.

We might return then to the image of the novel's first pages: Selden observing a mute Lily, vacillates and equivocates until he reaches a satisfying narrative conclusion. Wavering at the end of the novel between self-reproach and suspicion as he flicks through her papers, he can find no very elevating role for himself – until he recalls her farewell kiss. He decides that despite the 'spiritual fastidiousness' that kept him from her, 'he *had* loved her – had been willing to stake his future on his faith in her – and if the moment had been fated to pass from them before they could seize it, he saw now that, for both, it had been saved whole out of the ruin of their lives ... He knelt by the bed ... draining their last moment to its lees' (329). Wharton thus lends Selden a few grand sentiments to drape around his naked hypocrisy: his 'love' and his 'faith' were never given; nothing has been 'saved' for Lily; the 'last moments' are his, not hers – she is dead. As Cynthia Griffin Wolff says, 'we might want to reconsider the moral status of any narrator or any reader who would want to reduce human suffering to an artistically satisfying (albeit morally elevating) experience'.[58]

Selden's 'spiritual fastidiousness', his false assumption that the true essence of humanity is to be found by abandoning the material for some wholly 'other' world, in which 'meaning is *not* created and recreated culturally, but is transparent', is as damaging to Lily as is her consumption of dress. It would, as Elizabeth Wilson points out, be 'a world without fashion ... a world without discourses'[59] – a world without humanity. Inspired by Selden, the dress Lily chooses to express her 'true' self, the one dress Wharton allows us to see in full, is unreal in every sense. Finding no recognizable 'human fringes', Lily's audience had simply searched for the nearest frame of reference – in this case New York's 1905 equivalent of a strip-show. The meanings that Lily had intended to give to her appearance are visible enough – Gerty and Selden both understand – but the light that her intended meaning casts on the moral squalor of her audience only illuminates how it is able to destroy her.

Wharton does not 'strip' from Lily, in Swiftian disgust, those dresses whose consumption have been part of her destruction and whose presence has so far only been suggested by texture, light, colour and perfume. At the novel's end fragments of her spent wardrobe shimmer, like exquisite revenants in the dark, in substance almost nothing but recalling and suggesting everything. Neither good taste nor morality has a resting-place in the shifting patterns of modernity. Knowing what we know now of Lily's world, those shimmering 'gleams' cast their light down into the past giving a life to her dresses that no formal description could have achieved: Wharton has made us 'think' the beauty for ourselves. We regret the loss of the dresses even as we count their terrible cost.

–9–

The Missing Wedding Dresses: Samuel Richardson's *Pamela* to Anita Brookner's *Hôtel du Lac*

Discussing Walter Besant's misguided attempts to define a 'good' novel, Henry James, in 'The Art of Fiction', suggests that, for some (not James), a novel required a 'happy ending' – and he talked, we may recall, of 'a distribution at the last of prizes, pensions, husbands, wives, babies, millions, appended paragraphs and cheerful remarks'; such an ending was 'like that of a good dinner, a course of dessert and ices'.[1] A rewarding wedding, of at least two of the central characters, as James suggests, generally constituted the Realist Novel's final 'treat'. And surely the central confection of the dénouement – an occasion for the novelist's descriptive powers – would be the representation of that most important dress of all, the wedding dress?

Even now a dress-design show ends with a wedding dress. As the editor of *Brides' Magazine* writes – sponsoring a lavish book on the topic – 'no other raiment speaks so symbolically of promise, of the mysteries of good luck'. The author of the book herself speaks breathlessly of the bride's appearance as 'a reflection of everything her culture finds beautiful'.[2] Lily Bart in *The House of Mirth*, critical of everyone else at the van Osburgh wedding, was rapt at the bride's 'mystically-veiled figure'.

But in 1858 Anthony Trollope – arch-purveyor of 'happy endings' – ending his novel *Doctor Thorne* with two weddings, refused to describe any dresses:

> Beatrice was wedded and carried off to the Lakes. Mary, as she had promised, did stand near her ... She wore on that occasion – But it will be too much perhaps to tell the reader what she wore as Beatrice's bridesmaid, seeing that a couple of pages, at least, must be devoted to her own marriage-dress.... And now I find I have not one page – not half a page – for the wedding dress. But what matter? Will it not all be found in the columns of the *Morning Post*?[3]

Trollope's blurring of fictional and real teases the reader, but we might wonder just how often wedding dresses *do* feature as final descriptive flour-

157

Plate 11 James Tissot, *The Bridesmaid*. 1885. Leeds Museum and Art Gallery.

ishes, and whether their incidence or absence has significance. Elsewhere
Trollope provides dress descriptions when there is a point to be made – the
elaborate train of Mrs Proudie's dress, so disastrously pinioned by a sofa,
in *Barchester Towers*, for example. Does he assume that his readers are
over-familiar with wedding dresses and will be bored? That such accounts
are banally journalistic? Certainly, by 1850 the standard components of
the church-wedding – the white dress, veil, wreath of orange-blossom and
bouquet of flowers – had been in place almost half a century.

Trollope is reluctant to describe the predictable in the passage from
Doctor Thorne; but perhaps more important to him as a teller of traditional

tales, is that to offer such a description suggests there is more to be said, further complications which, when plots are unravelled, secrets revealed, lovers reconciled, is not the note wanted for an ending of 'desserts and ices'. Wedding dresses are described across the history of the novel, but paradoxically, they do not herald unalloyed bliss; they may not promise 'good luck' at all. They may even be very bad news indeed. In this final 'dress show', I want to return to that early distribution of prizes, Samuel Richardson's *Pamela* of 1741, in which 'Virtue' is 'Rewarded' in the marriage of the good girl to the rich aristocrat, and then to look at examples of wedding dresses over the next two centuries, to Virtue Unrewarded in Anita Brookner's *Hotel du Lac* of 1984.

Richardson had initially intended his invented correspondence between a young maidservant and her parents to serve as models of letter-writing for the upwardly aspiring classes; comments on dress were a useful supplementary guide to the polite life. In the book's final form, as a novel of contemporary domestic manners, Pamela's detailed accounts of dress contribute tangibility and visibility to the story's air of immediacy.

On the death of Pamela's mistress, her new master, Mr B., offers her a '[silk] suit of my lady's clothes ... four pair white cotton stockings, three pair fine silk ones'.[4] She feels uneasy about accepting such finery, especially the silks, and Mr B.'s subsequent behaviour justifies her disquiet. However, after attempted seductions, ambuscades and near-rapes, Mr B. is so impressed by Pamela's steadfast virtue that he offers marriage – though, as Aileen Ribeiro remarks, her virtue was less attractive to Mr B. than her acceptability in his world, 'an acceptability gained through natural virtues and applied intelligence'.[5] Mindful of her position, she wears homespun gowns and plain muslin to clarify her status. But for the marriage ceremony with Mr B., Pamela, in accordance with her change of rank, puts on the 'rich white satin night-gown that was my lady's' (PA 306) which she had earlier rejected.

The nightgown is, as Ribeiro says, a confusing garment and appears in a variety of situations – though it is never what we call a nightdress. It was made of a variety of fabrics, and could be an open or closed gown, and, though it had informal connotations, could be worn for quite grand occasions: Margaret Cavendish's wedding clothes of 1734, for example, included a nightgown, of white lustring, imbroidered all over the faceings with silver and purple'[6] – evidently a garment similar to Pamela's.

A public, religious ceremony was not legally required until the 1753 Marriage Act; weddings could take place anywhere, anytime, without banns or licence. Secret weddings abounded and as Lawrence Stone remarked in his study of eighteenth-century marriages, *Uncertain Unions*, 'very large numbers of perfectly respectable people could never be quite sure whether they were married or not'. The betrothal was the legally binding act, when settlements were agreed; the wedding was simply a confirmation of that agreement. The first of Hogarth's series of paintings, *Marriage à la Mode* of 1744, shows such a betrothal ceremony, in which the bride-to-be wears a simple white silk gown and cap. With little ceremony and few guests there was no reason to formalize dress. With the Marriage Act, church banns and a public ceremony became obligatory, and it is from this point that weddings begin to amass ritual finery. But a bride before 1753 still needed public acknowledgement of her status, and Pamela's first appearance as Mr B.'s wife is in fact at church. Mr B. has written to his mercer 'to send him patterns of the most fashionable silks'. Pamela asks him to select 'what befitted his own rank and condition' (PA 319), and when the silks arrive, Mr B. chooses 'six of the richest ... one was white flowered with silver most richly: and he was pleased to say, that, as I was a bride, I should appear in that the next Sunday' (PA 426). Mr B. has given her his mother's diamonds, and on Sunday they set off for church, Pamela 'dressed in the suit of white, flowered with silver, a rich head-dress, and the diamond necklace, earrings ... my dear Sir, in a fine laced silk waistcoat, of blue Paduasoy, and his coat a pearl-coloured fine cloth' (PA 441). Since Mr B is responsible for the silks and jewels, Pamela's decorum is unsullied.

These outfits are the wedding clothes, though the ceremony has already taken place. 'White and silver, in the second half of the century', according to Ribeiro, 'were the customary colours for upper-class brides, and could also be worn by their grooms';[7] choice of style was governed, as Madeleine Ginsburg says, 'by the time of day at which the ceremony took place and by the rank of the wearer'.[8] Pamela's dress is a formal day dress, to be worn on further occasions, or adapted for evening wear. The groom's present of pearls or diamonds, to be worn at the wedding, is already established, though we might note that neither flowers nor veil are mentioned. This careful dress-description is not in fact the novel's conclusion – Pamela has several volumes of hoops to jump through before bliss is unalloyed – but it is exceptional, as we shall see, in that it does herald Virtue's final reward.

The novel was a phenomenal success, but critics quickly pointed out that Pamela could be said to be holding out on Mr B. for status and financial gain – cool calculation is rewarded, not virtue. Richardson answered in 1748 with *Clarissa*, in which the heroine is persecuted by a worse rake, drugged, raped, and then, unable to live with the loss of her virtue but rejecting marriage, starves herself to death. Clarissa's preparations for death parallel those for marriage: 'never was bride so ready as I am. My wedding garments are bought. And though not fine and gaudy to the sight, though not adorned with jewels and set off with gold and silver ... yet will they be the easiest, the *happiest* suit, that ever bridal maiden wore'. By describing what is not there, Richardson simultaneously evokes the glamour of a wedding dress and denies it. Belford, writing to Lovelace, Clarissa's rapist, describes the dying Clarissa as 'up and dressed; in a white satin night-gown. Ever elegant; but now more so than I had seen her for a week past.'[9] In a reversal of Pamela's purchase of dresses, Clarissa sells her finery, infuriating Lovelace: 'As to selling her clothes, her laces, and so forth, it has, I own, a shocking sound to it.... Some disappointed fair ones would have hanged, some drowned themselves. My beloved only revenges herself upon her clothes.' (CA 496–7)

Clarissa's destruction of her physical state starts with her clothes – the cerements of the tomb are substituted for the adornments of the *jeune fille à marier*. Her view of the situation makes death her only option: as an *haute bourgeoise* heiress, she has need of neither Lovelace's status nor his money; to marry him would be to condone rape. No longer chaste, she is no longer marriageable; but for a girl of her class marriage is the only career. The white wedding dress becomes a shroud: and it is this image of the dress that is dominant in literature hereafter. Edith Wharton's Lily Bart, at the last, takes out of her trunk the white dress that reproduced the bridal Mrs Lloyd's dress – a dress once symbolic of hope, a herald now of death.

Lower down the eighteenth-century social scale there was an alternative to white satin: 'some wedding dresses were neither specialised nor particularly elaborate', according to Madeleine Ginsburg. The vicar, in *The Vicar of Wakefield* of 1766, opens his story by saying that he chose his wife 'as she did her wedding dress, not for a fine glossy surface, but such qualities as would wear well'.[10] His wife would have chosen a good-quality, sober-coloured day dress that would have a long afterlife. This latter mode would become the 'going-away' dress of the nineteenth-century, to be worn for the wedding-journey, but for the quiet family weddings of the earlier period, which could take place at any time of day and where ostentatious display could be considered immodest, the more informal, serviceable style was probably the norm.

Trollope's evasion of a final wedding account does in fact have several precedents. After prolonged romantic complications, in which dress plays a key part, Maria Edgeworth's eponymous Belinda, of 1801, is happily married. Cynical Lady Delacour, anticipating Trollope's teasing of his reader, asks Belinda 'shall I finish the novel for you?' Belinda objects to 'hurrying things toward the conclusion' and wants a fuller account, but Lady Delacour says that '[s]omething must be left to the imagination. Positively I will not describe wedding dresses, or a procession to church',[11] and concludes the novel with a parodic wedding-tableau – uncostumed. Belinda is a virtuous heroine; elaborate dress has been associated in the novel with the unhappy, badly-behaved Lady Delacour. Therefore, though rich dress befits Belinda's rank, the demands of 'virtue' leave the dress undescribed.

Despite pretty white-wedding conclusions to recent film versions of Jane Austen's novels, Austen also dispatches her brides summarily. From the sparse accounts given in the novels we might guess that the Austen bride agrees with the Vicar of Wakefield. Emma Woodhouse's wedding 'was very much like other weddings, where the parties have no taste for finery or parade; and Mrs Elton ... thought it all extremely shabby, and very inferior to her own. – "Very little white satin, very few lace veils; a most pitiful business."' But as the passage, and the novel, end with a declaration of the couple's 'perfect happiness',[12] one can assume that modesty and discretion on the part of author and bride secures married bliss. We might, however, note that veils as well as white satin are now associated with modish weddings, though what Mrs Elton has in mind is not the long face-concealing veil of later periods but the bonnet veils worn by female wedding guests.

Veils and scarves of lace, silk and muslin were fashionable for day and evening wear in 1816 – the date of *Emma* – and fashion historians agree that the wedding outfit was consolidated at this period. 'The great white wedding: a church crowded with friends and relatives; the bridegroom waiting at the altar; the blushing bride in veil and orange-blossom ... This was when it all happened, when all the jigsaw pieces ... came together to form the great white wedding tradition.'[13] 'The acceptance of virgin white as the most usual colour for formal wedding dress coincided with the age of sentiment',[14] not simply because of its chaste connotations, but because white muslin was almost *de rigueur* for formal occasions – as we saw in Austen's *Northanger Abbey*. The fashionable bride, therefore, as Anthea Jarvis says, would have worn 'drifting diaphanous veils and scarves ... white, high-waisted clinging dresses [as] part of the neo-classical look popular throughout Europe in the years following the French Revolution'.[15] Not only were the heavy brocades of the earlier period old-fashioned, they were also hard to get during the Napoleonic Wars: muslin was the fashionable and more practical substitute – but not a fabric that lent itself to much ornament. Penelope Byrde quotes from an account of

Figure 21 Veils and Scarves. *Lady's Monthly Museum*, Vol. 7, 1809. London: Vernor, Hood & Sharpe.

an Austen family wedding of 1814 – considered a quiet affair – where the bride wore a dress 'of fine white muslin, and over it a soft silk shawl, white, shot with primrose, with embossed white satin flowers and delicate yellow tints'.[16] Flowers ornament the shawl, but real or artificial flowers are not yet part of the image and this is borne out by fashion plates of the period. The orange-blossom wreath seems to have been imported into England from France around 1830 – a Mediterranean, pre-Christian symbol of fertility.

Roses were an alternative to orange-blossom: Mr Rochester, in *Jane Eyre*, declares he will 'attire my Jane in satin and lace, and she shall have roses in her hair, and I will cover the head I love best with a priceless veil'. But Jane is uncomfortable with these elements of an upper-class wedding, inappropriate to her self-image of an independent woman of modest means and unpretentious looks, the self for which she correctly believes she is loved – 'I shall not be your Jane Eyre any longer, but an ape in a harlequin's jacket.' Like Mr B., Rochester wants to put his bride in rich silks – 'the most brilliant amethyst dye and a superb pink satin', but 'I persuaded him to make an exchange in favour of a sober black satin and pearl-grey silk'.[17] When the wedding dress arrives Jane finds 'the priceless veil' concealed in the box and protests that Rochester has tricked her 'into accepting something costly', having herself prepared 'a square of unembroidered blond' (JE 229).

Like so much in *Jane Eyre*, this incident blends the rational with the uncanny. The plain veil becomes an almost superstitious token of Jane's independence and identity: misfortune follows her acceptance of Rochester's costly veil. That same night Jane sees a ghostly figure standing before her mirror in a white dress, 'whether gown, sheet or shroud, I cannot tell'; the figure throws Jane's veil over its head, then 'it removed my veil from its gaunt head, rent it two parts, and flinging both on the floor, trampled on them' (JE 242). Terrified, Jane loses consciousness, and in the morning, uncertain of the reality of the vision, allows Rochester to soothe her into believing it a dream. When Jane sees herself in front of the same mirror later, before the marriage ceremony, the 'dream'-image returns: 'I saw a robed and veiled figure, so unlike my usual self that it seemed almost the image of a stranger' (JE 244) – and for a moment we are unsure whether Jane sees herself or the unknown woman of her dream. It is at all events not a reassuring moment. Significantly she is wearing the veil that represents her own 'plain' identity; the mistress of Thornfield's costly veil has been destroyed by its legal owner, Bertha Rochester. The wedding, as we know, ends catastrophically: Jane is not married, and before she flees Thornfield, she 'take[s] off the wedding-dress and replace[s] it by the stuff gown [she] had worn yesterday' (JE 252). When she finally marries Rochester, we simply hear they had 'a quiet wedding' (JE 382) – conjugal happiness, babies and the restoration of Rochester's eyesight follow in short order in the remaining two pages.

Published in 1847, the same year as *Jane Eyre*, William Thackeray's *Vanity Fair* takes a darker view of the married state. Thackeray, as Jenni Calder says, 'was the first novelist to reject marriage as a happy ending'.[18] There are two heroines, Amelia Sedley and Becky Sharp, and therefore two weddings, both of which take place well before the end. How Becky married Rawdon Crawley, Thackeray says, 'is not of the slightest consequence to anybody':[19] for Becky the wedding is simply a necessary step on her road to social and financial advancement; and since it is a secret ceremony, undertaken with little sentiment on her part, there is no finery or fuss. For Amelia, on the other hand, her union with George Osborne is an event of longed-for joy, though the groom is less enthusiastic. An account of the wedding clothes is relayed to the narrator by the worshipful Captain Dobbin:

> The bride was dressed in a brown silk pelisse ... and wore a straw bonnet with a pink ribbon; over the bonnet she had a veil of white Chantilly lace, a gift from Mr Joseph Sedley, her brother. Captain Dobbin himself has asked leave to present her with a gold chain and watch ... and her mother gave her her diamond brooch – almost the only trinket that was left to the old lady. (VF 260)

The novel is set in the Napoleonic period, but Thackeray, in his preface, declared his intention to put his characters in 'present fashion' rather than disfigure his heroes and heroines by the 'hideous' costumes of 1815. The pelisse was a coat-dress, and, for Thackeray, usefully fashionable between 1817 and 1840, altering its shape according to changes in the fashionable silhouette. This dress is a sombre, serviceable garment, the Sedleys having fallen on hard times; thrift governs the choice of a straw bonnet, though the lace veil – the gift of rich Joseph – lends a touch of luxury to mark the occasion as a wedding. The gift of jewellery, traditionally that of the groom, is here the gift of the two who are genuinely fond of Amelia, a forewarning of the limits of George's affections, which soon begin to stray. His adulterous plans are, however, forestalled by his death on the field of Waterloo – either way, the marriage was ill-starred. The description of the dress is therefore not simply a matter of realistic scene-setting, but one in which each item has a bearing on past, present and future events.

When finally Amelia is united with Dobbin, she runs to him through rain 'in a dripping white bonnet and shawl' and disappears 'under the folds of the old cloak ... kiss, kiss, kiss and so forth' (VF 791). Thackeray makes a gesture of sorts to white weddings, but he undermines it with rain and mockery, and is disinclined to do much in the way of 'prizes': 'Grow green again, tender little parasite, round the rugged old oak to which you cling.' (VF 792) Dobbin has in fact fallen out of love with her; something, as we see in the novel's final paragraph, they learn to live with.

The close of Thackeray's *Pendennis* provides a discordant note in the history of bridal descriptions: there is no bride. On the wedding day of Laura Bell with Arthur Pendennis – the culmination of all her hopes and happiness – we see only Pen. Before changes in canonical law in 1886, allowing weddings to take place in the afternoon, the ceremony had to be over by noon: 'Early in the day, before eleven', the author of *The Habits of Good Society* tells us, 'the bride should be dressed, taking breakfast in her own room.'[20] But instead of describing this key emotional moment in a girl's life we are given 'Mr Arthur, attired in a new hat, a new blue frock-coat and blue handkerchief, in a new fancy waistcoat, new boots, and new shirt-studs ... [making] his appearance at a solitary breakfast-table'.[21] What all Pen's shiny new finery bodes for the happiness of Laura – or indeed how she is feeling, what she is doing or how she looks – is left to the imagination. But then we have to agree that Laura, for all her virtue, is of no interest whatever.

If Arthur has already run through Laura's money, at least he doesn't change his mind after breakfast, as did Miss Havisham's fiancé in Charles Dickens's *Great Expectations* of 1862. Twenty-five years after this catastrophe, Pip, the hero of the novel, enters Miss Havisham's darkened room and among the things he notices is her watch that 'had stopped at twenty minutes to nine o'clock',[22] the point at which – having had break-fast – a bride would be dressing for church; and the moment at which Miss Havisham received the letter breaking the engagement. Before noticing her watch, Pip takes in her strange figure:

> She was dressed in rich materials – satins and lace, and silks – all of white. Her shoes were white. And she had a long white veil dependent from her hair, but her hair was white. Some bright jewels sparkled on her neck and on her hands, and some other jewels lay sparkling on the table. Dresses, less splendid than the dress she wore, and half-packed trunks, were scattered about. She had not quite finished dressing for she had but one shoe on – the other was on the table near her hand – her veil was but half-arranged, her watch and chain were not put on, and some lace for her bosom lay with those trinkets, and with her hand-kerchief and gloves, and some flowers and a prayer book, all confusedly heaped about the looking-glass. (GE 57)

The problem for Thackeray in *Pendennis* and Dickens in *Great Expectations*, as realist novelists, is what Richard Altick calls 'lapses of time': they are not really historical novels, but in following the hero's career, these novels of necessity start some twenty years before their close. Descriptions of dress cannot therefore be too specific. There are enough standard components now to the wedding outfit, however, to make it identifiable as such, without assigning it a datable style. Wedding dresses conformed to the modes of the day, and not until skirts short-ened in the 1920s did the wedding dress and the fashionable formal dress part company. From about mid-century onward we find that veil and orange-blossom serve increasingly as shorthand for the whole ensemble. We might note here, however, that Miss Havisham's appear-ance is described twenty-five years after her non-wedding; Pip's child-hood meeting with her is described by the adult Pip, which takes us from

1862 back to 1815 as the original date of the dress, but nothing in Dickens's description – except perhaps the flowers – would look odd on a bride of 1815, 1840 or 1862.

The passage of time is all the same conveyed in Pip's re-view of the dress. As the adult Pip he says that not everything was visible at first, and what he noticed as he moved closer, was 'that everything ... which ought to be white, had been white long ago, and had lost its lustre, and was faded and yellow. I saw the bride within the bridal dress had withered like the dress, and like the flowers, and had no brightness left but the brightness of her sunken eyes' (GE 58). We have therefore Pip in 1862, remembering himself as a child in 1840 looking at a dress of twenty-five years before. What happened in 1815 to make the white dress such a macabre mockery of marriage in 1840, and how will it end? The threads of the distant past and of Pip's childhood past weave together to create the Pip of the novel's 'now' – to answer the mystery of the dress. This dress speaks above all other fictional wedding dresses of disaster past, present and yet to come. Miss Havisham did not marry her lover; the dress fixes her in a present hell of hatred, and it will cause her death – and Pip does not marry Estella.

The image moves the novel out of a realist mode into visual metaphor – the withered bride in her decay becomes an embodiment of the corrosiveness of the nineteenth-century marriage. If Dickens apparently endorses the marriage paradigm, his novels themselves describe unsatisfactory, unhappy, violent unions. The tormented women of these unions resist their roles but are locked into them, calling into question the institution of marriage. Calder points out that for Dickens marriage is ideally a refuge from a nasty world, and in *Great Expectations* Herbert Pocket and Wemmick escape into 'islands' with their domestic angels. But Dickens also attacks marriage 'as an instrument of society ... a collaboration with the world':[23] Miss Havisham assented to a commercial marriage, but unhappily she was also in love. She is thus ceaselessly in transit between the states of daughter and wife. All the elements of her wedding are in place; to accept a return to the unmarried state, to own to being unloved, to remove her dress, is to fail in the eyes of nineteenth-century society. Like her author, she cannot accept the wreck of her ideals by brute reality. There are no alternatives to marriage for a woman of her class; there can therefore be no future without the completion of this stage – nineteen minutes to nine o'clock cannot happen.

Miss Havisham 'goes mad' in white satin, a curiously persistent stereotype that is rarely questioned. Without any evidence from Shakespeare's text, we take for granted that Ophelia – another thwarted bride – goes

Figure 22 The White Wedding outfit. Louisa Tuthill, *The Young Lady's Home*, Philadelphia: Lindsay Blakiston, 1848.

mad in white. The source of this stereotype has not been traced, as far as I know: but turning to Walter Scott's *Bride of Lammermoor* of 1819 and its operatic offshoot, Donizetti's *Lucia di Lammermoor* of 1835, we might find in Scott's/Donizetti's image of an insane, murderous bride in white the figure who became, according to Fiona Robertson, 'a byword for emotional liberation'[24] for a generation of writers, composers and painters across Europe.

It may be Donizetti, not Scott, who is responsible. *The Bride of Lammermoor* is set in eighteenth-century Scotland, but, unlike in his heavily medievalized *Ivanhoe* of the same year, Scott does not give his central character, Lucy Ashton, historically specific dress. However, even the editor of the Oxford edition of the novel cannot escape the grip of the white dress, and recounting how a raven falls dead at the feet of Lucy and Ravenswood, she writes in the Introduction that 'its blood spatter[ed] Lucy's white gown' (BL xxi) – when Lucy is actually wearing azure silk and a plaid shawl. However, after she has been forced to renounce

Figure 23 The Modest Wedding outfit. J. W. Kirton, *Happy Homes and How To make Them*, London: John Kempster & Co., *c.*1855.

Ravenswood and accept Bucklaw, Lucy is 'splendidly arrayed [in] white satin and Brussels lace' (BL 318) for the wedding. She is found, after the murder of Bucklaw, in white night-clothes, 'torn and dabbled with blood … her features convulsed into a wild paroxysm of insanity' (BL 337). Whatever might have been the costume of the original Lucia of Donizetti's opera, it would be a brave director now who put his leading lady into any-thing other than white satin for the great Mad Scene. It is from this image, I suspect, that Bertha Rochester, Wilkie Collins's Anne Catherick, Miss Havisham – and countless others – spring.

Out of the ensemble of wedding garments, the veil emerges as a key symbol – as we saw in *Jane Eyre*. In *The Love Match* of 1847, by Henry Cockton (an obscure but representative 'Silver Fork' novelist) – the veil becomes the one thing needful to make an elopement more bridal. The hastily summoned bridesmaid, reviewing her wardrobe, says '"I must look a little like a bridesmaid … Miss Storr will wear a white veil, of course, Colonel Cartwright?" … "I should say not," said Mildmay, "seeing that that might excite some suspicion." "Well, then, as I've two beauties I'll wear one myself, and then take the other with me for her, She must look a *little* like a bride'".[25] 'The veil', according to *The Habits of Good Society*, 'should be of the same sort of lace as the dress', which 'should be of the first quality – Brussels or Honiton is the most delicate and becoming'.[26] Queen Victoria, promoting domestic industry, had worn Honiton lace for her wedding in 1840. She was probably 'the first British royal bride to wear a veil',[27] according to Penelope Byrde: lace, or lace over silk, and a lace veil with an orange-flower wreath became indispensable to a British wedding thereafter. The wedding itself, with its attendant *trousseau*, was now essentially a performance of conspicuous consumption. Jane Welsh Carlyle, when asked in 1862 how she enjoyed a wedding, replied that her feelings were mixed: "'Mixed?" the rector asked, "Mixed of what?" "Well," I said, "It looked to me something betwixt a religious ceremony and a – pantomime!"'[28]

Mary Braddon's treatment of dress in her early best-seller, *Lady Audley's Secret*, was dramatically pictorial, though by mid-career her descriptions of dress approached fashion-magazine jargon. *Taken at the Flood*, of 1884, is Braddon at neither her best nor her worst, but it describes two wedding outfits, lengthily enough to augur very bad luck indeed. Sylvia Carew, the pretty daughter of a schoolmaster, captures the heart of Edmund Standen, whose mother then threatens to disinherit him. They plight their troth but part. Sylvia then catches the eye of the wealthy, older Sir Aubrey Perriam and forgets Edmund. She has spent the first half of the novel yearning for pretty frocks, so she shops with zest for her marriage to Sir Aubrey, ignoring the unsuitability of a full white ensemble for the private ceremony Sir Aubrey has planned:

> She chose the best and choicest articles in Mr Ganzlein's emporium ... she must have twenty yards of this and seventeen of that, and ten yards of the broad Brussels lace, and three or four pieces of Madeira work for the underlinen ... That thick, corded silk of pearliest white, which she selected after much deliberation for the wedding dress, would do for a dinner dress afterwards ... Sylvia chose a dove-coloured silk and a delicate grey ... She bought a good deal of lace, some linen fine enough for a princess of blood Royal, a morning-dress or two of plain white cambric and a black silk mantle, and a warm shawl for travelling.[29]

We might note that while the wedding dress is still hand-sewn, other dresses are bought ready-made. The contemporary response of Braddon's predominantly female readers, however, would have mixed pleasurable vicarious consumerism with righteous disapproval at such ostentation. Knowledgeable readers would also have noted that Sylvia chooses a 'thick corded silk' that according to etiquette is too heavy[30] for a young bride.

If readers missed the warning, Braddon hammers the point home: 'Only on the very threshold of doom did Sylvia pause to consider what she was doing ... at this last moment she felt that her wedding dress was too fine for her wedding. There were to be no bridesmaids, no guests, no breakfast.' (TF 185) Her father complains that 'that white thing's quite out of place for a private wedding'; and Sir Aubrey 'gave a little start at the sight of the bride's white robes' (TF 186). This is not Sir Aubrey's last shock – Sylvia, on Edmund Standen's return, locks up her ailing husband in the attic, gives him out as dead, and prepares to marry her first love.

For her second wedding her French maid urges on her 'the most delicious chapeau of white chip, ostrich feathers and palest mauve, the faintest suggestion of half-mourning' (TF 360). The etiquette for widow-brides forbids 'any signs of the first bridal':[31] no white may be worn.[32] Sylvia's bonnet is thus a breach of propriety, though her wedding dress 'of pearl grey satin, trimmed with heavy Spanish point lace' (TF 361) conforms to the rule that widows 'should at church wear a coloured silk'.[33] However, the wedding is prevented, and secrets revealed, and like Jane Eyre, Sylvia strips off her dress 'the white satin slippers [another mistake] – the muslin underskirts ... as if they had been more loathsome than Cinderella's rags' (TF 373).

This is not the last view of her finery, however. Repentant Sylvia flees to France, where Edmund finds her on her deathbed. In a final Mad Scene, she sees her wedding dress: 'Such lovely point lace – fit for a duchess, but not too good for your wife ... let me get up and be dressed ... I know my wedding dress has come home.' (TF 407) And after one last kiss, she dies. Edmund is quickly rewarded with marriage to a forgettable girl in 'purest white' – which, with Sylvia's death, is Braddon's sop to Victorian conventions. The haste with which it is done, however, is a sign of changing views of marriage: Calder points to a tightening of attitudes on the one hand, but a promotion of wifely insubordination – even a rejection of marriage[34] – on the other. Braddon has evoked rebellious shades of Bertha Rochester, Jane Eyre, Lucia/Lucy and, in Sylvia's ghastly deathbed looks, something of Miss Havisham. The novel's prolix accounts of wedding dresses loudly signal disaster, as one might expect from a 'Sensation' novel, but they are also, inadvertently, a gift to the dress historian.

Touches of red on white – echoes of Lucia – are a *leitmotif* of Thomas Hardy's *Tess of the D'Urbervilles*. They are seen at the start, when Tess, on

May Day, wears a white dress with 'a red ribbon in her hair ... the only one of the white company who could boast of such a pronounced ornament',[35] and at the end, when a spreading patch of red on a white ceiling marks Alec D'Urberville's death at Tess's hands. The deployment of colours and clothes in Hardy's work, however, unlike that of Braddon, is metaphoric; dress in *Tess* is deliberately devoid of fashion – except once – for Tess is both an ironic and mythic embodiment of the novel's subtitle, 'A Pure Woman'. Angel Clare sees her as the incarnation of 'the old Elizabethan simile of roses filled with snow' (TU 209), her hands 'amid the immaculate whiteness of the curds ... showed themselves of the pinkness of a rose' (TU 239). Angel proposes marriage and orders the white wedding dress that will be the apotheosis of his vision of her; but Tess, looking at it, wonders if 'this robe should betray her by changing colour, as her robe had betrayed Queen Guénever' (TU 272). In her trustfulness she tells him of her seduction, and the death of her baby. Aghast, he spurns her: 'I thought I should secure rustic innocence as surely as I should secure pink cheeks' (TU 308) – the marriage is aborted and they part.

The dress that represented what Angel saw in Tess – a stereotyped virgin bride – is never worn, nor described. When they are reunited after Alec's murder Hardy places Tess within a realist not an idealizing frame. She has left the scene of murder 'in the costume of a well-to-do young lady ... over her hat and black feather a veil was drawn' (TU 476). At first Angel does not recognize her, 'even the ivory-handled parasol that she carried was of a shape unknown in the retired spot to which they had now wandered' (TU 476). The fashionable accessories place Tess in a late nineteenth-century context; in a Braddon novel they would have marked her as 'fallen', but here they become, in effect, wedding clothes, removed to consummate her love for Angel. But touched with black – a colour impermissible in wedding dresses – they are also anti-wedding clothes.

The morning after their night together in an empty house, the house's caretaker comes upon them, asleep, and is 'so struck with their innocent appearance and with the elegance of Tess's gown hanging across a chair, her silk stockings beside it, the pretty parasol and the other habits ... that her first indignation at the effrontery of tramps and vagabonds gave way to a momentary sentimentality over this genteel elopement' (TU 482). The caretaker is both right and wrong. Tess, in nineteenth-century terms, is a low-class Fallen Woman, a murderess fleeing the law, who breaks into a house and sleeps with a man not her husband: the caretaker is misled by her own class prejudices to judge Tess's social – and therefore moral status – by her clothes. But she is also right. Despite violating every aspect of the nineteenth century's image of womanhood, Tess's 'purity' remains intact – for, like fashionable, discarded clothes, Victorian attitudes to women were becoming redundant. The clothes *do* represent the consummation of love at the end of a story; but, ominously, they are described – therefore there is more and worse to come. Sure enough, in the remaining pages Tess is arrested, imprisoned and executed. Hardy turns the nineteenth century's ideals and narrative conventions about marriage on their head. Conventionally he rewards his beautiful and sympathetic heroine with a happy 'wedding' night; conventionally he punishes her sins by denying her marriage and killing her; unconventionally he telescopes these two conclusions into one. Henry James, simultaneously exploring similar themes in different contexts, concludes that marriage is impossible: as a character in a James story remarks, these were 'bad years in the matrimonial market'.[36]

We saw how Lily Bart, obedient to the imperatives of the nineteenth-century matrimonial market, still fails, and dies beside the trunk holding the 'bridal' dress that was always a fiction. Through the eyes of Newland Archer, in *fin de siècle* New York, Edith Wharton's *The Age of Innocence*, presents the traditional wedding scene in a misty haze of defunct clichés:

> The white and rosy procession was ... half way up the nave ... the music, the scent of the lilies on the altar, the vision of the cloud of tulle and orange blossoms floating nearer and nearer ... the eight pink bridesmaids, the eight black ushers: all these sights and sounds and sensations, so familiar ... so unutterably strange and meaningless in his new relation to them, were confusedly mingled in his brain ... their hands clasped under her veil. 'Darling!' Archer said – and suddenly the black abyss yawned before him and he felt himself sinking into it.[37]

The period described by Wharton in *The Age of Innocence* was one of unprecedented American wealth. And as the pages of American and European journals testify, this wealth found one of its showiest displays in the highly publicized weddings of Dollar Princesses. Editions of *The New York Herald* of 1895 covered Anna Gould's wedding to the Comte de Castellane and the Vanderbilt-Marlborough wedding in detail – both had very twentieth-century endings in divorce. The French magazine *Femina* ran a special four-page pictorial supplement on Alice Roosevelt's wedding in 1906. How marriage or ceremony ended I do not know, but Alice seems to have thrown caution, veil and orange blossoms to the wind, and introduced a modernist note to proceedings by performing 'The Cakewalk' in her wedding gown.[38]

These weddings took components of the traditional ceremony and reproduced them on a gargantuan scale – of which Archer's wedding to

May Welland is a modest version. Mrs Sherwood's guide to 'Social Usages', published in New York in 1884, describes brides as 'dressed in gorgeous array, generally in white satin, with veil of point lace and orange blossoms ... ushers first, two and two; then the bridesmaids, two and two; then some pretty children; and then the bride',[39] a pattern to which Archer and May conform. Wharton makes plain that with Archer's affections engaged elsewhere, the marriage is a mistake. The novel concludes inconclusively in the 1920s: Newland, still disabled by Old New York's 'social usages' that led him to marry May and forsake Ellen Olenska, cannot return to Ellen, even after May's death. No one has resorted to melodramatics or violence, the marriage has not been a tragedy, simply dull; but the violence done to the idea of romantic love, symbolized by the sights, scents and sounds of the traditional ceremony, is present in the brutal contrast of white tulle and orange blossom to the 'black abyss' that opens before Newland.

The world changed, Virginia Woolf said, around 1910 – the date of the Post-Impressionist exhibition in London, which, together with the impact of the Ballets Russes, radically altered the Western world's aesthetic values. Explanations for the changes in female dress at this time conflict: the effects of war, women in the workplace, the granting of suffrage, the aesthetic climate. Anne Hollander argues convincingly that 'the visual demands that govern change in the art of dress have more authority, more consistent and sustained power over all kinds of fashion, than practical and economic demands'. As we saw in the last chapter, the camera began to dictate the way people saw themselves: instead of the nineteenth century's assemblage of disparate and decorated parts, the desired dress-effect was now a single snapshot 'blur of chic'.[40]

Paul Poiret's designs had anticipated this change, but his creations were not easy to wear. The radical move came when Gabrielle Chanel, a music-hall *vedette*, took up with a sporting French aristocrat and his English friend 'Boy' Capel, and discovered a passion for riding and riding dress. By 1910, according to her biographer, her own clothes had simplified current modes, and sportswear became her catalyst for *the* style of the twentieth century: 'Avec elle commence une élégance à rebours: la fin des vêtements de parade ... Avec Chanel l'écurie détrône le pesage.'[41] (With her began an elegance that went against the grain: it was the end of clothing as display... With Chanel the stable usurped the Royal Enclosure). With Capel's help, she launched herself as a dressmaker and 'began to design some of the first modern fashions, in beige locknit and grey flannel ... The Chanel style was to become the paradigm of the twentieth century style'.[42]

If, as Elizabeth Wilson says, Chanel 'created the "poor" look, the sweaters, jersey dresses and little suits that subverted the whole idea of fashion as display',[43] what became of that supreme garment of display, the wedding dress? Parody or eccentricity seems to have been the initial reaction to what Cecil Beaton describes as Chanel's 'nihilistic' philosophy of dress – that 'clothes do not really matter at all, it is the way you look that counts'.[44] Poiret designed a dress for the 'bride of the future', which was actually made and worn in a Charles Cochrane revue of 1921 – the veil, survivor of the traditional ensemble, seems to have been this 'bride's' only garment.[45] Beaton recalls socialite Paula Gellibrand dressing as a nun for her wedding.[46] Cunnington's account of twentieth-century dress records some attempts at knee-length wedding dresses in the 1920s but the 'Picture' dress, drawing on medieval, eighteenth-century, and Victorian styles[47] prevails. In fact the wedding dress has fossilized into near-uniform, nostalgically retaining key attributes of 'romance' – veils, long skirts, tight bodices and orange blossom. Gestures to current modes are made – slashing the skirt from hem to thigh, or tearing the cloth 'punk' fashion – but essentially fashion and the wedding dress diverge around 1920.

How does the novel reflect these changes? In novels of the inter-war period weddings happen off-stage, if at all. Relations between the sexes are explored clinically, cynically, but rarely happily. Bitter nostalgia for what has been or might be characterizes the novels of Evelyn Waugh and Scott Fitzgerald, for example, but without wedding dresses. The wedding dress re-emerges in the fiction of post-Second World War America, which significantly saw a return to conservative attitudes toward women. Weddings, rather than being culminating moments, become incidents around which other things happen, for characters other than bride or groom – interestingly, the word 'wedding' figures repeatedly in book-titles, perhaps betraying some anxiety about the concept.

In Eudora Welty's *Delta Wedding* and Carson Mc Cullers' *Member of the Wedding*, of 1945 and 1946 respectively, two orphan girls see their chance to be part of the traditional family, at a marriage. The weddings are not important other than as 'MacGuffins'.[48] For Welty's Laura, the marriage of her pretty cousin, in an idyllic Southern plantation house, is a moment of blissful acceptance into a family at last: 'In twos the brides-maids began coming, they entered and arranged themselves in front of the boys ... then Laura came in ... at last she was out before everybody, one of the wedding party, dressed up like the rest in an identical flower-girl dress'. The bride's dress is like a 'little white cloud'.[49] Cheerful remarks, 'desserts and ices' conclude events.

McCullers's more hoydenish Frankie believes that the union of her brother to his bride will in fact celebrate *her* union with the couple. The clothes she prepares for the event are, however, badly wrong: the family-servant looks 'from the silver hair ribbons to the sole of the silver slippers.... She looked at the orange satin evening gown and shook her head ... "It don't do."' But to Frankie it is the bride who is wrong: 'There was no veil except a little veil that came down from the wedding hat and nobody was wearing fancy clothes. The bride was wearing a day-time suit ... there was from first to last, the sense of something terribly gone wrong'.[50] It is Frankie's belief in herself as central to the marriage for which she has dressed so festively that is mistaken, and she is devastated when the couple drive off without her. Although both novels, like many at this time, focus on an adolescent's developing consciousness, the wedding, its rituals and clothes conform to Victorian fictional patterns: the dress of successful brides and bridesmaids is indistinct – detail bodes ill.

The savage parody of the traditional courtship/marriage narrative of Vladimir Nabokov's *Lolita* of 1955 still shocks. Humbert Humbert falls in love with twelve-year-old Lolita, and marries her mother in order to gain access to the girl – 'love-at-first-sight' is followed by courtship, and then – true to form – a wedding:

> When the bride is a widow and the groom a widower ... when Monsieur wants to get the whole damned thing over with as quickly as possible and Madame gives in with a tolerant smile, the wedding is generally a 'quiet' affair. The bride may dispense with a tiara of orange-blossoms securing her finger-tip veil, nor does she carry a white orchid in a prayer book. The bride's little daughter might have added to the ceremonious uniting ... but I knew I would dare to be too tender with cornered Lolita ... it was not worth while tearing the child away from her beloved Camp Q.[51]

Like Richardson in *Clarissa*, Nabokov evokes the traditional components of a wedding, not only to deny but deride and destroy. The groom looks forward to 'cornering' and deflowering Lolita, not the bride – the perverse conclusion to a traditional succession of events. And as in *Clarissa*, wedding finery heralds death.

The crisis of Dorothy Baker's *Cassandra at the Wedding* of 1962 turns on the appearance of such finery, the attempt of the wedding dress to rejoin current fashion. Ambitious, intellectual Cassandra – a new kind of heroine who anticipates the feminist concerns of the 1970s – is to be an old-fashioned bridesmaid at her twin sister Judith's wedding. The story is told mainly by Cassandra – wittily but often disagreeably. As she journeys toward the event, it becomes clear that, without meeting her sister's fiancé, she hates him, and intends to prevent the marriage.

Sceptical of marriage, she has nonetheless chosen her dress carefully: 'It was a white dress, and it would probably do for the wedding. In fact, I don't even have to wonder about it – it was very simple and elegant and costly; it would do for anything anywhere.'[52] At home, she shows the dress to her sister and grandmother:

> The dress lay there quietly and unobtrusively, white against the white paper … I told them it was the kind of dress that doesn't give the best account of itself lying in a box … The way it fits is the thing. And the way it is made. 'This pleat, for instance,' I said. I turned it over and showed granny the beautiful tailor's tacks that held the pleat at the top and the bottom, and granny didn't say a thing. 'Pure silk,' I said, 'feel the weight of it. It crunches.' (CW 63)

The quiet white dress is in fact a ticking bomb – Judith's wedding gown is revealed as identical. Cassandra explodes in fury: '"That's no dress for a bride … it's too God-damned simple … Don't you know the bride is supposed to be gussied up? … Nobody gets married in anything decent. You wear something you wouldn't be caught dead in any place but your own wedding. And you never wear it again. You pack it away to show your dumb kids."' (CW 67). Cassandra insists that traditional weddings demand traditionally terrible dresses, dresses that have no place in contemporary life, but Judith replies with icons of avant-garde chic to persuade Cassandra she is wrong: 'Jane would undoubtedly have picked the same dress. So would the Bouvier sisters and Althea Gibson and the Duchess of Windsor' (CW 76) – that is, Jane, their dead young mother, the Bouvier sisters, Jacqueline Kennedy and Lee Radziwill, a famous black athlete, and Mrs Simpson, the ultimate American triumph over stuffy tradition – reinforcing Chanel's dictum that it is not the dress but the meaning you give to it that matters.

The ending is apparently 'happy' – Cassandra's suicide attempt is prevented, a Mad Scene in white averted – but much is left hanging in the air. Cassandra sourly concedes victory to tradition: 'Let nothing endanger the proper marriage … the non-irritating thesis that says nothing new and nothing true … So let's have the frilling wedding.' (CW 204) Fleeing the reception, however, Cassandra removes her Jackie Kennedy dress and returns to scholarly solitude – though that too is undercut by the young woman doctor, who had flown to her bedside and cared for her with a more than professional passion, and whose dialogue suggests another story.

'The romantic market is beginning to change',[53] Edith Hope's publisher warns her, at the start of Anita Brookner's *Hôtel du Lac* of 1984. Twenty years of sexual liberation and feminist writing lie between Baker's and Brookner's novels, but Freud's question as to what women want abides. 'It's sex for the young woman executive now,' the publisher says, 'to reassure her that being liberated is fun' (HL 26). Edith, thirty-nine, a successful romantic novelist, and clearly 'liberated' with her London flat and her lover, disagrees. She believes women 'prefer the old myths ... the tortoise and the hare' (HL 28). Aesop, she says, was writing for the tortoise market, and tortoises need that final 'prize' of dessert and ices.

Edith has gone to a Swiss hotel to recover from walking out on her wedding to Geoffrey. Events leading up to the wedding are revealed in parallel with her accounts of the hotel guests, in letters to her lover, David. The narrative moves between first-and third-person – much of it in free indirect discourse; our image of Edith, therefore, is constructed out of the way she sees herself, and only obliquely from other viewpoints. Mrs Pusey, for instance, whose vulgarities are retailed for David's amusement, thinks of Edith rather as 'sad', and as resembling Princess Anne (HL 35, 63) – an image of horse-faced dowdiness not at all consonant with Edith's self-image. On the other hand, Mr Neville's pursuit of Edith suggests she has her attractions.

Edith, the pattern of late twentieth-century female success, nevertheless tells Neville that happiness lies in the routine of marriage: 'to sit in a hot garden all day, reading, or writing, utterly safe in the knowledge that the person I love will come home to me in the evening. Every evening.' (HL 98) The wedding-*débâcle,* told in flashback, follows this scene.

On the morning of the wedding, as she puts on 'the fine stockings and the beautiful grey satin slip', she reflects on the planning of her outfit:

> [She] had gone to an elderly Polish dressmaker in Ealing with some fine blue-grey material ... And here she was, dressed in a very creditable Chanel copy, the jacket bound with dark blue and white silk braid. Mme Wienowska had also made her a plain round-necked blouse, which she wore with her Aunt Anna's pearls ... Her shoes were blue and white, and, she thought a little too high in the heel, and she carried her white gloves ... she was pleased with herself. She looked elegant, controlled. (HL 126)

Edith approves of herself, but the taxi-driver taking her to the registry office, assumes 'from her modest demeanour that she was one of the guests' (HL 130). Chanel's designs were bold blows for freedom in 1912: in 1984 an elderly dressmaker's copy of a Chanel suit in grey-blue – in a London of punk fashion and 'executive' shoulders – is almost ostentatiously restrained. The grey slip seems particularly unseductive, white gloves had not been seen for decades – and the account is ominously over-detailed.

Like many of the heroines I have described, a second-chance wedding seems likely. A groom improves perhaps, like Rochester; an alternative is offered, or a first-love returns. We return to the hotel, where Neville offers Edith an up-dated version of marriage, premised on the centrality of self: 'You have no idea how promising the world begins to look once you have decided to have it all for yourself.' (HL 94) Did Edith, in rejecting dull Geoffrey, also slough off her Chanel suit? Just before his proposal Neville suggests that Edith give up wearing Virginia Woolf cardigans – her style, it would seem then, is unchanged, and not to his liking. The Chanel suit abides, an image of timeless elegance; but to choose it with such deliberation is to plant one's fashion allegiances outside time. Classic fiction offers structures for character and plot that also are no longer consonant with modern life, yet Edith insists on the endurance of narratives that speak for the centrality of married love. Geoffrey promised routine without passion; Neville's Nietzschian vision was never compatible with Edith's romanticism, even without evidence of his treachery. What she has are fragments of love gleaned from David – irregular and unreliable. The novel ends with the word 'return' substituted for 'coming home', in an old-fashioned telegram to David. There is no 'home', no appended paragraphs or cheerful remarks. Virtue, modesty, decorum is unrewarded.

The incidence of weddings across the history of the novel is obviously legion, and despite my contention that oddly few dresses are involved, there are many more than I have described. The pattern outlined of happy fictional brides going on their way in – at the most – a blur of white, while carefully dressed brides head for disaster, is not susceptible of proof. But it suggests underlying imperatives that have something to do with our instinctive suspicion of dress and point also to the need many novelists feel to separate the ideal permanence of marriage from the vagaries of fashion. In literature, after the great white wedding was instituted, around 1840, and the dress started to detach itself from fashion and move toward uniform, a wedding-shorthand of veil, tulle and orange-blossom began to stand in for the whole. Long descriptions imply further complications and after mid-century these had anyway become the province of journalists, photographers and society columnists. Looking at the exhaustively described and illustrated account of the marriage of Muriel Stephenson to the son of the Earl of Carlisle, – one of *the* weddings of 1900, it is not only the scale of the event that is remarkable – and, with hindsight, unsustainable for all but royalty – but the intractability of

Figure 24 Muriel Stephenson's Wedding Gown, 1900.

Figure 25 Muriel Stephenson's Going-Away Costume, 1900.

Figure 26 Muriel Stephenson's Bridesmaid's Dress, 1900.

Figure 27 Muriel Stephenson's Attendants' Dress, 1900.

such material for a novelist. An off-centre 'little white cloud' is the best that can be managed for the twentieth-century fictional bride.

Fictional wedding dresses, then, chart the changing face of marriage in the modern world. Thackeray's novels covertly undermine the marriage-plot; and though Braddon found it necessary to keep traditional rewards and punishments for her readership, marriage nevertheless is a perilous undertaking in her fictions. Thomas Hardy demolished tradition and lost self-righteously respectable readers. Wedding dresses had become the-atrical costumes by the 1930s, fashioned into spun-sugar fantasies; any real relation to traditional meanings evaporated, and as a closure to the novel, the wedding was now a moribund cliché. Chanel's nihilistic ele-gance translated itself, for weddings, into understated jersey-crepe in greys and blues – no tulle, veil or blossom; little, in fact, to lend colour and excitement to a plot. Fashion and the traditional wedding dress were barely on speaking terms.

In a world where taboos about illegitimacy, relationships outside mar-riage, and same-sex partnerships have virtually disappeared, late twen-tieth-century fiction questions the need for marriage altogether – Baker's

The Hon. Oliver Howard, son of the Earl of Carlisle, was married on St. Patrick's Day at All Saints' Church, Ennismore Gardens, to Miss Muriel Stephenson, daughter of Mr. Russell Stephenson, and niece of Lady Dufferin. The officiating clergy were the Hon. Canon Bertrand P. Bouverie and the Rev. Ravenscroft Stewart. The bride, who was given away by her father, wore a handsome dress of rich white satin, made en princesse, and draped with very beautiful Brussels lace.

The six bridesmaids were, Lady Dorothy Howard, Lady Mary Walde-grave, Lady Bertha Anson, the Hon. Norah Strutt, Miss K. Cockburn, and Miss Rowan Hamilton. Their dresses were of white Oriental satin, the bodices arranged with fichus of white chiffon and sashes of green crêpe de chine falling in long ends at the side of the skirt. The yokes were of silk guipure, whilst the sleeves were plain and long. With these they wore pretty picture hats of black crinoline straw. The bridegroom presented them with shamrock brooches. The Hon. Geoffrey Howard was best man, and the Hon. George Howard, son of Lord Morpeth and nephew of the bridegroom, acted as train-bearer. A wedding breakfast was served at 56, Rutland Gate, and early in the afternoon the Hon. Mr. and Mrs. Oliver Howard left for Naworth Castle, Carlisle, the seat of the Earl of Carlisle. The bride had a going-away costume of dore-coloured faced cloth. The skirt was prettily tucked and stitched and finished near the hem with fourteen rows of narrow stitching. The bodice was pouched and had a large beautiful collar embroidered in chenille, whilst the vest was of tucked chiffon. With this she wore a hat and cape to correspond. The numerous and handsome presents included, from H.R.H. the Princess Louise, Marchioness of Lorne, a diamond star and fur collar; from the Marquis of Lorne, a diamond crescent brooch; from the Marquis and Marchioness of Dufferin and Ava, a dressing case; the Countess of Carlisle, diamond tiara, &c., &c. The bride's wedding dress, travelling gown, and bridesmaids' frocks were made by Miss Doyle, of 21A, Sloane Street.

Figure 28 Newspaper Account of Muriel Stephenson's Wedding, 1900.

heroine yields to a chic, updated version of the dress, but hints at other pathways, other possibilities and ends oddly by dropping a white sock into San Francisco Bay. Brookner draws our attention to classic dress, classic plots and their lamentable modern substitutes, but sees no answers to the questions raised by her awkward, unfashionable truths, and no comfort either in upholding them.

My final 'catwalk' procession of wedding dresses retraces the chronological ground of this study, from *Roxana* to *The House of Mirth* – coincidentally, both these novels end with a 'masquerade' dress hidden in a trunk; and neither heroine marries, although both hoped to. Wedding dresses seem to have followed an independent route in fiction, however: they do not operate for the writer as other dresses do. After 1820 they acquire discrete meanings and increasingly fixed forms which allow little flexibility or ambiguity of interpretation. Only when the author insists on describing a wedding outfit is our attention – or our suspicion – aroused.

How then have images of dress operated in fiction? The question of a novelist's intention in a work of fiction is not one that can be answered easily, but images of dress, 'unpacked' and unfolded, open up a text, as we have seen, revealing underlying structures and patterns that illumine the whole and allow insights into the 'unseen' that lies beneath the 'seen', in terms of both plot and meaning. Reviewing the two centuries of dress in fiction, what seems to emerge is an unexpected consistency in the fiction writer's employment of dress. Anne Hollander points out that literature's 'mirroring' of dress 'has been less visual than moral, emotional and spiritual'.[54] The authors I have considered have nonetheless found ways to evoke the 'look' of the clothes they represent. Defoe, while recognizably recording an early eighteenth-century fashion, and referring to details of dress, also conveyed the experience of wearing dress; he used dress as a metaphor, a class or economic-marker, and as a sexual or moral statement. And most strikingly, as we moved to the catastrophe, he conveyed a sense of the occult 'alterity' of dress, its subterranean power.

A key issue has often been the relation of dress to aesthetic and ethical values – how far are the surfaces we live with, contrived as they are to produce certain effects, also false? Roxana, the courtesan, started and ended her journey by reaching for the meanings that sober stuffs, touched with white, would lend her: did she then deceive? As Henry James observes of Mrs Headway – who despite her murky past is insistently in white – 'people don't change their nature, but they change their desires, their ideal, their effort': and, he might have added, their clothes.

Roxana finally wanted to be virtuous, but this conflicted with her inability to relinquish her loved Turkish dress. Love of dress – and by association, a concern for dress in art or literature – is still regularly dismissed as female and frivolous. Jane Austen's Catherine, conventional and candid in white muslin, was enchanted by Henry Tilney's unconventional, unsexist conversation on dress, books and art. Her candour, reflected in dress, saved her from the greed that underlay the deceptions of the fashionable Thorpes. Dress, for Austen, has its proper place in life as in conversation or in art. Thackeray's Pen, on the other hand, was to the last much possessed by dress, but in control of it, displaying his attractions knowingly, and getting away with it. Even Thackeray's own approval of more manly looks was overwhelmed by the sheer glamour of his creation. The novel's moral ground here seems provocatively unstable.

Roxana's near-criminal employment of multiple identities and disguises was, like Braddon's Lucy Audley, almost successful but finally catastrophic. Unlike Roxana's first-person narration, we never 'go behind' Lady Audley, but by leaving details of dress increasingly indistinct, and invoking subversive images from art, Braddon suggested that beneath her heroine's chameleon appearance lay a potential for action ultimately more threatening than pushing redundant husbands down wells. The development of the novel in the West, as my study has constantly underlined, runs parallel to the rise of capitalism, and Defoe's and Braddon's novels use dress as economic markers. While the reader's sympathies became engaged with Roxana's zestful independence within a male, sexual/economic exchange-system, Braddon subverted her own explanation for Lucy's murderous reaction to that system at its height, and left us with questions unanswered.

The impact of Puritanism was reality, not history, to Roxana and to Defoe's readers – puritan dress had powerful – even dangerous – connotations, and Roxana mimicked its meanings at her peril. To George Eliot's Dorothea and Edith Wharton's Lily, Puritanism was part of their genetic or national heritage. Dorothea's rejection of the exuberance of 1830s' modes in favour of puritanical grey and white was in part instinctive, but also revealed inconsistent, self-dramatizing aspects to her search for an authentic style. More endearingly, however, the style suited her and enhanced her attractions for the opposite sex. Her choice in dress was finally consistent with her nature – unlike Roxana's 'masquerade' of Puritanism – and she was rewarded with the man of her choice. Eliot acknowledges that this a relatively tepid conclusion, but interestingly, posterity has judged that Dorothea has one of fiction's finest wardrobes.

In throwing off her overblown mourning, Dorothea frees herself from being defined in terms of the dead husband who had been so hostile to her true self – 'dress', as Elizabeth Wilson has said, 'is the frontier between the self and the not-self'.[55] Roxana and Lily Bart kept the dresses they should have discarded; beautiful, treacherous not-selves that haunt and destroy. There is no place for the seductions of a Turkish *houri* in a good Protestant housewife's luggage. Lily's faith in the connotations of pure bridal white and High Art was fatally naive in a corrupt society where wealth is the only measure of value: she overlooked the truth that Roland Barthes points to, that 'clothes live in close symbiosis with their historical context'.[56]

If, as Anne Hollander concludes, the study of dress 'has no real substance other than in *images* of clothes', I would suggest that clothes in fiction enhance those images: clothes in fiction are clothes in action, clothes experienced and clothes observed. To look at dress in literature needs many different spectacles, for dress is endlessly polyvalent and changing: the result may be obliquity, confusion and ambiguity, but as Elizabeth Wilson says, to avoid reductivism or normative moralizing about dress, 'we must attempt it'.[57] Dress's triumphant, paradoxical secret is that while we dismiss it as frivolous, chronically restless and ephemeral, it outlives us – in museums, art and, as my book has attempted to make plain, in literature. 'There is something eerie', Wilson believes, 'about a museum of costume': it holds 'congealed memories of … daily life'.[58] Dressed in fiction, clothes of the past are warmed into life, metamorphosed into a kind of poetry. Roland Barthes believed that clothing constitutes 'an excellent poetic object; first, because it mobilises with great variety all the qualities of matter: substance, form, color, tactility, movement, rigidity, luminosity; next, because touching the body and functioning as its substitute and its mask, it is certainly the object of a very important investment; this "poetic" disposition is attested to by the frequency and the quality of vestimentary descriptions in literature'.[59] The poor hero of one of literature's first and greatest short stories, Gogol's 'The Overcoat', longing and saving up for a coat, thinks of this coat as if he were married to it, 'as if some pleasant life's companion had agreed to walk down the path of life with him'[60] – his is a warm, convivial garment, existing largely in his imagination, and waiting, like a patient fiancée, for the moment of their union. Elizabeth Wilson thinks of the clothes in museums waiting poignantly 'for the music to begin again'. Literature, I hope I have shown, provides one of the ways for the music to begin.

Notes

Chapter 1 Dressing for the reader

1. Elizabeth Bowen, 'Dress', in *Collected Impressions* (New York: Knopf, 1950) p. 112.
2. Quoted in Kathryn Hughes, *George Eliot: The Last Victorian* (London: Fourth Estate, 1998) p. 352.
3. Mrs Ellis, *The Daughters of England* (London: Fisher & Son, 1842) p. 227.
4. Anon., *The Habits of Good Society* (London: James Hogg, ?1853) p. 130.
5. Thomas Carlyle, *Sartor Resartus* (Oxford: Clarendon 1913 [1834]) p. 51.
6. Anne Hollander, *Seeing Through Clothes* (Berkeley: University of California Press, 1993) pp. 450, 448.
7. See Michael Carter, *Fashion Classics* (Oxford: Berg, 2003).
8. Daniel Roche, *The Culture of Clothing*, trans. Jean Birrell (Cambridge: Cambridge University Press, 1999) p. 4.
9. Virginia Woolf, *A Room of One's Own* (London: Triad Grafton, 1987 [1929]) p. 70.
10. John Harvey, *Men in Black* (London: Reaktion, 1996) p. 17.
11. Roche, *Culture of Clothing*, p. 19.
12. George Orwell, *Orwell and the Dispossessed* (Harmondsworth: Penguin Books, 2001 [1933]) p. 158.
13. Carol Shields, *Dressing Up for the Carnival* (New York: Viking, 2000) p. 1.
14. Mrs Ellis, *Wives of England* (London: Charles Griffin & Co., ?1840) pp. 243–4.
15. Henry James, *Literary Criticism, Vol. 1, American Writers; English Writers* (New York: Library of America, 1984) p. 24.
16. Richard Altick, *The Presence of the Present* (Columbus: Ohio State University Press, 1991) pp. 275–338.
17. Tony Tanner, *Jane Austen* (Houndmills: Macmillan Education, 1986) pp. 60–4.
18. Aileen Ribeiro, *The Art of Dress* (New Haven: Yale University Press, 1995).
19. Hollander, *Seeing Through Clothes*, p. 424.
20. Honoré de Balzac, 'Traité de la vie élégante' (Paris: Arléa, 1998 [1830]) pp. 22–3.
21. Judith Watt, *Fashion Writing* (Harmondsworth: Penguin, 1999) p. x.
22. Roland Barthes, 'The Diseases of Costume', in *Critical Essays* (Evanston: Northwestern University Press, 1979) p. 46.
23. Hollander, *Seeing Through Clothes*, p. 424.

24. Henry James, *Literary Criticism*, Vol. 2, *French Writers; Other European Writers* (New York: Library of America, 1984) p. 148.
25. Jonathan Bate, *The Song of the Earth* (Cambridge, MA: Harvard University Press, 2000) p. 1.
26. Eleanor Wachtel, 'Henry James: A Discussion with Cynthia Ozick, Sheldon Novick and Susan Griffin', an interview in *The Henry James Review* 19, iii (1998) p. 319.
27. See Steven Connor's article, 'Making an Issue of Cultural Phenomenology', *Critical Quarterly* 42, 1 (Spring, 2000) p. 3.
28. Ann Buck, 'Clothes in Fact and Fiction, 1825–1865' *Costume*, 17, (1983) p. 89.

Chapter 2 The Fatal Dress: Daniel Defoe's Roxana

1. Terry Castle, *Masquerade and Civilization* (Stanford: Stanford University Press, 1986) p. 57.
2. Daniel Defoe, *Roxana: The Fortunate Mistress*, ed. John Mullan (Oxford: Oxford University Press, 1996 [1724]) pp. 173–4. All further quotations are from this edition, and cited in parentheses in the text.
3. David Blewett, *Defoe's Art of Fiction* (Toronto: University of Toronto Press, 1979) p. 143.
4. Castle, *Masquerade*, pp. 75, 76.
5. Blewett, *Defoe's Art*, p. 129.
6. John J. Richetti, *Defoe's Narratives* (Oxford: Clarendon, 1975) p. 36.
7. See the reproduction of original title page, Oxford University Press edition.
8. Quoted in Blewett, *Defoe's Art*, p. 121.
9. John J. Richetti, Introduction, *The Cambridge Companion to the Eighteenth Century Novel*, ed. J. Richetti (Cambridge: Cambridge University Press, 1996), p. 5.
10. John Mullan, Introduction, *Roxana: The Fortunate Mistress* (Oxford: Oxford University Press, 1996 [1724]), p. xxii.
11. Ronald Paulson, 'Consumption and Literacy', in A. Bermingham and J. Brewer (eds) *The Consumption of Culture: 1600–1800*, (London: Routledge, 1995) p. 387.
12. Anne Hollander, *Seeing Through Clothes* (Berkeley: University of California Press, 1993), pp. 370, 371.
13. Mullan, Introduction, p. xxi.
14. Richetti, *Defoe's Narratives*, p. 209.
15. Lou Taylor, *Mourning Dress* (London: Allen & Unwin, 1983), p. 103.
16. Ibid., p. 106.
17. Jane Ashelford, *The Art of Dress* (London: National Trust, 1996), p. 98.
18. John Sekora, *Luxury* (Baltimore: Johns Hopkins University Press, 1977), pp. 23, 76.
19. Ibid., p. 73.
20. Richetti, *Defoe's Narratives*, p. 195.

21. Linda Colley, *Captives* (London: Jonathan Cape, 2002) p. 45.
22. Ibid., p. 4.
23. Ibid., p. 105.
24. Ruth Bernard Yeazell, *Harems of the Mind* (New Haven: Yale University Press, 2000) p. 1.
25. Aileen Ribeiro, *Dress in Eighteenth Century Europe* (New Haven: Yale University Press, 2002) p. 265.
26. Quoted in Marcia Pointon, *Hanging the Head* (New Haven: Yale University Press, 1993) p. 154.
27. Charles Saumarez Smith, *Eighteenth Century Decoration* (London, Weidenfeld & Nicolson,1993), p. 78.
28. Aileen Ribeiro, *Dress and Morality* (London: Batsford, 1986), p. 95.
29. Castle, *Masquerade* p. 56.
30. Ibid., p. 63.
31. G. J. Barker-Benfield, *The Culture of Sensibility* (Chicago: University of Chicago Press, 1992) p. 175.
32. Christopher Flint, *Family Fictions* (Stanford: Stanford University Press 1998), p. 156.
33. John Dryden, 'Ode for St. Cecilia's Day', 1687.
34. Castle, *Masquerade* p. 119.
35. Milan Kundera, *L'Ignorance* (Paris: Gallimard, 2003), p. 35 (My translation)
36. Tony Tanner, *Adultery in the Novel* (Baltimore: Johns Hopkins University Press, 1979) pp. 3, 4.

Chapter 3 Talk about Muslin: Jane Austen's *Northanger Abbey*

1. Hilaire Belloc, *Selected Cautionary Verses* (Harmondsworth: Penguin, 1968) pp. 61, 58.
2. Jane Austen, *Love and Friendship* (London: The Women's Press, 2000 [1789]) p. 28.
3. Alistair Duckworth, *The Improvement of the Estate* (Baltimore: Johns Hopkins University Press, 1971) p. 91.
4. Penelope Byrde, *Jane Austen Fashion* (Ludlow: Excellent Press, 1999) p. 13.
5. Ibid., p. 28.
6. Jane Austen, *Northanger Abbey* (Harmondsworth: Penguin, 1995 [1818]) p. 26. All further quotations are from this edition and cited in parentheses in the text.
7. Aileen Ribeiro, *The Art of Dress: Fashion in England and France, 1750–1820* (New Haven: Yale University Press, 1995) p. 70.
8. Deirdre Le Faye, (ed.), *Jane Austen's Letters* (Oxford: Oxford University Press, 1997) pp. 6, 146, 256.
9. Ibid., pp. 237, 273.
10. Tony Tanner, *Jane Austen* (Houndmills: Macmillan Education, 1986) p. 601.
11. Fanny Burney, *Evelina*, Boston: Bedford/St. Martin's, 1997 [1778]) p. 73.

12. Henry James, *Literary Criticism: American Writers; English Writers* (New York: Library of America, 1984) p. 24.
13. Stana Nedanic, 'Romanticism and the Urge to Consume', in Maxine Berg (ed.), *Consumers and Luxury*, (Manchester: Manchester University Press, 1999) p. 210.
14. Maxine Berg, 'New Commodities, Luxuries and their Consumers in Eighteenth Century England', in Berg, *Consumers and Luxury*, p. 66.
15. Duckworth, *Improvement*, pp. 83–4.
16. Marilyn Butler, Introduction, in Jane Austen, *Northanger Abbey* (Harmondsworth: Penguin, 1995 [1818]) p. xxv.
17. Tanner, *Jane Austen*, p. 63.
18. Butler, Introduction to *Northanger Abbey*, p. xlii.
19. Tanner, *Jane Austen*, p. 60.
20. Ibid., p. 63.
21. Le Faye, *Letters*, p. 343.

Chapter 4 Unrepentant Dandies: William *Thackerery's Pendennis*

1. Christopher Breward, *The Hidden Consumer* (Manchester: Manchester University Press, 1999) p. 2.
2. J. Munns and P. Richards (eds), *The Clothes that Wear Us* (Newark: University of Delaware Press, 1999) p. 23.
3. Ellen Moers, *The Dandy* (London: Secker & Warburg, 1960) p. 21.
4. *The Habits of Good Society, A Handbook of Etiquette for Ladies and Gentlemen* (London: James Hogg, ?1853) p. 144.
5. Moers, *The Dandy*, p. 17.
6. William Thackeray, *Pendennis*, ed. John Sutherland (Oxford: Oxford World Classics,1999 [1850]) p. 1. All further quotations are from this edition and cited in parentheses in the text.
7. Moers, *The Dandy*, p. 14.
8. Barbara Hardy, *The Exposure of Luxury* (London: Peter Owen, 1972) p. 12.
9. Richard Altick, *The Presence of the Present* (Columbus: Ohio State University Press, 1991) p. 10.
10. Quoted in ibid., p. 179.
11. William Thackeray, *The Adventures of Philip*, ed. George Saintsbury (Oxford: Oxford University Press, n.d. [1860]) note, p. 650.
12. 'Skeleton' suits were relaxed all-in-one cloth garments for small boys – the top buttoning onto loose trousers – which, around 1790 replaced the stiff, impractical replicas of the adult male outfit.
13. Anita Brookner, *The Genius of the Future* (London: Phaidon, 1971) p. 60.
14. Altick, *Presence*, p. 244.
15. Ibid., p. 287.
16. It was in 1850, in fact, that Thackeray, on a visit to America, dismayed the

infant Henry James by remarking on his jacket – 'in England, if I were to go there, I should be addressed as Buttons'. Quoted in F. W. Dupee, *Henry James: The Autobiography* (London: Hutchison, 1956) p. 52.

17. Alison Adburgham, *A Punch History of Manners and Modes* (London: Hutchinson, 1961) pp. 35–6.
18. *Habits*, p. 140.
19. Moers, *The Dandy*, p. 148.
20. Ibid., p. 153.
21. Ibid., p. 155.
22. Brookner, *Genius*, p. 83.
23. Hardy, *Exposure*, p. 17.
24. C. Willett Cunnington, *Feminine Attitudes in the Nineteenth Century* (London: Heinemann, 1935) pp. 80, 93, 95.
25. Anne Hollander, *Sex and Suits* (New York: Kodansha International,1994) p. 101.
26. William Thackeray, 'Men and Coats', in *The Complete Works* Vol. 13 (London: Smith, Elder, & Co., 1899) pp. 611, 600–1.
27. Anne Hollander, *Seeing Through Clothes* (Berkeley: University of California Press, 1993) p. 424.
28. *The Habits of Good Society*, p. 146.
29. Nearly thirty years later, Henry James was to describe Frederick Winterbourne watching Daisy Miller – a female version of Pen in her instinct for dress and teasing eroticism: she has 'the *tournure* of a princess', he marvels. We might see here a switch of Sex Objects from the pre-Victorian Dandy to the late Victorian Femme Fatale.
30. Hardy, *Exposure*, p. 136.
31. Ibid., p. 37.
32. *Habits*, p. 156.
33. Mario Praz, *The Hero in Eclipse* (Oxford: Oxford University Press, 1969) p. 210.
34. John Sutherland, 'Introduction' to *Pendennis* (Oxford: Oxford University Press, 1994 [1850]) p. xxviii.
35. Henry James, *The Critical Muse: Selected Literary Criticism* (Harmondsworth: Penguin, 1987) p. 190.
36. *Habits*, pp. 143, 155.
37. Quoted in Andrew Berry, 'Reasons for being Nice and Having Sex', *London Review of Books*, 6 February, 2003, p. 36.
38. Vauxhall Gardens closed in 1859, its magic destroyed by the rivalry of gas-lit Cremorne Gardens. Cremorne itself lasted only another twelve years, closed by the forces of moral disapproval.
39. Quoted in Hardy, *Exposure*, p. 119.
40. Praz, *Hero*, pp. 240, 243.
41. Moers, *The Dandy*, p. 207.
42. Quoted in ibid., p. 210.
43. Sutherland, 'Introduction', p. xxvii.
44. Hollander, *Sex and Suits*, p. 100.

45. Stendhal, *Scarlet and Black*, trans. G. Scott Moncrieff (London: Dent, 1962 [1830]) p. 310.

46. Moers, *The Dandy*, p. 205.

47. W. M. Thackeray, 'Roundabout Papers', *The Complete Works* (Oxford: Oxford University Press, n.d. [1860]) pp. 440, 433.

Chapter 5 The Woman in White and the Woman in Colour: Wilkie Collins's Woman in White and Mary Braddon's *Lady Audley's Secret*

1. John Harvey, *Men in Black* (London: Reaktion Books, 1995) pp. 195, 196.

2. Introduction to M. E. Braddon, *John Marchmont's Legacy*, ed. T. Sasaki (Oxford: Oxford University Press, 1999 [1867]) p. xii.

3. Harvey, *Men in Black*, p. 206.

4. Wilkie Collins, *The Woman in White* (Oxford: Oxford University Press, 1996) pp. 20, 28.

5. Harvey, *Men in Black*, p. 208.

6. Jennifer Carnell, *The Literary Lives of M. E. Braddon* (Hastings: Sensation Press, 2000) p. 154.

7. Mary Braddon, *Lady Audley's Secret*, ed. D. Skilton (Oxford: Oxford University Press, 1987 [1862]) p. 11. All further quotations are from this edition and cited in parentheses in the text.

8. Mary Braddon, *Phantom Fortune* (London: Maxwell, 1884) p. 256.

9. Henry James, *Literary Criticism: American Writers; English Writers*(New York: Library of America, 1984) pp. 744–5.

10. Cited in George Hughes, *Reading Novels* (Nashville: Vanderbilt University Press, 2002), p. 58.

11. See Carnell, *Literary Lives*, Appendix One, pp. 287–375.

12. Carnell, *Literary Lives*, p. 178.

13. Alan Bowness et al., *The Pre-Raphaelites* (London: Tate Gallery/Penguin, 1984), p. 190.

14. Jan Davis Schipper, *Becoming Frauds* (Lincoln, NE: Writer's Club Press, 2002) p. 20.

15. Lyn Pykett, *The Improper Feminine* (London: Routledge, 1992) pp. 89, 81, 82.

16. Nina Auerbach, *Woman and the Demon* (Cambridge, MA.: Harvard University Press, 1982) p. 107.

17. Clair Hughes, *Henry James and the Art of Dress* (Houndmills: Palgrave, 2001) p. 11.

18. Virginia Morris, *Double Jeopardy* (Lexington: University of Kentucky Press, 1990) p. 162.

20. Andrew Wilton et al., *The Age of Rossetti, Burne-Jones and Watts* (London: Tate Gallery Publishing, 1997), p. 123.

21. John Ruskin, *The Times*, 24 May 1854, quoted by Judith Bronkhurst, Tate Gallery exhibition catalogue, 1984, p. 121.

22. There were now, in fact, numerous women art-collectors – Ellen Heaton, Lady Trevelyan, Martha Combe – and coincidentally, they collected Pre-Raphaelite and Aesthetic works rather than mainstream art.

23. Carnell, *Literary Lives*, pp. 196–7.

24. See Wilton, *Age of Rossetti*.

25. Biography, Rossetti Archive Website, http://jefferson.village.virginia.edu: 2002.

26. Ibid.

27. Wilton, *Age of Rossetti*, p. 19.

28. Pykett, *Improper Feminine*, p. 101.

29. Wilton, *Age of Rossetti*, p. 19.

30. Rossetti Archive, Production History of *Fazio's Mistress*.

31. Wilton, *Age of Rossetti*, p. 97.

32. Ibid., p. 102.

Chapter 6 Mind and Millinery: George Eliot's *Middlemarch*

1. Henry James, *Literary Criticism*, Vol.1, *American Writers; English* (New York, Library of America, 1984) p. 847.

2. George Eliot, 'Silly Novels by Lady Novelists', in *Selected Essays*, ed. A. Byatt (Harmondsworth: Penguin, 1990) p. 140.

3. George Eliot, *The Mill on the Floss* (London: Dent, 1966 [1860]) p. 312.

4. Richard Altick, *The Presence of the Present* (Columbus: Ohio State University Press, 1990), p. 161.

5. Gillian Beer, *George Eliot* (London: Harvester Press, 1986) p. 148.

6. George Eliot, *Adam Bede*, ed. S. Gill (Harmondsworth: Penguin, 1980 [1859]), p. 224.

7. G. H. Lewes, 'Recent German Fiction', in S. Regan (ed.), *The Nineteenth Century Novel: A Critical Reader*, (London: Routledge, 2001) p. 37.

8. Eliot, 'Silly Novels', p. 149.

9. Kathryn Hughes, *George Eliot: The Last Victorian* (London: The Fourth Estate, 1998) p. 288.

10. Thomas Carlyle, *Sartor Resartus* (Oxford: Clarendon, 1913 [1834]) pp. 51, 47.

11. James, *Literary Criticism*, Vol. 1, p. 1005.

12. Hughes, *Last Victorian*, p. 341.

13. Ibid., p. 362.

14. James, *Literary Criticism*, Vol. 1, pp. 931, 1006.

15. George Eliot, *Romola* (Oxford: Oxford University Press, 1998 [1863]), p. 117.

16. Hughes, *Last Victorian*, p. 358.

17. Anne Hollander, *Seeing Through Clothes* (Berkeley: University of California Press, 1993) p. 433.

18. Ellen Moers, *Literary Women* (London: The Women's Press, 1986), p. 194

19. George Eliot, *Middlemarch*, ed. B. G. Hornback (New York: Norton, 2000 [1871/72]), p. 5. All further quotations are from this edition and cited in

parentheses in the text.

20. Karen Chase, *Eros and Psyche: The Representation of Personality in Charlotte Brontë, Charles Dickens, George Eliot* (London: Methuen, 1984) p. 139.

21. Ibid., pp. 139–40.

22. Anon., *Saturday Review*, 7 December 1872, 733–4, quoted in *Middlemarch* (New York: Norton, 2000), p. 573.

23. Willett Cunnington in *English Women's Clothing in the Nineteenth Century* (London: Faber & Faber, 1938, p. 109) mentions no fewer than ten different styles of sleeve for the year 1830.

24. Hollander, *Seeing Through Clothes*, p. 361.

25. W. J. Harvey, 'An Introduction to *Middlemarch*', in P. Swinden (ed.), *Middlemarch: Casebook Series*, (London: Macmillan, 1972), p. 199.

26. Laurence Lerner, 'Dorothea and the Theresa-Complex', in *Middlemarch: Casebook Series*, ed. Patrick Swinden (London: Macmillan, 1972), p. 229.

27. Mrs Craik, *A Woman's Thoughts about Women* (London: Hurst & Blackett, n.d. 1st edn. 1858), p. 3.

28. *The Bible Pattern of a Good Woman*, of 1867, for example, by Mrs Balfour, offered moral guidance and pious anecdotes to the lower-middle classes, drawing heavily on Biblical references.

29. Ed. Gordon Haight, *The George Eliot Letters*, I (New Haven: Yale University Press., 1954) p. 66.

30. T. R. Wright, '*Middlemarch* as a Religious Novel', in B. Hornback (ed.), *Middlemarch*, (New York: Norton, 2000) p. 641.

31. Sarah Lewis, *Woman's Mission* (London: John W. Parker, 1840) p. 11.

32. Elizabeth Helsinger, et al., *The Woman Question*, Vol. 1, (Chicago: University of Chicago Press, 1989) p. 5.

33. Lewis, *Woman's Mission*, pp. 40, 50, 119, 120.

34. Ibid., p. 130.

35. Moers, *Literary Women*, pp. 174, 180.

36. Quoted in ibid., p. 180.

37. Hollander, *Seeing Through Clothes*, p. 421.

38. James, *Literary Criticism*, Vol. I, p. 960.

39. John Harvey, *Men in Black* (London: Reaktion, 1996) p. 212.

40. Cunnington, *English Women's Clothing*, pp. 15, 89.

41. C. Willett Cunnington, *The Perfect Lady* (London: Max Parrish, 1948) p. 17.

42. Ibid., p. 17.

43. Mrs Chapone, *Letters*; Dr Gregory *A Father's Legacy* (London: J. Walker & Edwards, 1816 [1774]) p. 165.

44. Chapone; Gregory, p. 140.

45. Chapone; Gregory, p. 149.

46. Mary Wollstonecraft, *Vindication of the Rights of Women* (Harmondsworth: Penguin, 1982 [1792]) p. 111.

47. Countess Blessington (ed.), *The Keepsake* (London: Longman, Brown, 1842).

48. Richard Altick, 'Anachronisms in *Middlemarch*: A Note', *Nineteenth Century Fiction* 33 (1978) pp. 366–72.

49. J. C. Flügel, *The Psychology of Clothes* (London: 1930).

50. Beer, *George Eliot*, p. 124.

51. Lewis, *Women's Mission*, Chapters 11 and 12.

52. Beer, *George Eliot*, p. 62.

53. Lou Taylor, *Mourning Dress* (London: Allen & Unwin, 1983) p. 30.

54. Ibid., pp. 203, 204.

55. Clair Hughes, *Henry James and the Art of Dress* (Houndmills: Palgrave, 2001), p. 84.

56. Cunnington, *The Perfect Lady*, p. 16.

57. Cunnington, *English Women's Clothing*, p. 124.

58. Carlyle, *Sartor Resartus*, p. 37.

59. Wright, cited in *Middlemarch*, Norton edn, p. 642.

60. Quoted in Quentin Bell, *On Human Finery* (London: Hogarth Press, 1976) p. 11.

61. Barbara Hardy, 'The Surface of the Novel', in P. Swinden (ed.), *Middlemarch: Casebook Series*, (London: Macmillan, 1972) p. 219.

62. Ibid., p. 220.

63. Hollander, p. 364.

64. Melissa Gregory, 'James and Domestic Terror', *Henry James Review*, 25(2), Spring 2004, pp. 146–167. This article examines James's images of male terrorisation of women through aesthetic and intellectual brutality. Casaubon's descendant Gilbert Osmond is Gregory's central example.

65 George Eliot, 'Margaret Fuller and Mary Wollestonecraft', in *George Eliot: Selected Essays* (1990 [1856] p. 333.

66. Harvey, *Men in Black*, p. 202.

67. V. S. Pritchett, 'The Living Novel', in Patrick Swinden (ed.), *Middlemarch: Casebook Series* (London: Macmillan, 1972) p. 102.

68. Honoré de Balzac, *Traité de la vie elégante* (Paris: Arléa, 1998 [1830]) p. 19. (My translation)

69. Charles Baudelaire, 'Le Peintre de la vie moderne', *Oeuvres Complètes*, ed. Marcel Ruff (Paris: Editions du Seuil, 1968) p. 553. (My translation)

Chapter 7 Shades of White: Henry James's 'The Siege of London' and 'The Author of Beltraffio'

1. Henry James, *Literary Criticism*, Vol. 1, *American Writers; English & American Writers* (New York: Library of America, 1984) p. 63.

2. Virginia Woolf, in *The Times Literary Supplement*, 20 November 1919. Quoted in Patrick Swinden, (ed.), *Middlemarch: Casebook* (Houndmills: Macmillan, 1972) p. 101.

3. James, *Literary Criticism*, Vol. 1, p. 497.

4. Ibid., p. 907.

5. Ibid., p. 53.

6. James, *Literary Criticism*, Vol. 2, *French Writers; Other European Writers* etc, (New York: Library of America, 1984) p. 97.

7. James, *Literary Criticism*, Vol. 1, pp. 606, 608.

8. James, *Literary Criticism,* Vol. 2, p. 1107.

9. Henry James, *The Complete Notebooks*, eds Leon Edel and Lyall Powers (Oxford: Oxford University Press, 1987) p. 13.

10. James, *Literary Criticism,* Vol. 1, p. 53.

11. Henry James, *Complete Short Stories, 1874–1884* (New York: Library of America, 1999 [1884]) p. 566. All further quotations are from this edition and cited in parentheses in the text.

12. J. L. Sweeney (ed.), *The Painter's Eye* (Madison: University of Wisconsin Press, 1989) p. 26.

13. Tony Tanner, *Henry James: Life and Work* (Amherst: University of Massachusetts Press, 1985) p. 24.

14. In the 1908 New York Edition James substituted San Pablo for San Diego, the latter having lost the edge in lawlessness and doubtful dealings. Mrs Headway becomes a 'Texan belle' and has adventures in New Mexico, a result presumably of James's last trip to the States in 1905.

15. James may have intended Mrs Headway to be a less melodramatic, more cheerful version of Trollope's terrifying American, Mrs Hurtle, in *The Way We Live Now* of 1875, who, having shot one faithless lover, pursues a young Englishman across the Atlantic with a view to marriage.

16. Eric Homberger, *Mrs Astor's New York* (New Haven: Yale University Press, 2002) p. 4.

17. Ibid., p. 20.

18. Lionel Trilling, 'Manners, Morals and the Novel' in *The Liberal Imagination* (London: Secker & Warburg, 1951) p. 209.

19. Peggy McCormack, *The Rule of Money* (Ann Arbor: University of Michigan Research Press, 1990) p. 32.

20. Milton Rugoff, *Prudery and Passion* (London: Hart Davies, 1971) p. 38.

21. Sweeney, pp. 140, 141.

22. Henry James, *Daisy Miller* and *An International Episode* (New York: Harper and Bros, 1892) p. 11.

23. Clair Hughes, *Henry James and the Art of Dress* (Houndmills: Palgrave, 2001) p. 16. See also Sweeney, p. 140, n., and Viola Hopkins Winner, *Henry James and the Visual Arts* (Charlottesville: University of Virginia Press, 1970) pp. 87, 88.

24. Hughes, *Art of Dress*, p. 17.

25. John Kimmey, *Henry James and London* (New York: Peter Lang, 1991) p. 71.

26. See Henry James, *Washington Square*, ed. B. Lee (Harmondsworth: Penguin, 1984 [1881]), chapters 4, 5 and 8.

27. This seems to have been a current catch-phrase. Yum-Yum, in Gilbert and Sullivan's *The Mikado* of 1885, coyly refers to herself as 'a child of nature'.

28. Kimmey, *Henry James and London*, p. 73.

29. Deborah Davis, *Strapless: John Singer Sargent and the Fall of Madame X* (New York: Tarcher/ Penguin, 2003).

30. Ibid., p. 54.

31. Ibid., p. 95.
32. Ibid., p. 124.
33. Henry James, *Letters,* vol. 3 ed. Leon Edel (Cambridge MA: Harvard University Press, 1980) p. 43.
34. Sweeney, *Painter's Eye*, p. 226.
35. James, *Letters,* iii, p. 43; Sweeney, *Painter's Eye*, p. 226.
36. Davis, *Strapless*, p. 168.
37. Dress straps were clearly an issue. Mrs Haweis, doyenne of advice books on personal appearance, traces the plunge of the 1880s' bodice to 'the detestable strap'. Mrs H. R. Haweis, *The Art of Beauty* (London: Chatto & Windus, 1883) p. 83.
38. Anne Hollander, *Seeing Through Clothes*, (Berkeley: University of California Press, 1993) p. 424.
39. Elizabeth Bowen, *Collected Impressions* (New York: Knopf, 1950) p. 111.
40. James's Letter to Edmund Gosse, 1883, quoted in Fred Kaplan, *The Imagination of Genius* (New York: William Morrow, 1992) p. 271.
41. James, *Literary Criticism*, Vol. 1, pp. 63–4.
42. James, 'The Author of *Beltraffio*' in *Complete Stories, 1874–1884*, p. 865. All further quotatons are from this edition, and cited in parentheses in the text.
43. Rictor Norton, 'The Life of John Addington Symonds'. *The Life and Writings of John Addington Symonds*, http://www.infopt.demon.co.uk/symonds.htm
44. Wendy Graham suggests that identification with Robert Louis Stevenson is equally possible. Ambient's exhausted appearance, his velvet jacket and loose shirt, certainly recall Stevenson rather than Symonds. See *Graham, Henry James's Thwarted Love* (Stanford: Stanford University Press, 1999) pp. 32, 33.
45. James, *Complete Notebooks*, p. 25.
46. Jonathan Freedman, *Professions of Taste* (Stanford: Stanford University Press, 1990) p. xvi.
47. Ibid., p. 136.
48. Alan Sinfield, *The Wilde Century* (London: Cassell, 1994) p. 85.
49. Eric Haralson, *Henry James and Queer Modernity* (Cambridge: Cambridge University Press, 2003) p. 55.
50. Andrew Wilton et al., *The Age of Rossetti, Burne-Jones* and *Watts – Symbolism in Britain* (London: Tate Gallery Publishing, 1997) pp. 11–33.
51. Ibid., pp. 17, 18.
52. Letter to Edmund Gosse, in Kaplan, *Imagination of Genius*, p. 271 (see n40 above).
53. Haralson claims the narrator is 'unforeseen' in the notebooks (see Haralson, *Queer Modernity*, p. 81), but his role is in fact described at some length, though he is unnamed. (James, *Notebooks*, p. 26)
54. James, *Notebooks*, p. 25.
55. Haralson, *Queer Modernity*, p. 65.
56. James, *The Author of 'Beltraffio' And Other Tales*, p. 61.
57. Eve Kosofsky Sedgwick, *Epistemology of the Closet* (Harmondsworth: Penguin,

1990) p. 185.

58. Sinfield, *Wilde Century*, p. 62.
59. C. Hughes, *Henry James*, p. 65.
60. Sinfield, *Wilde Century*, p. 68.
61. Hilary Fraser et al., *Gender and the Victorian Periodical* (Cambridge: Cambridge University Press, 2003) p. 100.
62. Penelope Byrde, *Nineteenth-century Fashion* (London: Batsford, 1992) p. 72.
63. Elizabeth Wilson, *Adorned in Dreams* (London: Tauris, 2003) p. 3.
64. Henry James, *The Aspern Papers*, ... (New York: Charles Scribner's & Sons, 1909) p. 296.
65. Peter Rawlings, 'Telling Tales: Henry James and the Civil War', paper given at the M.M.L.A. Conference, Chicago, November 2003.
66. James, *Aspern Papers*, p. xxi.
67. Ibid., p. 307.
68. Tanner, p. 12.
69. Michael Carter, *Fashion Classics* (Oxford: Berg, 2003), p. 155.

Chapter 8 Consuming Clothes: Edith Wharton's *The House of Mirth*

1. Edith Wharton, *A Backward Glance* (London: Century Hutchinson, 1987 [1934]) p. 191.
2. See Clair Hughes, *Henry James and the Art of Dress* (Houndmills: Palgrave, 2001) Chapter 8.
3. R. B. Lewis and Nancy Lewis (eds), *Letters of Edith Wharton* (London: Simon & Schuster, 1988) pp. 96–7.
4. Robert L. Heilbroner, *The Worldly Philosophers* (New York: Touchstone, 1995) p. 217.
5. Edith Wharton, *The House of Mirth* (Harmondsworth: Penguin, 1993 [1905]) p. 3. All further quotations are from this edition and cited in parentheses in the text.
6. George Hughes, in *Reading Novels* (Nashville: Vanderbilt University Press, 2002), notes how description in the nineteenth-century novel is given extra weight when delivered by 'experts' such as teachers, doctors, travellers and guides. See *Reading Novels*, p. 58.
7. Edith Wharton, *A Backward Glance*, p. 208.
8. C. W. Cunnington, *English Women's Clothing in the Present Century* (London: Faber & Faber, 1952) p. 68.
9. Michael Carter, *Putting a Face on Things* (Sydney: Power Publications, 1997) pp. 111, 142.
10. Fiona Clark, *Hats* (London: Batsford, 1985) p. 44. See also Caroline R. Milbank, *New York Fashion* (New York: Harry N. Abrams, 1989) p. 52.
11. Anon. Review in *The Independent*, 10, July, 1905, p. 113. Cited in *The House of Mirth*, ed. Ammons (1990 [1905]) p. 308.

12. Anne Hollander, *Seeing Through Clothes* (Berkeley: University of California Press, 1993) p. 421.

13. Ibid., p. 422.

14. Wharton, *A Backward Glance*, p. 1.

15. See Clair Hughes, *Henry James*, p. 3, 8.

16. Wharton, *A Backward Glance*, p. 47.

17. Mrs Haweis, *The Art of Beauty* (London: Chatto & Windus, 1883) pp. 3, 5.

18. Quoted in Lois Banner, *American Beauty* (New York: Knopf, 1983) p. 101.

19. Wharton, *A Backward Glance*, p. 11.

20. Quoted in Eleanor Dwight, 'Wharton and Art", in C. Singley (ed.), *A Historical Guide to Edith Wharton*, (Oxford: Oxford University Press, 2003) p. 191.

21. Wharton, *A Backward Glance*, p. 207.

22. Heibroner, *Worldly Philosophers*, p. 217.

23. Theodore Veblen, *The Theory of the Leisure Class* (Harmondsworth: Penguin, 1994 [1899]), pp. 168, 169.

24. Ibid., p. 42.

25. Martha Banta, 'Wharton's Women: In Fashion, In History, Out of Time', in C. Singley (ed.), *Edith Wharton: A Historical Guide*, (Oxford: Oxford University Press, 2003) p. 52.

26. Jane Ashelford, *The Art of Dress* (London: National Trust, 1996) p. 242.

27. Milbank, *New York Fashion,* p. 48.

28. Cynthia Griffin Wolff, 'Lily Bart and the Beautiful Death', in *The House of Mirth*, ed. Ammons (New York: Norton, 1990) p. 338.

29. 'On November 17, 1905, a front-page story listed John D. Rockefeller as being richer than the rich monarchs; "His Annual Income $30,000,000 Nearly Equal to Those of All Europe's Crowned Heads Combined".' Hebe Dorsey, *The Age of Opulence* (New York: Harry N. Abrams, 1986) p. 18.

30. J. P. Sartre, *La Nausée* (Paris: Gallimard, 1938) p. 187.

31. C. Willett Cunnington, *The Perfect Lady* (London: Max Parrish, 1948) p. 66.

32. Henry James, *Literary Criticism*, Vol. 2, p. 132.

33. Cunnington, *English Women's Clothing,* pp. 55, 61.

34. Hollander, *Seeing Through Clothes*, p. 451.

35. Dorsey, *Age of Opulence*, p. 124.

36. Ashelford, *Art of Dress*, p. 252.

37. Ibid., p. 248.

38. Martha Banta, 'The Excluded Seven', in D. McWhirter (ed.), *Henry James's New York Edition*, (Stanford: Stanford University Press, 1995) p. 356.

39. Elizabeth Wilson, *Adorned in Dreams*, (London: Tauris, 2003) p. 103.

40. Banta, 'Wharton's Women', p. 52.

41. Veblen, *Theory of the Leisure Class*, pp. 172, 173.

42. Wharton sheds an interesting light, via Aunt Peniston, on the new importance of the couturier-artist: Bertha has to spend 'a day with [her couturier] at his villa at Neuilly'(109) before he will take an order. See Wharton *House of Mirth*, Penguin edn.

43. Cynthia Griffin Wolff, Introduction to Wharton, *The House of Mirth* (Harmondsworth: Penguin, 1993) p. xix.
44. Ibid., p. xxii.
45. Hollander, *Seeing Through Clothes*, p. 311.
46. Ibid., p. 330
47. Ibid., p. 324.
48. Wolff, 'Lily Bart and the Beautiful Death', in *The House of Mirth*, ed.Elizabeth Ammons (New York: Norton, 1990) p. 321.
49. Helen Campbell, *The American Girl's Home Book of Work and Play* (New York: G.P. Puttnam's Sons, 1883) pp. 93, 94.
50. From an article in *The International Herald Tribune*, 10 July 2004, p. 7.
51. Maureen Howard, 'The Bachelor and the Baby', in M. Bell (ed.), *The Cambridge Companion to Edith Wharton*, (Cambridge: Cambridge University Press, 1995) p. 148.
52. Dorsey, *Age of Opulence*, p. 19.
53. Ibid., pp. 160, 165.
54. Ashelford, *Art of Dress*, p. 253.
55. Milbank, *New York Fashion*, p. 52.
56. Clark, *Hats*, p. 44.
57. Candace Waid, *Edith Wharton's Letters from the Underworld* (Chapel Hill: University of North Carolina Press, 1991), p. 37.
58. Wolff, 'Lily Bart and the Beautiful Death', p. 339.
59. Wilson, p. 58.

Chapter 9 The Missing Wedding Dresses: Samuel Richardson's *Pamela* to Anita Brookner's *Hôtel du Lac*

1. Henry James, 'The Art of Fiction', *The Critical Muse: Selected Literary Criticism*, ed. Roger Gard (Harmondsworth: Penguin,1987) p. 190.
2. Maria McBride-Mellinger, *The Wedding Dress* (New York: Random House, 1993) pp. 8, 9.
3. Anthony Trollope, *Doctor Thorne* (London: Dent, Everyman, 1993 [1858]) II, pp. 310, 317.
4. Samuel Richardson, *Pamela*, Vol. 1 (London: Dent, 1960 [1741]) pp. 7, 8. All further references are to this edition and cited in parentheses in the text.
5. Aileen Ribeiro, *Dress in Eighteenth-century Europe* (New Haven: Yale University Press, 2002) p. 168.
6. Cited in ibid., p. 40.
7. Ibid., p. 202.
8. Madeleine Ginsburg, *Wedding Dress: 1740–1970* (London: HMSO, 1981) p. 2.
9. Samuel Richardson, *Clarissa* (London: Dent, 1967 [1745]) Vol. 4, pp. 303, 324. All further quotations are from this edition and cited in parentheses in the text.
10. Oliver Goldsmith, *The Vicar of Wakefield* (Oxford: Oxford University Press, 1992 [1766]) p. 9.

11. Maria Edgeworth, *Belinda* (Oxford: Oxford University Press, 1995 [1801]) pp. 477, 478.
12. Jane Austen, *Emma* (Oxford: Oxford University Press, 1998 [1816]) 440.
13. Ann Monsarrat, *And the Bride Wore...* (London: Gentry Books, 1973) p. 108.
14. Ginsburg, *Wedding Dress*, p. 1.
15. Anthea Jarvis, *Wedding Clothes and Customs* (Liverpool: Merseyside County Museums, 1985) p. 3.
16. Penelope Byrde, *Jane Austen Fashion* (Ludlow: Excellent Press, 1999) p. 86.
17. Charlotte Brontë, *Jane Eyre* (New York: Norton, 2001 [1847]) p. 221. All further quotations are from this edition and cited in parentheses in the text.
18. Jenni Calder, *Women and Marriage in Victorian Fiction* (London: Thames & Hudson, 1976) p. 26.
19. William Thackeray, *Vanity Fair*, ed. J. M. Stewart (Harmondsworth: Penguin, 1968 [1847]) p. 195. All further quotations are from this edition and cited in parentheses in the text.
20. *The Habits of Good Society* (London: James Hogg, ?1853) p. 368.
21. William Thackeray, *Pendennis*, ed. John Sutherland (Oxford: Oxford University Press, 1999 [1850]) p. 792.
22. Charles Dickens, *Great Expectations*, ed. C. Mitchell (Harmondsworth: Penguin, 1996) p. 58. All further quotations are from this edition and cited in parentheses in the text.
23. Calder, *Women and Marriage*, p. 108.
24. Sir Walter Scott, *The Bride of Lammermoor*, ed. Fiona Robertson (Oxford: Oxford University Press, 1998 [1819]) p. x. All further quotations are from this edition and cited in parentheses in the text.
25. Henry Cockton, *The Love Match* (London: W. M. Clark, 1847) p. 325.
26. *Habits of Good Society*, p. 369.
27. Penelope Byrde, *Nineteenth-century Fashion*, (London: Batsford, 1992) p. 149.
28. Quoted in Monsarrat, *And the Bride Wore*, p. 109.
29. Mary Braddon, *Taken at the Flood* (London: Maxwell, 1884) p. 181. All further quotations are from this edition and cited in parentheses in the text.
30. *Habits of Good Society*, p. 369.
31. Mrs Sherwood, *Manners and Social Usages* (New York: Harper Bros., 1884) p. 71.
32. A Member of the Aristocracy, *Manners and Rules of Good Society* (London: Frederick Warne, 1892) p. 130.
33. Sherwood, *Manners*, p. 71.
34. Calder, *Women and Marriage*, pp. 165–6.
35. Thomas Hardy, *Tess of the D'Urbervilles* (Harmondsworth: Penguin, 1982 [1891]) p. 51. All further quotations are from this edition and cited in parentheses in the text.
36. Henry James, *Complete Short Stories* (New York: Library of America, 1999) Vol. 2, p. 133.
37. Edith Wharton, *The Age of Innocence* (New York: Collier Books, 1993 [1920]) p. 185.

38. 'Le Mariage de Miss Roosevelt', *Femina* (Paris: 1906) 4 unnumbered pages.
39. Sherwood, *Manners*, p. 67.
40. Anne Hollander, *Seeing Through Clothes* (Berkely: University of California Press, 1993) pp. 312, 331.
41. Edmonde Charles-Roux, *Le Temps de Chanel* (Paris: Editions de La Martinière, 2004) p. 74.
42. Elizabeth Wilson, *Adorned in Dreams* (London: Tauris, 2003) p. 40.
43. Ibid., p. 40.
44. Cecil Beaton, *The Glass of Fashion* (London: Weidenfeld & Nicolson, 1954) pp. 162, 163.
45. Martin Battersby, *Art Deco Fashion* (London: Academy Editions, 1984) p. 70.
46. Beaton, *Glass*, p. 142.
47. C. Willett Cunnington, *English Women's Clothing in the Present Century* (London: Faber & Faber, 1952) pp. 219, 255, 273.
48. Alfred Hitchcock's term for the plot's dynamic object. See Chapter 5.
49. Eudora Welty, *Delta Wedding* (London: Virago, 1982 [1945]) pp. 211, 213.
50. Carson McCullers, *The Member of the Wedding* (Harmondsworth: Penguin, 1962 [1946]) pp. 106, 171.
51. Vladimir Nabokov, *Lolita* (Harmondsworth: Penguin, 1995 [1955]) p. 74.
52. Dorothy Baker, *Cassandra at the Wedding* (London: Virago, 1982 [1962]) p. 7. All further references are to this edition and are cited in parentheses in the text.
53. Anita Brookner, *Hôtel du Lac* (London: Jonathan Cape, 1984) p. 26. All further quotations are from this edition and cited in parentheses in the text.
54. Hollander, p. *Seeing Through Clothes*, 418.
55. Wilson, p. 3.
56. Quoted in M. Carter, *Fashion Classics* (Oxford: Berg, 2003) p. 160.
57. Wilson, p. 11.
58. Ibid., p. 1.
59. Roland Barthes, *The Fashion System*, (New York: Hill, 1983) p. 236. I am indebted to Mick Carter for drawing my attention to this comment.
60. Nikolai Gogol, *The Collected Tales*, trans. R. Pevear and L. Volkhonsky, (London: Granta, 2003) p. 406.

Bibliography

Adburgham, A. (1961), *A Punch History of Manners and Modes*, London: Hutchinson.

Altick, R. (1978), 'Anachronisms in *Middlemarch*: A Note', *Nineteenth Century Fiction*, 33.

—— (1991), *The Presence of the Present*, Columbus: Ohio State University Press.

Ashelford, J. (1996), *The Art of Dress*, London: National Trust.

Auerbach, N. (1982), *Woman and the Demon*, Cambridge, MA: Harvard University Press.

Austen, J. (1995 [1818]), *Northanger Abbey*, Harmondsworth: Penguin.

—— (1998 [1816]), *Emma*, Oxford: Oxford University Press.

—— (2000 [1779]), *Love and Friendship*, London: The Women's Press.

Baker, D. (1982 [1962]), *Cassandra at the Wedding*, London: Virago.

Balfour, Mrs (1867), *The Bible Pattern of a Good Woman*, London: S. W. Partridge.

Balzac, H. de. (1998 [1830]), *Traité de la vie elégante*, Paris: Arléa.

Banner, L. (1983), *American Beauty*, New York: Knopf.

Banta, M. (1995), 'The Excluded Seven', in D. McWhirter (ed.), *Henry James's New York Edition*, Stanford: Standord University Press.

—— (2003), 'Wharton's Women: In Fashion, In History, Out of Time', in C. Singley (ed.), *Edith Wharton: A Historical Guide*, Oxford: Oxford University Press.

Barker-Benfield, G. J. (1992), *The Culture of Sensibility*, Chicago: University of Chicago Press.

Barthes, R. (1983 [1967]), *The Fashion System*, New York: Hill.

—— (1979) 'The Diseases of Costume', *Critical Essays*, Evanston: Northwestern University Press.

Bate, J. (2000), *The Song of the Earth*, Cambridge, MA: Harvard University Press.

Battersby, M. (1984), *Art Deco Fashion*, London: Academy Editions.

Baudelaire, C. (1968), *Oeuvres complètes*, ed. M. Ruff, Paris: Editions du Seuil.

Beaton, C. (1954), *The Glass of Fashion*, London: Weidenfeld & Nicolson.

Beer, G. (1986), *George Eliot*, London: Harvester Press.

Bell, M. (ed.), (1995), *The Cambridge Companion to Edith Wharton*, Cambridge: Cambridge University Press.

Bell, Q. (1976), *On Human Finery*, London: Hogarth Press.

Belloc, H. (1968 [1907]), *Selected Cautionary Verses*, Harmondsworth: Penguin.

Berg, M. (ed.), (1999), *Consumers and Luxury*, Manchester: Manchester University Press.

Bermingham, A. and Brewer, J. (eds) (1995), *The Consumption of Culture; 1600–1800*, London: Routledge.

Blessington, Lady M. (1842), *The Keepsake*, London: Longman Brown.

Blewett, D. (1979), *Defoe's Art of Fiction*, Toronto: University of Toronto Press.

Bowen, E. (1950), *Collected Impressions*, New York: Knopf.

Bowness, A. et al. (1984), *The Pre-Raphaelites*, London: Tate Gallery/Penguin.

Braddon, M. (1884), *Taken at the Flood*, London: Maxwell.

—— (1884), *Phantom Fortune*, London: Maxwell.

—— (1987 [1862]), *Lady Audley's Secret*, ed. D. Shilton, Oxford: Oxford University Press.

Breward, C. (1999), *The Hidden Consumer*, Manchester: Manchester University Press.

Brontë, C. (2001 [1847]), *Jane Eyre*, ed. R. J. Dunn, New York: Norton.

Brookner, A. (1971), *The Genius of the Future*, London: Phaidon.

—— (1984), *Hôtel du Lac*, London: Jonathan Cape.

Buck, A. (1983), 'Clothes in Fact and Fiction, 1825–1865', *Costume*, 17.

Burney, F. (1997 [1778]), *Evelina*, ed. K. Straub, Boston: Bedford/St. Martin's.

Byrde, p. (1992), *Nineteenth-century Fashion*, London: Batsford.

—— (1999), *Jane Austen Fashion*, Ludlow: Excellent Press.

Calder, J. (1976) *Women and Marriage in Victorian Fiction*, London: Thames & Hudson.

Campbell, H. (1883), *The American Girl's Home Book of Work and Play*, New York: G. P. Puttnam's Sons.

Carlyle, T. (1913 [1834]), *Sartor Resartus*, Oxford: Clarendon.

Carnell, J. (2000), *The Literary Lives of M. E. Braddon*, Hastings: Sensation Press.

Carter, M. (1997), *Putting a Face on Things*, Sydney: Power Publications.

—— (2003) *Fashion Classics*, Oxford: Berg.

Castle, T. (1986), *Masquerade and Civilization*, Stanford: Stanford University Press.

Chapone, H. (1816 [1779]), *Letters*, London: J. Walker & Edwards.

Charles-Roux, E. (2004), *Le Temps de Chanel*, Paris: Editions de La Martinière.

Chase, K. (1984), *Eros and Psyche: The Representation of Personality in Charlotte Brontë, Charles Dickens, George Eliot*, London: Methuen.

Clark, F. (1985), *Hats*, London: Batsford.

Cockton, H. (1847), *The Love Match*, London: W. M. Clark.

Colley, L. (2002), *Captives*, London: Jonathan Cape.

Collins, W. (1996 [1861]), *The Woman in White*, Oxford: Oxford University Press.

Connor, S. (2000), 'Making an Issue of Cultural Phenomenonology', *Critical Quarterly*, 42, 1, Spring.

Craik, Mrs (n.d. 1st edn. 1858), *A Woman's Thoughts about Women*, London: Hurst & Blackett.

Cunnington, C. W. (1935), *Feminine Attitudes in the Nineteenth-century*, London: Heinemann.

—— (1938), *English Women's Clothing in the Nineteenth-century*, London: Faber & Faber.

—— (1948), *The Perfect Lady*, London: Max Parrish.

—— (1952), *English Women's Clothing in the Present Century*, London: Faber & Faber.

Davis, D. (2003), *Strapless: John Singer Sargent and the Fall of Madame X*, New York: Tarcher/Penguin.

Defoe, D. (1996 [1724]), *Roxana: The Fortunate Mistress*, ed. J. Mullan, Oxford: Oxford University Press.

—— (1987 [1724]), *Roxana: The Fortunate Mistress*, ed. D. Skelton, Harmondsworth: Penguin.

Dickens, C. (1996 [1861]), *Great Expectations*, ed. C. Mitchell, Harmondsworth: Penguin.

Dorsey, H. (1986), *The Age of Opulence*, New York: Harry Abrams.

Duckworth, A. (1971), *The Improvement of the Estate*, Baltimore: Johns Hopkins University Press.

Dupee, F. W. (1956), *Henry James: The Autobiography*, London: Hutchison.

Dwight, E. (2003), 'Wharton and Art', in C. Singley (ed.), *A Historical Guide to Edith Wharton*, Oxford: Oxford University Press.

Edgeworth, M. (1995 [1801]), *Belinda*, ed. W. R. Nicoll, Oxford: Oxford University Press.

Eliot, G. (1966 [1860]), *The Mill on the Floss*, London: Dent.

—— (1980 [1859]), *Adam Bede*, ed. S. Gill, Harmondsworth: Penguin.

—— (1990), *Selected Essays*, ed. A. S. Byatt, Harmondsworth: Penguin.

—— (1998 [1863]), *Romola*, ed. A. Brown, Oxford: Oxford University Press.

—— (2000 [1872]), *Middlemarch*, ed. B. G. Hornback, New York: Norton.

Ellis, Mrs (1842), *The Daughters of England*, London: Fisher & Son.

—— (?1840), *The Wives of England*, London: Charles Griffin & Co.

Flint, C. (1998), *Family Fictions*, Stanford: Stanford University Press.

Flügel, J. C. (1930), *The Psychology of Clothes*, London.

Fraser, H., Green, S. and Johnston, J. (2003), *Gender and the Victorian Periodical*, Cambridge: Cambridge University Press.

Freedman, J. (1990), *Professions of Taste*, Stanford: Stanford University Press.

Ginsburg, M. (1981), *Wedding Dress: 1740–1970*, London: HMSO.

Gogol, N. (2003), *The Collected Tales,* London: Granta Books.

Goldsmith, O. (1992 [1766]), *The Vicar of Wakefield*, Oxford: Oxford University Press.

Graham W. (1999), *Henry James's Thwarted Love*, Stanford: Stanford University Press.

Gregory, Dr (1816 [1774]), 'A Father's Legacy to his Daughters', London: Walker and Edwards.

Gregory, M. (2004) 'James and Domestic Terror', *Henry James Review*, 25(2), Spring.

The Habits of Good Society (?1853), London: James Hogg.

Haight, G. (1954), *The George Eliot Letters*, New Haven: Yale University Press.

Haralson, E. (2003), *Henry James and Queer Modernity*, Cambridge: Cambridge University Press.

Hardy, B. (1972a), *The Exposure of Luxury*, London: Peter Owen.

Hardy, B. (1972b), 'The Surface of the Novel', in P. Swinden (ed.), *Middlemarch: Casebook Series*, London: Macmillan.

Hardy, T. (1982 [1891]), *Tess of the D'Urbervilles*, ed. A. Alvarez, Harmondsworth: Penguin.

Harvey, J. (1995), *Men in Black*, London: Reaktion.

Harvey, W. J. (1972 [1966]), 'An Introduction to *Middlemarch*', in P. Swinden (ed.), *Middlemarch: Casebook Series*, London: Macmillan.

Haweis, Mrs (1883), *The Art of Beauty*, London: Chatto & Windus.

Heibroner, R. L. (1995), *The Worldly Philosophers*, New York: Touchstone.

Helsinger, E., Sheets R. and Veeder, W. (1989), *The Woman Question*, Chicago: University of Chicago Press.

Hollander, A. (1993), *Seeing Through Clothes*, Berkeley: University of California Press.

—— (1994), *Sex and Suits*, New York: Kodansha International.

Homberger, E. (2002), *Mrs Astor's New York*, New Haven: Yale University Press.

Howard, M. (1995), 'The Bachelor and the Baby', in M. Bell (ed.), *The Cambridge Companion to Edith Wharton*, Cambridge: Cambridge University Press.

Hughes, C. (2001) *Henry James and the Art of Dress*, Houndmills: Palgrave.

Hughes, G. (2002), *Reading Novels*, Nashville: Vanderbilt University Press.

Hughes, K. (1998), *George Eliot: The Last Victorian*, London: The Fourth Estate.

James, H. (1892 [1879 and 1881]), *Daisy Miller* and *An International Episode*, New York: Harper and Bros.

—— (1937 [1909]), *The Aspern Papers; The Turn of the Screw; The Liar; The Two Faces*, New York: Charles Scribner's & Sons.

—— (1937 [1909]), *The Author of 'Beltraffio' And Other Tales*, New York: Charles Scribner's & Sons.

—— (1980), *Letters*, ed. Leon Edel, Cambridge MA: Harvard University Press.

—— (1984), *Literary Criticism*, Vol. 1, *American Writers; English Writers*, New York: Library of America.

—— (1984), *Literary Criticism*, Vol. 2, *French Writers; Other European Writers; The Prefaces*, New York: Library of America.

—— (1984 [1881]), *Washington Square*, ed. B. Lee, Harmondsworth: Penguin.

—— (1987) *The Critical Muse: Selected Literary Criticism*, ed., R. Gard, Harmondsworth: Penguin.

—— (1987), *The Complete Notebooks*, eds L. Edel and L. Powers, Oxford: Oxford University Press.

—— (1999 [1884]), *Complete Short Stories, 1874–1884* New York: Library of America.

Jarvis, A. (1985), *Wedding Clothes and Customs*, Liverpool: Merseyside County Museums.

Kaplan, F. (1992), *The Imagination of Genius*, New York: William Morrow.

Kimmey, J. (1991), *Henry James and London*, New York: Peter Lang.

Kundera, M. (2003), *L'Ignorance*, Paris: Gallimard.

Le Faye, D. (ed.) (1997), *Jane Austen's Letters*, Oxford: Oxford University Press.

Lerner, L. (1972 [1967]), 'Dorothea and the Theresa-Complex', in P. Swinden (ed.) *Middlemarch: Casebook Series*, London: Macmillan.

Lewes, G. H. (2001) 'Recent German Fiction', in S. Regan (ed.), *The Nineteenth Century Novel: A Critical Reader*, London: Routledge.

Lewis, R. B. and Lewis, N. (eds). (1988) *Letters of Edith Wharton*, London: Simon & Schuster.

Lewis, S. (1840), *Woman's Mission*, London: John W. Parker.

McBride-Mellinger, M. (1993), *The Wedding Dress*, New York: Random House.

McCormack, P. (1990), *The Rule of Money*, Ann Arbor: University of Michigan Research Press.

McCullers, C. (1962 [1946]), *The Member of the Wedding*, Harmondsworth: Penguin.

McWhirter, D. (1995), *Henry James's New York Edition*, Stanford: Stanford University Press.

A Member of the Aristocracy (1892), *Manners and Rules of Good Society*, London: Frederick Warne.

Milbank, C. R. (1989), *New York Fashion*, New York: Harry. Abrams.

Moers, E. (1960), *The Dandy*, London: Secker & Warburg.

—— (1986), *Literary Women*, London: The Women's Press.

Monsarrat, A. (1973), *And the Bride Wore ...*, London: Gentry Books.

Morris, V. (1990), *Double Jeopardy*, Lexington: University Press of Kentucky.

Mullan, J. (1996 [1724]), 'Introduction', *Roxana: The Fortunate Mistress*, Harmondsworth: Penguin.

Munns, J. and Richards, P., (eds). (1999), *The Clothes that Wear Us*, Newark DE: University of Delaware Press.

Nabokov, V. (1995 [1955]), *Lolita*, Harmondsworth: Penguin.

Norton, R., 'The Life of John Addington Symonds', *The Life and Writtings of John Addington Symonds,*, http;www.infopt.demon.co.uk/symonds.htm

Orwell, G. (2001 [1933]), 'Down and Out in Paris and London', in P. Davison (ed.), *Orwell and the Dispossessed*, Harmondsworth: Penguin.

Pointon, M. (1993), *Hanging the Head*, New Haven: Yale University Press.

Praz, M. (1969), *The Hero in Eclipse*, Oxford: Oxford University Press.

Pritchett, V. S. (1972 [1947]), 'The Living Novel', in P. Swinden (ed.), *Middlemarch: Casebook Series*, London: Macmillan.

Pykett, L. (1992), *The Improper Feminine*, London: Routledge.

Ribeiro, A. (1986), *Dress and Morality*, London: Batsford.

—— (1995), *The Art of Dress*, New Haven: Yale University Press.

—— (2002), *Dress in Eighteenth Century Europe*, New Haven: Yale University Press.

Richardson, S. (1960 [1741]), *Pamela*, London: Dent.

—— (1967 [1745]), *Clarissa*, London: Dent.

Richetti, J. J. (1975), *Defoe's Narratives*, Oxford: Clarendon.

—— (1996), 'Introduction', in J. Richetti (ed.), *The Cambridge Companion to the Eighteenth Century Novel*, Cambridge: CambridgeUniversity Press.

Roche, D. *The Culture of Clothing*, trans. J. Birrell (Cambridge: Cambridge University Press.

Rugoff, M. (1971), *Prudery and Passion*, London: Hart Davies.

Saumarez Smith, C. (1993), *Eighteenth Century Decoration*, London: Weidenfeld & Nicolson.

Sartre, J. P. (1938), *La Nausée*, Paris: Gallimard.

Schipper, J. D. (2002), *Becoming Frauds*, Lincoln: NE: Writer's Club Press.

Scott, W. (1998 [1819]), *The Bride of Lammermoor*, ed. F. Robertson, Oxford: Oxford University Press.

Sedgwick, E. K. (1990), *Epistemology of the Closet*, Harmondsworth: Penguin Books.

Sekora, J. (1977), *Luxury*, Baltimore: Johns Hopkins University Press.

Sherwood, Mrs (1884), *Manners and Social Usages*, New York: Harper Bros.

Shields, C. (2000), *Dressing Up for the Carnival*, New York: Viking.

—— (2002), *Unless*, London: Fourth Estate.

Sinfield, A. (1994), *The Wilde Century*, London: Cassell.

Singley, C. (ed.) (2003), *A Historical Guide to Edith Wharton*, Oxford: Oxford University Press.

Stendhal (1962 [1830]), *Scarlet and Black*, trans. G. Scott Moncrieff, London: Dent.

Sweeney, J. L. (ed.) (1989), *The Painter's Eye*, Madison: University of Wisconsin Press.

Swinden, P. (ed.) (1972), *Middlemarch: Casebook*, Houndmills: Macmillan.

Tanner, T. (1979), *Adultery in the Novel*, Baltimore: Johns Hopkins University Press.

—— (1985), *Henry James: Life and Work*, Amherst: University of Massachusetts Press.

—— (1986), *Jane Austen*, Houndmills: Macmillan Education.

Taylor, L. (1983), *Mourning Dress*, London: Allen & Unwin.

Thackeray, W. (1968 [1847]), *Vanity Fair*, Ed. J. L. M. Stewart, Harmondsworth: Penguin.

—— (1999 [1850]), *Pendennis*, ed. J. Sutherland, Oxford: Oxford University Press,

—— (n.d. [1860]), *The Adventures of Philip*, ed. George Saintsbury, Oxford: Oxford University Press.

—— (n.d. [1860]), 'Roundabout Papers', *The Complete Works*, Oxford: Oxford University Press.

Trilling, L. (1951), 'Manners, Morals and the Novel', *The Liberal Imagination*, London: Secker & Warburg.

Trollope, A. (1993 [1858]), *Doctor Thorne*, London: Dent.

Wachtel, E. (1998), 'Henry James: A Discussion with Cynthia Ozick, Sheldon Novick and Susan Griffin', *The Henry James Review*, 19(3), Johns Hopkins University Press.

Veblen, T. (1994 [1899]), *The Theory of the Leisure Class*, Harmondsworth: Penguin.

Waid, C. (1991), *Edith Wharton's Letters from the Underworld*, Chapel Hill: University of North Carolina Press.

Watt, J. (1999), *Fashion Writing*, Harmondsworth: Penguin.

Welty, E. (1982 [1945]), *Delta Wedding*, London: Virago.

Wharton, E. (1987 1934]), *A Backward Glance*, London: Century Hutchinson.

—— (1990 [1905]), *The House of Mirth*, ed. E. Ammons, New York: W. W. Norton.

—— (1993 [1920]), *The Age of Innocence*, New York: Collier Books.

—— (1993 [1905]), *The House of Mirth*, ed. C. G. Wolff, Harmondsworth: Peguin.

Wilson, E. (2003), *Adorned in Dreams*, London: Tauris.

Wilton, A., Upstone, R., Bryant, B., Newall, C., Stevens, M., Wilson, S. (1997), *The Age of Rossetti, Burne-Jones and Watts – Symbolism in Britain*, London: Tate Gallery Publishing.

Winner, V. H. (1970), *Henry James and the Visual Arts*, Charlottesville: University of Virginia Press.

Wolff, C. G. (1993), Introduction to E. Wharton, *The House of Mirth*, Harmondsworth: Penguin.

Wollstonecraft, M. (1982 [1792]), *Vindication of the Rights of Women*, Harmondsworth: Penguin.

Woolf, V. (1988 [1928]), *Orlando*, London: Triad Grafton.

—— (1987 [1929]), *A Room of One's Own*, London: Triad Grafton.

Wright, W. J. (2000 [1984]), 'Middlemarch as a Religious Novel', in B. Hornback (ed.), *Middlemarch*, New York: Norton.

Yeazell, R. B. (2000), *Harems of the Mind*, New Haven: Yale University Press.

Index